Irit Back is a researcher, lecturer and Head of African Studies at Tel Aviv University. She is the author of *Islam and Post-Colonial Identity in West Africa* (2005) and various articles on conflict resolution and contemporary Islam in Africa.

'Most of the academic and policy literature in relation to Africa in general and to the specific topics at hand relies almost entirely on Western resources. In contrast, Back's excellent research analyzes Sudanese resources such as internet sites and newspapers in addition to Arabic and Middle Eastern newspapers. Hence it offers a more balanced understanding of issues involved with intervention in intrastate conflicts in general, and Sudanese reactions to this intervention in particular ... in its details, the study of the intervention in Darfur greatly contributes to our understanding of the development of the notion of non-intervention during Africa's post-colonial history. In its broader context, it offers important insights into African new peace and security architecture in issues such as the sovereignty of the state, the legitimacy of violent and oppressive regimes, and the right to protect the African citizen in cases of grave violations of human rights.'

Galia Sabar, Professor of African Studies,
Tel Aviv University

INTERVENTION AND SOVEREIGNTY IN AFRICA

Conflict Resolution and International Organizations in Darfur

IRIT BACK

I.B. TAURIS
LONDON · NEW YORK

Published in 2016 by
I.B.Tauris & Co. Ltd
London • New York
www.ibtauris.com

International Library of African Studies 52

ISBN: 978 1 78453 250 5
eISBN: 978 0 85772 971 2

A full CIP record for this book is available from the British Library
A full CIP record is available from the Library of Congress

Library of Congress Catalog Card Number: available

Typeset in Garamond Three by OKS Prepress Services, Chennai, India
Printed and bound by CPI Group (UK) Ltd, Croydon, CR0 4YY

MIX
Paper from responsible sources
FSC www.fsc.org FSC® C013604

To my parents, Rachel and Shraga, who survived genocide, and then went on to create a better world

CONTENTS

ACRONYMS AND ABBREVIATIONS

APF	African Peace Facility
AMIB	African Union Mission in Burundi
AMIS	African Union Mission in Sudan
AMISOM	African Union Mission in Somalia
ASF	African Standby Force
AU	African Union
AUHIP	African Union High Level Implementation Panel
CFC	Ceasefire Committee
CPA	Comprehensive Peace Agreement
DDDC	The Darfur-Darfur Dialogue and Consultation
DPA	Darfur Peace Agreement
ECOMOG	ECOWAS Ceasefire Monitoring Group
ECOWAS	Economic Community of West African States
GoS	Government of Sudan
GoSS	Government of South Sudan
ICC	International Criminal Court
ICISS	International Commission on Intervention and State Sovereignty
ICU	Islamic Courts Union (Somalia)
IDPs	Internally Displaced People
IGAD	Intergovernmental Authority on Development

IGASOM	IGAD Peace Support Mission in Somalia
INPFL	Independent National Patriotic Front of Liberia
LAS	League of Arab States
LRA	Lord's Resistance Army (Uganda)
MILBOS	Military Observers
MONUC	United Nations Organization Mission in the Democratic Republic of the Congo
NIF	National Islamic Front
NPLF	National Patriotic Front of Liberia
OAU	Organization of African Unity
RUF	Revolutionary United Front
SLM/A	Sudan Liberation Movement/Army
SPLA/M	Sudan People Liberation Army/Movement
TCCs	Troop-Contributing Countries
TFG	Transitional Federal Government (Somalia)
TDRA	Transitional Darfur Regional Authority
UNAMID	United Nations-African Union Mission in Darfur
UNAMIR	United Nations Assistance Mission for Rwanda
UNITAF	Unified Task Force (Somalia)
UNMIS	United Nations Mission in Sudan
UNOC	United Nations Operation in Congo
UNOMIL	United Nations Observer Mission in Liberia
UNOSOM	United Nations Operation in Somalia

TIMETABLE OF EVENTS IN DARFUR (AND RELATED EVENTS) 2004–10

2004

April – Humanitarian Ceasefire Agreement on the Conflict in Darfur (signed in N'Djamena, Chad).

April – Agreement between GoS, SLM/A, and JEM to convene and hold peace talks (signed in N'Djamena, Chad). First AMIS troops arrive in Darfur.

May – Agreement with the Sudanese parties on the Modalities for the establishment of the Ceasefire Commission and the Deployment of Observers in Darfur (signed in Addis Ababa, Ethiopia).

May – The PSC calls on the Commission to take all necessary measures to ensure effective implementation of the 8 April ceasefire agreement, including deployment of an African Union Mission in Darfur.

June – The first six AU military observers are deployed to the Ceasefire Commission in Darfur.

June – US Congress defines the events in Darfur as genocide.

August – The Abuja talks commence under AU auspices.

August – The African Union deploys the first Rwandan troops in Darfur, tasked with monitoring the ceasefire.

September – UN Security Council sets up an independent commission of inquiry into Darfur.

November – Protocol between GoS, SLM/A, and JEM on the Improvement of the Humanitarian Situation in Darfur (signed in Abuja, Nigeria).

October–December – Third and Fourth rounds of Abuja talks.

2005

January – Comprehensive Peace Agreement between GoS and the SPLM (signed in Naivasha, Kenya).

March – UN Security Council refers Darfur to ICC.

March – The AU PCS decides to support transition to a United Nations peacekeeping force in Darfur.

May – First discussion of handing over AMIS to the UN.

July – Government of National Unity established. John Garang dies in helicopter crash.

October – Haskanita Conference organized by Minni Minnawi.

September–November – Sixth and Seventh rounds of Abuja talks.

2006

January – AU rejects Sudan's bid to chair the organization.

May – The Darfur Peace Agreement (DPA) is signed in Abuja, Nigeria, by the Government of Sudan (GoS) and the Sudan Liberation Movement/Army (represented by Minni Minnawi).

June – The Ceasefire Commission (CFC) holds its first meeting.

August – Minni Minnawi is appointed senior assistant to the president.

November – The UN, AU, LAS, the European Union, and several nations meet in Addis Ababa for high-level consultations on Darfur.

The parties authorize the UN and the AU to restart the political process, strengthen the ceasefire, and make peacekeeping more effective.

December – The Secretariat of the Darfur-Darfur Dialogue (DDDC) begins operations.

December – The secretary-general appoints Jan Eliasson to the position of special envoy for Darfur.

2007

January – The AU rejects Sudan's second bid to chair the organization.

February – The Joint Mediation Team, consisting of special envoys on Darfur, Jan Eliasson of the UN, and Dr Salim A. Salim of the AU, goes on its first mission to Sudan to reinvigorate the peace process.

April – The ICC pre-trial chamber issues arrest warrants for Ahmad Muhammad Harun, who served as Sudan's minister of state for the interior from April 2003 to September 2005, and former Janjaweed senior commander Ali Kushayb.

May – The special envoys finalize the roadmap for peace negotiations on Darfur.

May – Mr Rodolphe Adada, former foreign minister of the Republic of Congo, and General Martin Luther Agwai, former army chief of Nigeria, are formally appointed as joint UN–AU special representative and force commander, respectively, of the proposed hybrid mission.

June – The UN and AU Special Envoys on Darfur present their combined report and roadmap on Darfur to the UN Security Council.

June – The Government of Sudan endorses the proposal to deploy an AU–UN hybrid operation in Darfur.

July – Mr Adada assumes charge as the head of AMIS in Khartoum pending assumption of duties as head of the hybrid mission.

July – The UN and AU special envoys on Darfur convene a meeting of Darfur stakeholders in Tripoli, Libya. The meeting endorses the AU–UN to lead the peace process as well as the roadmap on Darfur.

July – The UN Security Council adopts Resolution 1769 authorizing an international peacekeeping force in Darfur under Chapter VII of the UN Charter.

August – The UN and the AU sign the additional protocol on the heavy support package (HSP) in Addis Ababa, Ethiopia.

October – Political Negotiations on Darfur commence in Sirte, Libya.

December – Transfer of authority from AMIS to the AU–UN Hybrid Operation in Darfur (UNAMID).

2008

January – The joint United Nations–African Union hybrid force (UNAMID) takes over peacekeeping responsibilities in Darfur from the African Union Mission in Sudan (AMIS).

March – Dakar Agreement between Chad and Sudan on the normalization of their relations.

May – Omdurman and Khartoum attacked by JEM.

June – Djibril Bassolé, foreign minister of Burkina Faso, is chosen as joint AU–UN mediator for the AU–UN peace talks, replacing the joint mediation team of Salim Ahmed Salim and Jan Eliasson.

July – Indictment of President al-Bashir by the chief prosecutor of the ICC.

November – Sealed indictment of Darfur rebel commanders over the Haskanita attack on AU peacekeepers.

2009

February – Agreement of Good Will and Confidence Building for the Settlement of the Problem in Darfur (signed by GoS and JEM in Doha, Qatar).

March – ICC arrest warrant was issued against Sudanese President Omar al-Bashir. Sudanese government revokes licences of and expels ten international nongovernmental organizations immediately following the arrest warrant.

July – The AU summit in Sirte, Libya, issued a decision that AU members should not cooperate with the ICC in serving its arrest warrant against Sudanese President Omar al-Bashir.

2010

January – Professor Ibrahim Gambari, formerly UN under-secretary-general and special advisor to the secretary-general on Iraq, formally assumes his duties as UNAMID's new Joint Special Representative (JSR).

February – The Government of the Sudan and the Justice and Equality Movement (JEM) sign the Darfur ceasefire agreement in Doha, Qatar.

April – Sudan's first democratic national and regional elections held in 24 years. Omar al-Bashir wins 68.24 percent of the national votes. Salva Kiir Mayardit wins 92.99 percent of the votes for president of the country's southern region.

July – The ICC issues a second arrest warrant for Sudanese President al-Bashir, this time on charges of genocide.

November – The registration process begins for the referendum on South Sudan's self-determination. A total of 13 registration centres open in the Darfur states.

December – The Sudanese government's negotiating team pulls out of the Doha peace process.

ACKNOWLEDGMENTS

I would like to thank the Moshe Dayan Center for Middle Eastern and African Studies, the Tami Steinmetz Center for Peace Research, Tel Aviv University, the Minerva Center for Human Rights, Tel Aviv University, the Open University of Israel, and the Vital Capital Fund for their financial and academic support.

I would like also to thank my editor, Renée Hochman, for her dedication and patience, and Ofir Winter, my research assistant, for his intensive efforts. Above all, I would like to thank the moral and intellectual support of my beloved family – my husband Eyal and my daughters, Noa, Mika, and Tamara.

INTRODUCTION

Since the establishment of the Organization of African Unity (OAU) in 1963, the principle of non-intervention in the internal affairs of independent states has been a focal point in African discourse on unity. Two events that occurred early in the twenty-first century marked a significant change in African discourse on intervention in intrastate conflicts. The first was the establishment of the African Union (AU), a pan-continental organization that replaced the OAU in 2002. The second event was the outbreak of the conflict in Sudan's Darfur region. The connection between these events was revealed in the 2004 AU resolution to send an observer force to Darfur. Established in May 2004, the African Union Mission in Sudan (AMIS) deployed its first contingents in Darfur in June of that year. The mandate of AMIS, considered the first pan-African peacekeeping effort, was extended several times, until it was finally replaced by UNAMID, a joint UN–AU force.

This book analyzes the changes in African discourse on intrastate conflicts triggered by recent changes. Exploration of the historical context of this discourse and its response to earlier conflicts such as the genocide in Rwanda makes it possible to assess continuity and change in African discourse within the present conflict in Darfur. This examination concentrates on the changes in approach that were revealed through the AU's intervention in Darfur compared to previous cases of intervention (or non-intervention) in intrastate conflicts, and analyzes the manifestation of these changes in diplomatic efforts and action on the ground.

This book, which offers a comprehensive study of the impact of AU intervention in Darfur on contemporary attitudes on state sovereignty versus intervention in intrastate conflicts, should contribute to our understanding of changes in contemporary Africa, a region that faces major developments such as democratization and new commitments to human rights, and is concurrently challenged by increasing violence and state incapacity to protect its citizens or maintain basic law and order.

The first chapter of the book introduces the African context of the evolution of the non-intervention principle, from the establishment of the OAU until the outbreak of the conflict in Darfur. Using analyses of previous cases, such as the intervention of the Economic Community of West African States (ECOWAS) in Sierra Leone and Liberia, and non-intervention by the OAU throughout the genocide in Rwanda, the first chapter of this book outlines the foundation for the historic AU decision to deploy a peacekeeping force in Darfur.

Chapter 1 also clarifies the conceptual building blocks of this book, concentrating primarily on the issue of state sovereignty versus intervention. The discussion on intervention in the internal affairs of states focuses on the principle of Responsibility to Protect (R2P),[1] whose emergence coincided with the outbreak of the conflict in Darfur. Two main issues concerning R2P should be noted. First, the International Commission of State Sovereignty and Intervention (ICISS) recognized three circumstances in which this principle should be activated: "when a particular state is clearly either unwilling or unable to fulfill its responsibility to protect", "when a particular state [. . .] is itself the actual perpetuator of crimes or atrocities", or "where people living outside a particular state are directly threatened by actions taking place there". In 2005, all three conditions clearly existed in the case of the relations between the Government of Sudan (GoS) and its Darfur region, and therefore valid grounds to implement the R2P principle in Darfur were in place. Second, one of the paragraphs of the Outcome Document, drafted by ICISS during the 2005 UN World Summit, clearly indicates that intervention in support of regional organizations is "appropriate" where "peaceful means be inadequate and national authorities are manifestly failing to protect their populations from genocide, war crimes, ethnic cleansing and crimes against humanity". Therefore, AU intervention in Sudan and the subsequent joint efforts of the UN and the AU can be considered as an important test-case of the R2P principle and its effectiveness.

Chapter 2 introduces the background to the conflict. A review of the history of Darfur through its relationship with Sudan, first as a colony and later as an independent state, is followed by an analysis of the national and regional events that led to the escalation of violence in Darfur from a resource-driven conflict to crimes against humanity. The analysis focuses on the growing mechanisms of hate and racism that led to the outbreak of the contemporary conflict, and the complex challenges these mechanisms posed for peacekeeping missions and other attempts at humanitarian intervention. The chapter also places the conflict in Darfur within the broader discussion on global governance and the new wars of the post-Cold War era.[2]

Chapter 3 describes the concrete developments that prompted the establishment of a special AU force for Darfur, and follows the Mission's operations from its initial deployment to the transition to a hybrid force. This chapter analyzes the mechanisms that played a role in the AU decision-making process on intervention in intrastate conflicts, with specific reference to the decision-making process on intervention in Darfur. Two aspects of this process are discussed in detail: (a) the relations between different AU organs that were responsible for shaping organizational policy on intervention in intrastate conflicts, such as the Assembly of the Nation, the Peace & Security Council, and the Conflict Management Division; and (b) the diverse actors and interests within the African Union that were involved in the decision-making process concerning Darfur. One issue that is discussed at length is the multiple memberships of AU member states in various pan-African organizations, such as the African Union and the League of Arab States (LAS), and subregional organizations, such as the Intergovernmental Authority on

Development (IGAD), and their formative influence on member states' positions on intervention in intrastate conflicts. That the direct involvement of these subregional organizations may be responsible for more effective intervention in intrastate conflicts is an argument that warrants careful examination.

Chapter 4 analyzes the AU's massive diplomatic efforts to devise a solution to the ongoing conflict in Darfur. AU mediation efforts were unprecedented in scope, especially during what became known as the Abuja talks, which extended over the greater part of two years, and culminated in the signing of the Darfur Peace Agreement (DPA) in May 2006. This long, exhaustive negotiation process involving numerous stakeholders highlights the complex nature of the conflict, and the unattainability of an enduring solution (proven by the ultimate failure of the DPA). Nonetheless, a detailed analysis of this process, the AU's first comprehensive effort to reach a viable solution to a complex intrastate conflict, holds important lessons for other conflicts beyond Darfur.

Chapter 5 focuses on the Government of Sudan's (GoS) reactions to AMIS's presence. The AU's over-reliance on the GoS was one of the main reasons for the organization's failure to effectively end the conflict. While this argument is clearly supported by GoS reactions to AU initiatives, this chapter illustrates how AU diplomatic efforts motivated the GoS to change its position in several cases, including its position on the transition from a continental to an international peacekeeping force in Darfur. To extend existing academic and policy literature, which is based almost exclusively on Western resources, this chapter presents a comprehensive analysis of local Sudanese resources including Internet sites and newspapers, as well as Arabic and Middle Eastern newspapers, such as *Al-sharq Al-awsat*. As such, this book offers a more balanced understanding of issues related to intervention in intrastate conflicts in general, and specifically, Sudanese reactions to intervention. It is important to note that all the translations from Arabic to English in this book are the author's.

Chapter 6 focuses on the transition from AMIS to UNAMID in 2007–8, and examines the international climate that led to the decision to establish the AMIS, the allegations that international equivocation caused the conflict to deteriorate into one of the worst humanitarian crises in recent decades, and the transition to UNAMID. Despite the lack of historical perspective necessary to comprehensively analyze the strengths and shortcomings of UNAMID, its potential as a model for a partnership between continental and international organizations in future peacekeeping missions warrants acknowledgement.

Chapters 7 and 8 discuss the impact of recent events within and beyond Sudan on UNAMID in particular and African attitudes toward intervention in intrastate conflicts in general. Since the International Criminal Court (ICC) issued an arrest warrant for Sudanese President Omar al-Bashir in March 2009, state sovereignty and intervention in internal affairs have become much more sensitive issues for both Sudanese and Africans. Chapter 7 elaborates on the different positions emerging on these issues, such as the claim against neo-colonial attitudes toward Africa and the re-emerging demand for "African Solutions to African Problems" in the case of war crimes and war criminals. Chapter 8 discusses the recent widespread anti-governmental uprisings in the Arab world (commonly known as the Arab Spring), which have contributed a new degree of relevance and complexity to the state sovereignty versus intervention debate.

As the first comprehensive effort to analyze the role of the African Union's mission in Darfur, this book hopes to create greater understanding of changing African positions on intervention in intrastate conflicts in twenty-first century Africa. Despite the intractable nature of the Darfur conflict, an analysis of the achievements and shortcomings of AMIS and UNAMID operations in Darfur since 2004, and the intensive diplomatic efforts to resolve the conflict, suggests that these intervention efforts represent a new orientation in African attitudes toward sovereignty versus intervention in intrastate conflicts. Baba Gana Kingibe, head of AMIS in 2005, stated that AMIS was the first ever African initiative of this magnitude by Africans in solidarity with their African brothers and sisters under the new AU principle of non-indifference to conflicts and related situations within member states.[3] This book concludes with a careful examination of this argument.

In its broader context, this study of African intervention in Darfur and of the ongoing operation of the peacekeeping force there offers important insights into African discourse on issues such as the legitimacy of violent and oppressive regimes, and the right to protect African citizens from grave violations of human rights.

CHAPTER 1

SOVEREIGNTY VERSUS INTERVENTION IN AFRICA: HISTORICAL AND IDEOLOGICAL BACKGROUND

In the early 1960s, at the peak of the African states' independence phase, Ghana's President Kwame Nkrumah's popular cry to establish a "United States of Africa" seemed to be facing a major challenge.[1] The second and third clauses of the Convention of the Organization of African Unity (OAU), an organization founded in 1963, dealt with the principles of non-intervention in the internal affairs of independent states and respect for state sovereignty and territorial integrity. As most African states gained independence from colonial rule, it became evident that the sovereign African states' commitment to these principles served as a source of legitimacy for their disregard of intrastate conflicts, in spite of clear evidence of grave human rights violations.[2] The OAU's unwillingness to formulate a clear joint position on such violations first emerged with regard to the Nigerian–Biafran War between 1967 and 1970, and was reflected repeatedly in the organization's response to numerous cases of intrastate conflicts in the 1970s.[3]

In the 1980s and the 1990s, however, the OAU states' fierce commitment to the principle of non-intervention developed some cracks. After close to two decades of adherence to non-intervention, critical discourse in the OAU demanded instituting a "culture of accountability" to replace the instrumental role of non-intervention in promoting a "culture of impunity" for heads of state who committed atrocities.[4] The demand to promote human rights issues instead of a commitment to the interests of the sovereign states and régimes produced the African (Banjul) Charter of Human Rights of Peoples, adopted in 1981, and the framework for an African Commission on Human Rights.[5] Despite this shift, its practical effect on OAU policy on intrastate conflicts appeared negligible.

The firm institutionalization of the OAU's norm of non-intervention was more clearly revealed during the Liberian civil war between 1989 and 1997 (and, subsequently, between 1999 and 2003). In contrast to most African states, Liberia had never been subject to European colonial rule. Nevertheless, the 144-year period of political, economic, and social domination of the Americo-Liberian ruling oligarchy (mostly freed slaves from the United States) and its combined policy of authoritarianism and ethnic deprivation, was widely considered "Black Colonialism". Thus, Samuel Doe's *coup d'état* in April 1980 was viewed as a genuine national revolution symbolizing the end of the Americo-Liberian hegemony and the transition of power to the indigenous people of Liberia.[6] Soon after the *coup d'état* it became clear, however, that the old oligarchy had been replaced by an ethnic junta that had no intention of establishing a democratic republic with equal representation for Liberia's 16 ethnic groups, and was not averse to using violent and oppressive measures to establish its dominance.

Opposition groups quickly formed to challenge the new regime's oppressive and dictatorial measures. The rebel attack of the National Patriotic Front of Liberia (NPLF), comprising Libyan-trained Liberian dissidents led by Charles Taylor, in Nimba County on 24 December 1989, was considered the starting point of Liberia's civil war. By June 1990, NPLF forces reached the outskirts of Monrovia and controlled most of the state's territory, but Taylor's promises to restore full constitutional democracy through free and fair elections and rebuild the Liberian economy were crushed almost immediately by NPLF acts of pillage and plunder among the civilian population. During that period, Prince Johnson established a second opposition group, the Independent National Patriotic Front of Liberia (INPFL). The three military forces turned on each other, leading to the total destruction of Liberia, and, as warlords dominated different parts of the country, ethnic slaughter reached a massive scale and created a huge refugee problem, which also affected Liberia's neighboring countries and raised concerns about regional stability. With the collapse of the Liberian state, and the grave internal and external implications of the situation, attention focused on the issue of who should be in charge in Liberia.

Although the then chairman of the OAU, Yoweri Museveni of Uganda, advocated intervention in the Liberian conflict, the continental organization "merely dusted up its articles on noninterference in the internal affairs of member-nations".[7] The response of the regional Economic Community of West African States (ECOWAS) was completely different. As early as May 1990, ECOWAS heads of state met in Banjul, Gambia, and established the ECOWAS Ceasefire Monitoring Group (ECOMOG). That ECOWAS was strongly committed to intervene in the Liberian domestic conflict was evident from its explanation for the establishment of a Standing Mediation Committee:

> The wanton destruction of human life and property and the displacement of property [. . .] the massive damage of various forms being caused by the armed conflict to the stability and survival of the entire Liberian nation; and concern [. . .] about the plight of foreign nationals, particularly citizens of the Community who are seriously affected by the conflict; and considering that law and order in Liberia had broken down [. . .] to find a peaceful and lasting solution to the conflict and put an end to the situation which is seriously disrupting the normal life of innocent citizens in Liberia.[8]

ECOMOG's mission in Liberia was to achieve an immediate ceasefire, establish an interim administration in Monrovia, and set in motion a process of nation wide elections that ECOMOG would also monitor;[9] yet it soon became clear that the cease fire monitoring and diplomatic efforts were insufficient to resolve the chaotic situation in Liberia. In July 1990, a blueprint for an ECOWAS military intervention was announced, and the first ECOMOG force landed in Monrovia the following month. The force's failure to control the situation on the ground paved the way for United Nations Security Resolution 866, adopted in September 1993.

> Since the role foreseen for UNOMIL [United Nation Observers Mission in Liberia] is to monitor and verify the implementation of the [Cotonou] Agreement, its concept of operation necessarily must be parallel of that of ECOMOG [. . .] UNOMIL would thus [. . .] deploy observer teams in concert with ECOMOG deployment, including border crossings, airports and seaports [. . . In short], UNOMIL and ECOMOG would collaborate closely in their operations.[10]

This resolution was considered precedential as it determined a joint framework of cooperation between the UN and ECOWAS, and, more broadly, it created a foundation for coordination between international and regional organizations regarding intervention in domestic conflicts in Africa. While an evaluation of the failures and successes of the joint ECOMOG–UNOMIL (United Nations Observer Mission in Liberia) force is beyond the scope of this book,[11] several lessons from this case are important for an understanding of future developments. First, as the first intervention by a regional organization in a domestic conflict, the joint ECOMOG–UNOMIL force defined a basic framework for future interventions. Second, internal controversies and acrimony within ECOWAS, such as the conflicting views of Côte d'Ivoire and Burkina Faso on the legitimacy of intervention in internal conflicts, was one of the main causes of the intervention's ineffectiveness, and consequently prolonged the civil conflict and its devastating consequences.[12] The polarized debate over the intervention's legality and procedures, which ultimately undermined ECOWAS's efforts to protect civilians, recurred in subsequent cases of intervention in intrastate conflicts, including the African Union (AU) intervention in Darfur. Finally, as the first relatively successful partnership between a regional African organization and the UN since the failure of the United Nations Operation in Congo (UNOC) in the 1960s, the Liberian case offers a useful empirical benchmark for evaluating subsequent cases of task-sharing between the UN and the regional organization, such as in Sierra Leone.[13]

In fact, African intervention in the civil conflict in Sierra Leone, which lasted from 1991 until 2002, reflected many of the achievements and failures of Liberia. Similarly to other colonies, the small former British colony in West Africa suffered from over-exploitation of its natural resources and underdevelopment. After its independence in 1961, Sierra Leone experienced political instability, poor economic development, and insufficient external aid, even compared to other African states, and, by 1991, Sierra Leone had dropped to lowest position on the UN Human Development Index.[14] That year, a group named the Revolutionary United Front (RUF), led by former army corporal Foday Sankoh and supported by Charles Taylor of Liberia, instigated massive attacks against civilians. The rebels' ideological motives, which initially focused on justice and democracy, were soon channeled into attempts to seize control of the country's economic resources, especially its rich diamond fields. By 1995, the year the National Provisional Ruling Council was installed, country wide destruction reached overwhelming proportions, with thousands of killings, and hundreds of thousands of refugees and internally displaced persons (IDPs). The devastation not only crushed the economy, which racked up an external debt equal to 177 percent of the GNP, but also caused the total destruction of infrastructures, including 70 percent of the country's schools and the almost total elimination of healthcare centres.[15] RUF's horrific violence against civilians was characterized by barbaric acts that included the widespread use of sex slaves, child soldiers, and especially mass amputations of civilians, which came to be known as the symbol of that war.[16]

Despite grave reports of humanitarian violations in Sierra Leone, the UN refused to acknowledge the situation there as a "complex political emergency"[17] that requires a system-wide aid response by the international community that might include coordination and collaboration between UN agencies, donor governments, NGOs, and military establishments. Moreover, the UN allocated only a limited amount of financial aid to the country, an act that caused relief agencies to refer to the situation in Sierra Leone as the "forgotten emergency".[18] In stark contrast to international unwillingness to act in Sierra Leone, a South African mercenary company called Executive Outcomes deployed a small force to Sierra Leone in 1995. With its superior equipment and training, the force pushed back RUF fighters from key areas such as Freetown and the diamond fields within weeks. This small force proved the importance of an immediate response in the early stage of the conflict, and had the November 1996 Abidjan ECOWAS peace negotiators not demanded their expulsion, the Executives Outcomes might have made a difference in ultimate resolution of the conflict. Analyzing the subsequent developments in Sierra Leone, Ian Smillie and Larry Minear admitted in retrospect that the force's expulsion (a negotiating condition of the peace talks), compounded by the International Monetary Fund's (IMF) rejection of a request for US $1.8 million to maintain the force, was a fatal mistake. This amount later proved to be the daily cost of maintaining peacekeeping forces in Sierra Leone.[19]

The important lessons learned from international inaction in the initial phases of the civil war and failure to support a successful intervention proved to be relevant for future conflicts for several reasons.[20] First, from a regional perspective, the civil war in Sierra Leone clearly illustrated the dangers of a spillover effect. From the onset it was evident that the conflict in Sierra Leone was interwoven with the conflict in Liberia. Close ties between Charles Taylor and the RUF fueled the Sierra Leone war to create what was described as a "post-Cold War proxy war".[21] The growing number of refugees seeking asylum in Sierra Leone's neighbouring countries was another aspect of the regionalization of this internal conflict. As such, ECOWAS felt compelled to provide solutions to these acute problems to prevent the conflict from spilling over beyond state borders; the organization's commitment to resolve the IDP problem also relates to the second lesson.

Second, "African Solutions to African problems" became a rallying cry in response to the international community's failure to address the growing refugee and IDP population, control widespread hunger and disease, and stop unchecked violence in Sierra Leone. The UN Security Council was unable to pass effective resolutions concerning Sierra Leone, and only partially carried through on its financial promises. United States mediation efforts led to the dubious Lomé Agreement of 1999, forcing Sierra Leone President Tejan Kabbah to include RUF fighters as potential members of the government, award an "absolute and free pardon and reprieve to all", and grant the vice presidency to RUF commander Foday Sankoh. Such results reinforced the appreciation that Africans must be more active in their own affairs.[22] The "African solutions to African problems" cry was soon translated into the establishment of ECOMOG II in 1999, and the ECOWAS Peace Plan for Sierra Leone was announced the following year in Conakry. Still, it remained debatable whether the "African solutions" cry was more than a hollow slogan. The civil war in Sierra Leone ended only with the establishment in 1999 of the United Nation Mission in Sierra Leone (UNAMSIL),[23] and direct British military intervention, and not as a result of African efforts.[24]

Third, an analysis of the relations within ECOWAS and the organization's policy on Sierra Leone demonstrated the importance of cooperation within regional organizations and its impact on the effectiveness of intervention. Nigerian dominance in ECOWAS dictated the country's prominent role in the diplomatic efforts to settle the conflict, as well as its contribution to ECOMOG troops and financial aid. In some cases, Nigeria's dominance drew criticism from other ECOWAS members such as Ghana. Nigeria's pro-democratic intervention, reflected in its promise to reinstate President Kabbah in 1998, sparked fierce criticism against the efforts of a military regime (Nigeria) to impose democracy on another state.[25] Today, after more than a decade of democracy in Nigeria (and elsewhere in Africa), it is important to re-examine interventions of this type and their significance as precedents for the future.

The case of Sierra Leone offered further evidence of the marginalization of Africa's security needs in the post-Cold War era, particularly compared to international attention and peacekeeping efforts directed to Kosovo and East Timor in the same period.[26] From this perspective, the cry for "African solutions" expressed a genuine need to resolve Africa's internal security needs. It is not surprising that it was the genocide in Rwanda in 1994, rather than the violent conflicts in Liberia or Sierra Leone, which appears to be the major event responsible for changing African attitudes toward the principle of non-intervention.

The events in Rwanda differed from previous cases of intrastate conflicts in post-colonial Africa in their intensity and their cruelty: In a span of approximately 100 days, more than 800,000 Tutsis (and Hutus suspected as moderates) were murdered. The background and the events surrounding the genocide in Rwanda are widely discussed elsewhere.[27] While these events triggered an international debate on the international community's responsibility to protect civilians in the event of grave violations of human rights, an analysis of intervention patterns in the case of Rwanda confirms that the criticism directed against the international community's conduct was justified. Although international efforts to prevent the ethnic clashes had been in place before the conflict in Rwanda escalated to genocide, during the actual perpetration of the atrocities the international community ignored its commitment to the "Never Again" promise, and failed to uphold its commitment to "prevent and to punish" genocide.[28]

The first United Nations Assistance Mission for Rwanda (UNAMIR), a force of 2,500 peacekeepers, was established in 1993, when the Arusha Accords were signed between the rival groups in Rwanda. UNAMIR's mediating efforts, however, proved to be incapable of stopping the growing ethnic hatred that rapidly erupted into genocide. In UN headquarters, reports from the UNAMIR force were received in many cases with indifference: When UNAMIR commander General Romeo Dallaire sent a fax to UN headquarters in January 1994 warning of an impending genocide in Rwanda and stressing that the Hutu government was compiling lists of Tutsis and training militia men to kill them, his superiors in New York dismissed his concerns.[29]

On 6 April, the plane carrying Rwandan president Juvénal Habyarimana was shot down in an attempted assassination, an event that allegedly triggered the genocide. Following that event, ten Belgian peacekeepers were disarmed, tortured, and shot and hacked to death. They had been told not to resist violently by the UN force commander, as this would have breached their mandate. In response, Belgium decided to withdraw its peacekeepers from UNAMIR. The UN Security Council spent eight hours discussing the Rwandan crisis, but the resolution condemning the killing omitted the word "genocide": had the term been used, the UN would have been legally obliged to act to "prevent and punish" the perpetrators.

Despite clear evidence of a mass murder and the growing waves of refugees from Rwanda to its neighboring countries, it was not until 17 May that the Security Council admitted that acts of genocide may have been committed and adopted a resolution to send 6,800 troops and policemen to Rwanda with powers to defend civilians.[30] Ironically, even this relatively modest force was never deployed due to a disagreement between the UN and the United States over funding for the soldiers and their equipment.

Generally speaking, the American administration's approach to involvement in humanitarian missions in Africa was deeply connected to the failure of Operation Restore Hope in Somalia, and the death of American soldiers there in 1992 (discussed in Chapter 6 and 8).[31] As a result, US involvement in the activities of the UN and other humanitarian organizations in Rwanda remained limited. Moreover, the United States was one of the main brokers behind the Security Council's decision to reduce UNAMIR from 2,500 troops to 250, retaining only a small force to broker a ceasefire agreement between Rwandan government forces and the Rwandan Patriotic Front (RPF).[32] This decision was adopted only days after the plane carrying Rwandan president Habyarimana was shot down. Many observers, including General Dallaire himself, claimed that the presence of a force of at least 5,000 personnel with a broader mandate and sufficient equipment could have made a significant difference to the Rwandan genocide.[33]

The internationalization of the lessons of the Rwandan genocide was part of the broader post-Cold War discourse on state sovereignty versus intervention in internal affairs, and the derived concept of humanitarian intervention. International criticism of the OAU's failure to respond effectively to the Rwandan genocide[34] compelled African state leaders to reconsider their commitment to the principle of non-intervention. The principle of state sovereignty advocated by the OAU had a long history: This principle of international political order was established by the Treaty of Westphalia of 1648 and was reconfirmed by the 1933 Montevideo Convention on the Rights and Duties of States. With the establishment of the UN after World War II, the principle of respect for state sovereignty was extended beyond the frontiers of the Western world. Article 2(1) of the UN Charter referred to the sovereign equality of all organization members, thus abolishing the previous dichotomy between "insiders" (the imperial powers exerting dominance) and the "outsiders" (the colonies dependent on decisions by imperial masters), because virtually every person on earth had become a citizen of a sovereign state.[35]

Interwoven with the issue of respect for state sovereignty was the question of what was entailed in the jurisdiction of the member states. Article 2(7) provided that "Nothing contained in the present Charter shall authorize the United Nations to intervene in matters that are essentially within the domestic jurisdiction of any State or shall require the Members to submit such matters to settlement under the present Charter"; yet, what is "*essentially* within the domestic jurisdiction" remained to be clarified. Specifically, Article 2(7) failed to define whether respect for state sovereignty and state jurisdiction automatically serves as a barrier against intervention in a state's internal affairs even when a state fails to uphold its responsibility to protect its citizens.

Thomas Weiss argued, "For the first 45 years, the Charter regime privileged state sovereignty over human rights, with a significant exception of white-minority rule in Rhodesia and Apartheid in South Africa. But the balance shifted in the 1990s."[36] The changes in the discourse on state sovereignty versus intervention in domestic affairs were the result of the changing international order in the post-Cold

War era: The disintegration of the Soviet Union and Yugoslavia triggered a re-evaluation of issues related to the sanctity of borders and illegitimacy of secession.

Another change in this debate resulted from a decline in interstate wars that were related to superpower interests, and an increase in intrastate conflicts in the 1990s, which was considered a violent decade. The spread of intrastate violence was not limited to Africa, where conflicts erupted in Liberia, Sierra Leone, and Rwanda, mentioned above; conflicts also occurred in the Balkans and Srebrenica. Together, these conflicts emphasized the inability of failed or weak states to handle spreading acts of violence committed against their civilians. The rise in non-combat casualties during wartime attested to the growing prevalence of intrastate violence. From 1945 to 1980, civilians accounted for 64 percent of all wartime casualties; this figure rose to 90 percent in the 1990s.[37] Massive human rights violations were also accompanied by rising numbers of people fleeing areas of violence (the implications of the soaring refugee and IDP populations are discussed below, with reference to Darfur). The increasing numbers of domestic conflicts, the rise in non-combat casualties, and the soaring refugee and IDP problem promoted awareness that the changing trajectory of violent conflicts demanded that the discussion on the norm of sovereign inviolability be re-opened.

The appointment in 1993 of Francis Deng as representative of the UN secretary-general on internally displaced persons resulted in a detailed report, written with his colleague Roberta Cohen in 1998. On the need to reconsider the issue of sovereignty, they wrote:

> Sovereignty cannot be used as a justification for a mistreatment of populations. When governments fail to meet their obligations to beleaguered populations, such as internally displaced, they are expected to request outside assistance to help them fulfill their responsibilities. Should they refuse to accept such assistance, the international community can and should assert its concern, and step in when the government had failed to discharge its responsibility.[38]

The concept of "sovereignty as responsibility", asserted in Cohen and Deng's report, was further elaborated the following year in a popular article published by UN Secretary-General Kofi Annan in the *Economist*. In this article, entitled "Two Concepts of Sovereignty", Annan did not challenge the idea of sovereignty as the legitimate basis for international order, yet claimed that the legitimacy of humanitarian intervention in a sovereign state should be based on recognition of two concepts of sovereignty: the sovereignty of the state and the sovereignty of individuals:

> State sovereignty, in its most basic sense, is being redefined – not least by the forces of globalisation and international co-operation. States are now widely understood to be instruments at the service of their peoples, and not vice versa. At the same time individual sovereignty – by which I mean the fundamental freedom of each individual, enshrined in the charter of the UN and subsequent international treaties – has been enhanced by a renewed and spreading consciousness of individual rights. When we read the charter today, we are more than ever conscious that its aim is to protect individual human beings, not to protect those who abuse them.[39]

One year later, addressing the UN 2005 World Summit, Annan stated, "In essence, the problem is one of responsibility: In circumstances in which universally accepted human rights are being violated on a massive scale, we have the responsibility to act."[40] Such observations by Cohen, Deng, and Annan on the limits of sovereignty and the right to intervene expressed the shifting nature of the discourse on humanitarian intervention, and the emergence of Responsibility to Protect (R2P) doctrine.

Although this principle is not grounded in a generally accepted legal foundation for humanitarian intervention, the concept has several potential, albeit tenuous, sources of legal support in international law, including Article II of the UN Charter. Even the Charter itself employs the term "use or threat of force" instead of "intervention". Thomas Weiss asks:

> Did the Charter's prohibitions on the unilateral or use of force prohibit intervention altogether, or was intervention subsumed by the system of collective use of force? Was there an interpretation of the term "intervention" that would render the concept an exception to the Charter's prohibition on the use of force against the territorial integrity and political independence of a state? Does the Charter prohibit the use of force without the authorization of the Security Council even under exceptional circumstances?[41]

The Cold War balance of power, with much of the world aligned with one of the two superpowers, tended to restrict the extent of intervention in intrastate conflicts in order to prevent the escalation of domestic disputes into larger confrontations. The few cases of intervention in the Cold War era can be classified as one of two types: In the first category, which includes interventions such as Belgium's intervention in the Congo (1960) and the United States' intervention in the Dominican Republic (1965), interventions typically served the interests of the superpowers and their allies, and the concept of humanitarian intervention was merely an excuse for military invasion. The second category includes cases in which a stronger state invaded its weaker neighbor to overthrow a destabilizing regime, such as the case of India's invasion of East Pakistan (1971) and Tanzania's invasion of Uganda (1979). The invading country typically justified its actions as pre-emptive self-defence.[42]

Since the end of the Cold War, humanitarian intervention has become much more prevalent. The evolving role of the UN and the Security Council, no longer restrained by their former veto-induced paralysis, has resulted in a significant expansion of peacekeeping operations around the world. In contrast to the period from 1948 to 1978, when the UN deployed 13 peacekeeping missions, the UN has undertaken 47 peacekeeping operations in more than 15 countries since the end of the Cold War.[43] In addition to increased deployment frequency, UN peacekeeping missions have become better equipped and larger (several forces with 20,000 peacekeepers or more), and their mandate has been clearly defined as the protection of civilians.

In some cases, UN peacekeeping missions were deployed without state consent. In financial terms, for example, the current annual cost per operation has risen to US$1.6 billion, a stark contrast to the UN's total peacekeeping operations budget of US$300 million for the entire decade of the 1980s.[44] The signing of the Rome Statute of 1998, which led to the establishment of the International Criminal Court (ICC) and the International Criminal Tribunals (ICTs) for the former Yugoslavia and Rwanda, symbolized a new global commitment to protect civilians against the atrocities of their governments.

At the same time, numerous theories on humanitarian intervention were developed to address a wide range of related topics, encompassing both theoretical issues, such as the classification of internal conflicts (according to many international conventions genocide, but not civil war, obligates humanitarian intervention), and practical issues such as the status of refugees and IDPs.[45] These theories are discussed below, in connection to the conflict in Darfur.

Of all the concepts to emerge from humanitarian intervention theory, Responsibility to Protect is one of the most widely known doctrines, and one that developed a language of its own. The events in Rwanda, Srebrenica, and East Timor in the 1990s, combined with the new terminology regarding sovereignty as responsibility, prompted aspirations to create an effective framework to deal with cases where governments are unable to protect their populations, or where governments even instigate or participate in attacks against civilians. The term Responsibility to Protect was first coined in 2001 by the International Commission on Intervention and State Sovereignty (ICISS), which published a report entitled *The Responsibility to Protect*. The Commission, whose 12 representatives were carefully selected to equally represent the economic and security interests of both the North and the South, was co-chaired by Gareth Evans of Australia and Mohamed Sahnoun of Algeria. Canada was selected as the host country of the independent Commission to further ensure the neutrality of its operations and recommendations. The ICISS's new emphases represented a comprehensive attempt to harmonize contradicting concepts such as state sovereignty and intervention, and to reconcile state sovereignty with respect for human life.[46]

Addressing issues of state sovereignty and state responsibility to protect its citizens, the Commission's report explicitly declared:

> Sovereign states have a responsibility to protect their own citizens from avoiding catastrophe – from mass murder and rape, from starvation – but when they are unwilling or unable to do so, the responsibility must be borne by the broader community of states. The nature and dimensions of that responsibility are argued out, as are all the questions that must be answered about who should exercise it, under whose authority, and when, where and how.[47]

The Commission's recommendations were echoed in the 2004 UN High Panel on Threats, Challenges, and Change, particularly in the areas of prevention, timely response, and peace building,[48] and in the 2005 UN World Summit Outcome Document, which symbolized the transition from the concept of humanitarian intervention to the concept of R2P. This document embraces three temporal phases of the Responsibility to Protect: the responsibility to prevent, the responsibility to react, and the responsibility to rebuild. With respect to the first phase, for example, the 2005 Summit Outcome Document attempts to define events that require immediate intervention, including three categories of threat or actual use of coercion: military force, economic sanctions and arms embargos, and international criminal prosecution. The Outcome Document also stresses the importance of the immediacy of the response, and offers practical recommendations to establish early warning systems,[49] a recommendation that is elaborated in Chapter 2 in the context of the events in Darfur.

Despite hopes to draft a globally accepted document delineating the responsibilities of the international community and governments to protect their populations against various forms of atrocities, the discourse on the legal aspects of R2Pand its actual implementation still remain in an embryonic stage. Carsten Stahn, professor of International Criminal Law and Global Justice at the University of Leiden, for example, ponders whether the R2P is mere political rhetoric or an emerging legal norm.[50] Analyzing the contents of the four main documents that constitute the legal foundation for Responsibility to Protect (the ICISS Report of 2001; Report of the High-Level Panel on Threats, Challenges, and Change, entitled "A More Secure World: Our Shared Responsibility"; the report of the secretary-general, entitled "Implementing the Responsibility to Protect"; and the 2005 Summit Outcome Document), Stahn concludes that the main commitment in all these documents still leans toward the principles of the sovereign state's responsibility to protect its citizens. The debate on the conditions for intervention of outside forces in the case of weak sovereignty or even when proof of state participation in atrocities against its citizens actually exists, remains couched in ambiguity and indecisiveness.[51] Moreover, Stahn claims, no official authority has been designated to implement R2P; as a result, the Security Council retains almost exclusive discretion in implementation decisions.[52] Stahn's suggestion to examine whether the transition from the concept of humanitarian intervention to the concept of the Responsibility to Protect is merely "old wine in a new bottle" has particular relevance to Africa in the post-Cold War era.

The hope that the end of the Cold War would bring an enduring peace that would translate into economic development dissipated almost immediately in light of events in Liberia, Rwanda, and Sierra Leone, and it soon became apparent that one of the consequences of the diminishing bipolar politics was Africa's marginalization on the international community's agenda. Conflicts in Africa were now considered secondary to developments in "more important" areas, such as the former Soviet Union and former Yugoslavia in the 1990s, and Iraq and Afghanistan in the early twenty-first century. Even today, although the UN's largest peacekeeping forces and budgets are designated for Africa, these missions are still limited compared to the international forces stationed in Iraq and Afghanistan.[53] These global changes reignited discussions of the idea of "African solutions to African problems", a concept that had featured in OAU discourse in the past, yet was re-evaluated when the organization transformed into the AU.

The transformation of the OAU to the AU in 2002 signified the member states' desire to establish a more effective model for an

African Union, one that would resemble the European Union and deal more effectively with Africa's acute economic, political, and ethical problems.[54] Compared to the former organization's ambiguous commitment to the principle of "peaceful dispute settlement", the new organization seemed to have added checks and balances and other monitoring mechanisms that potentially made it a "more effective, democratic, and autonomous organization".[55]

The Constitutive Act of the AU was the core instrument for achieving goals such as peace, security, and stability in Africa. On the issue of intervention in intrastate conflicts, Article 4(h) of the Constitutive Act defined "the right of the Union to intervene in a member state pursuant to a decision of the Assembly in respect of grave circumstances, namely war crimes, genocide and crimes against humanity".[56] Another mechanism established to prevent, control, and resolve conflicts in the continent was the Peace and Security Council (PSC). Comprising 15 rotating members, the PSC was established to coordinate all responses to events involving grave human rights violations. Through the PSC, the AU also authorized the establishment of the African Standby Force (ASF), whose roles and abilities are discussed below. Despite the AU's innovative legislation and regulation, which were designed to deal with these situations, the organization's commitment to the principles of state sovereignty, territorial integrity, and state independence was not clearly defined. As Kelechi A. Kalu, director of the Center of African Studies in Ohio State University, claims, "Despite these improvements, the AU has inherited many of the problems of its predecessor."[57]

The outbreak of the conflict in Darfur was one of the first major challenges that faced the fledgling organization. The AU's decision to send a military and police force to Darfur, and the organization's declared commitment to a policy of "non-indifference", reflected changing perspectives on African unity in general, and, more specifically, changing attitudes to the commitment to the principle of non-intervention in the internal affairs of sovereign states.[58]

Based on the existing R2P documents, the conflict in Darfur appeared to meet all the conditions necessary for intervention. First, the International Commission on Intervention and State Sovereignty recognized three circumstances in which this principle should be activated: "when a particular state is clearly either unwilling or unable to fulfill its responsibility to protect", "when a particular state [. . .] is itself the actual perpetuator of crimes or atrocities", or "where people living outside a particular state are directly threatened by actions taking place there".[59] In 2005, all three conditions clearly existed in the case of the relations between the Government of Sudan (GoS) and its Darfur region, and therefore valid grounds for implementing R2P existed. Second, one of the paragraphs of the Outcome Document clearly indicates that it may be "appropriate" for regional organizations to support intervention when "peaceful means be inadequate and national authorities are manifestly failing to protect their populations from genocide, war crimes, ethnic cleansing and crimes against humanity".[60]

The case of the AU's intervention in Darfur, and the subsequent combined efforts of the UN and the AU, can be considered an important test-case for evaluating the effectiveness of regional organizations in resolving conflicts, both on their own and in collaboration with international organizations, in view of the evolving role of regional organizations in conflict resolution since the 1990s, as Janice G. Stein claimed:

> Regionalization has become an especially important focus of conflict resolution. As the UN increased its activity, so too did regional organizations. Since 1990, regional organizations have conducted ten peace operations designed to resolve conflict in Africa. Within Europe, NATO and the EU have led peace operations. Moreover, of the nine UN operations created since 1999, all but one – the "classical" operation between Ethiopia and Eritrea – were closely affiliated with regional organization and regional powers. Since the end of the Cold War, the UN has moved from becoming the primary actor to providing legitimacy for others.[61]

In the case of the AU intervention in Darfur, however, it is also important to explore whether the principle of defending civilian victims of human rights violations in sovereign states is compatible with the notion of "African solutions to African problems". In other words, did the decision to send an African force to Darfur create a genuine change in African attitudes on non-intervention in the internal affairs of the African states, or was the AU intervention in Darfur merely another effort by this pan-continental organization to create an appearance of intervention, while effectively defending the legitimacy of the Sudanese government and condoning the perpetration of war crimes, and even genocide, in Darfur? To address this complicated question, some historical background to the development of the conflict in Darfur is warranted.

CHAPTER 2

DARFUR: FROM RESOURCE-BASED CONFLICTS TO CRIMES AGAINST HUMANITY

Obscurity surrounding early rumours of an armed conflict developing in Darfur created a sense of confusion in global consciousness for two main reasons. First, the name "Darfur" had low recognition worldwide. The region had been occasionally mentioned in global communications with reference to sporadic events, such as the intervention of Libya and Chad in Sudan, and the spread of famine in the Sahel. Second, in the same year, 2003, peace talks were taking place between Sudan's two warring factions: the northern Sudan government and the southern Sudan People's Liberation Movement (SPLM) in Naivasha, Kenya. The hopes for ending one of the longest (1955–72 and 1983–2005) and most brutal civil wars in post-colonial Africa created a "feel-good factor" that helped the Sudanese government refute initial rumors about an armed conflict developing in its western region.[1]

In the first few months of 2004, news about the escalation of violent clashes in Darfur appeared in the global media with increasing frequency.[2] Clashes between the Government of Sudan (GoS) and two local Darfur groups, the Sudan Liberation Army (SLA) and the Justice and Equality Movement (JEM), were becoming more intense. The GoS initially responded to SLA victories directly, through air raids on Darfurian villages, and indirectly, through involvement in the activities of the quasi-governmental Janjaweed militias.[3] In spite of repeated efforts by the African Union and the international community to put an end to the crisis in Darfur, the conflict still continues today. Since its outbreak, the conflict in Darfur has caused the loss of lives of an estimated 250,000 to 400,000 individuals and has created more than two million refugees and IDPs. The extent of casualties, combined with evidence of ethnic cleansing, has branded the crisis in Darfur as one of the gravest humanitarian crises in the first decade of the twenty-first century.[4]

The international media tends to portray the conflict as a struggle between "Arabs" and "Africans", reflecting a rather simplistic and dichotomous understanding of the roots of conflict in Darfur. In practice, however, "One finds that Darfurians, like their co-nationals in northern Sudan, consist of many shades of blackness, varying degrees of religious adherence to the Islamic tenets decreed by theocratic leaders in Khartoum, and varying claims to 'Africanity' and 'Arabness'."[5] Influential political scientist and commentator Mahmood Mamdani argued, "The problem with the public discussion of Darfur and Sudan is not simply that we know so little; it is also the representation of what we do know."[6] To introduce a more nuanced perspective of the roots of the present conflict, Alex de Waal, a well-known scholar on Sudan, suggests focusing on Darfurian identity, with reference both to the history of Darfur and to its position within the greater geographical and political entity of Sudan.[7]

The existence of Darfur as a sovereign political entity can be traced to the late Middle Ages. In the seventeenth century, Fur leader Sultan Suleiman (*Solung-dungo*; literally, "pale face") led Fur warriors in a series of battles from the mountains to the plains, and occupied and Islamized the local population. The massive occupation led to the establishment of the Keyra Fur Sultanate, which was accompanied by cultural assimilation of the Fur identity.[8] The Darfurian polity has thus from the onset been dominated by a fluctuating interplay of ethnic and religious identities.

As in other political entities in Africa and elsewhere, the population of Darfur is a mixture of people who are considered the original inhabitants of the land (such as the Fur) and various waves of immigrants. Despite Darfur's relative isolation, created by the Sahara Desert and by the malaria- and tsetse-stricken Kordofan region, ties between Darfur and the outside world have existed for thousands of years, both with the West, through the trans-Saharan trade route, and with the Egyptian oasis to the east. Islam pervaded Darfur from both directions. In contrast to the first wave of Islamic conquests in North Africa in the seventh century, which established communities both orthodox and Arabized, the gradual and decentralized nature of Islamic incursion into Darfur (and Sudan in general) embodied diverse Islamic influences and approaches to the relations between Islam and the "other", especially the African. These ancient approaches still feature in contemporary discourse about "Arabs" and "Africans" in Darfur.

In the first centuries of Islam, the term *bilad al-Sudan* (the land of Sudan) referred to the "land of the black man", an area that was typically considered coinciding with sub-Saharan Africa. This geographical distinction was also synonymous with the religious distinction between *dar al-Islam* (the land under Islam) and *dar al-harb* (the land under the sword), and the social distinction between the believer, the *kufr* (un-believer), and the *ʿabid* (slave). As enslavement was prohibited among Muslims within *dar al-Islam,* the vast "land of Sudan" provided a constant supply of slaves for the great Arab empires. At the same time, Islam gradually penetrated the Darfur region through waves of migration from the al-Jazeera (Nile Valley) area and from the west African kingdoms of Kanem, Bornu, and Sokoto. These waves of migration created local identities that were defined both racially, such as the Arab-descended Baggara and African-descended Zaghawa, and vocationally, such as the distinction between Arab nomads and African farmers. Until the nineteenth century, relations between racial-ethnic groups were determined by resource-based conflicts over land, water, and grazing plots. Sufi Islam, which prevailed in this region, bridged the gaps between orthodox Islam and traditional beliefs and customs to create a hybrid ethno-racial society in Darfur.[9] The sovereign political entity of Darfur gradually became an African "divine kingdom" and, at the same time, an Islamic polity.

In the nineteenth century, Sudan lost its political sovereignty, first to Egyptian occupation and subsequently to joint Egyptian–British rule. Although Darfur retained its political independence, Sudan's loss of sovereignty had a significant impact on Darfur, especially with regard to its socio-ethnic composition. Two major groups that migrated to this area gradually transformed the traditional patterns of co-existence in Darfurian society. The first were the riverine *awlad al-bilad* (the children of the land), mostly merchants from the al-Jazeera area. The importance of this group to future developments in Darfur is discussed below in this chapter. The second group comprised migrants from West Africa, notably Hausa traders and Fulani holy men and pilgrims, locally named *fallata*. Many west Africans who resented the British occupation fled to Darfur, others were imported there as agricultural workers or chose to remain there en route to Mecca. It was the "holy men" of this group who spread Sufism, which fused a millennial perception and an anti-colonial agenda, a combination that influenced the establishment of the Mahdiyya movement (1883–98) in Sudan. This movement was one of the reasons that British attention focused on Darfur.[10]

Initially, British colonial interests lay in the Nile Valley, and Darfur was considered a peripheral territory, annexed only in 1916 to discourage expansion of the Mahdiyya movement in Darfur, and as a pre-emptive move to thwart French demands to annex Darfur to their colony in Chad.[11] Applying a divide-and-rule policy, British concerns of ethnic chaos prompted the Native Administration to delineate internal districts, or *dar*, some of which had an ethnic basis, while others were completely arbitrary.

Darfur's fragmented post-1916 political composition seemed uniquely suited for implementing the British colonial system of Indirect Rule and Native Administration. British officials indeed invested extensive efforts to establish ties with and delegate authority to local *shaykhs* and *nazirs*, creating, in the words of G. D. Lampen, the governor of Darfur in the 1920s, "an orgy of fining and imprisonment, when the most flagrant injustice and nepotism and selling of posts were allowed".[12] Yet, in addition to bad practices of government, it seems that the worst legacy of the British rule in Darfur was its blatant failure to provide for the future and its inaction in education and economic development, which ultimately led to acute underdevelopment in Darfur.

Indeed, it seems that the legacy of four decades of British colonial rule in Darfur concentrated in two areas: the formalization of internal boundaries and underdevelopment. According to de Waal,

> The British conquest of Darfur [...] represented a clear break with the past. Darfur was ruled by an external Leviathan which had no economic interest in the region and no ideological ambition other than saving of trouble. Darfur was annexed when the basic determinants of British policies in Sudan had already been established, and the main decisions were all taken with scant reference to Darfur.[13]

The consequences of Darfur's underdevelopment were clearly revealed in the 1955 census, considered to be Sudan's first scientific national census.[14] According to the census results, Darfurians comprised almost 18 percent of the population in North Sudan and 13 percent of the Sudan's total population. From an ethno-religious perspective, the census revealed that "375,000 of Darfur's people were Arabs (of whom, 269,000 were Baqqara) and 785,000 were 'Westerners' (Fur, Masalit), and that Arabic had become the first language of roughly one-third of those considered ethnic Fur."[15] The census also revealed the full extent of Darfur's marginalized development, even compared to other impoverished areas of Sudan. "In terms of the highest school attended (by people over the age of puberty), no province in the Sudan, including even the South, had a lower percentage for intermediate school than Darfur: 0.2 percent; the figure for women was 0."[16] On the eve of independence, only three vernacular elementary schools existed in all of Darfur (in El Fasher, Nyala, and Umm Kadada). Darfurian participation rates in higher education institutions in the north were insignificant. No development plans were ever implemented during the colonial era in other areas, including advanced agriculture or transportation infrastructure.[17]

Darfur's marginalization persisted even after Sudan's independence in 1956, as national and international attention focused on the developing conflict between the North and the South. Darfur's marginalization, the low priority attributed to the region in the national interests of the independent nation, and the region's resulting underdevelopment, seem to have had little impact on its ethnic–racial inter-group relations. Indeed, it seemed that the traditionalist norms of internal migration and the patterns of economic and political patriarchy that prevailed in the pre-colonial period persisted until the late 1970s.

The civil war between the deprived South and the politically dominant North erupted even before the British ceded colonial control in 1955, and continued uninterrupted until 1972, when the first phase of the war ended. In this period, persistent impoverishment and underdevelopment were exacerbated by chronic political instability. Although a cease fire accord was signed between the rivals under the autocratic military rule of Jaafar al-Nimeiri (1969–85), and the South was, to some extent, guaranteed autonomy, it became apparent that the government of Khartoum had no practical intention of fulfilling its promises toward the South, and the civil war was renewed in 1983 and continued until 2005. This, the longest civil war in post-colonial Africa, accounted for approximately two million deaths and four million refugees and IDPs.

While the underlying causes of the ongoing civil war and the complex structure of racial/ethnic identities in the North and the South are beyond the scope of this book, there appear to be many similarities between the ethnic-racial discourse developed in the South and in the West of Sudan and its impact on the attitudes of the northern-based elites toward Sudan's "non-Arab" citizens. The affinity between the country's South and West had, in fact, already been predicted in the 1980s by John Garang, the visionary leader of the SPLA/M. He cautioned,

> It is often forgotten that the Sudan is not just North and South. The Sudan is also West, East and Center, no matter what

> definitions you wish to attach to these labels [. . .] All patriots must appreciate the reality that we are a new breed of Sudanese; we will not accept being fossilized into sub-citizens in the "Regions".[18]

Kelechi A. Kalu aptly described the situation:

> The personalisation of power by the Muslim Arabs in Khartoum and their efforts to create a homogeneous Sudanese culture without requisite development infrastructures exacerbated the needs and desire for ethnic ties and consciousness. These expectations for ethnic unity were manifested in the formation of different groups who hoped to achieve for themselves what the dominant group within the central government historically denied them-effective and significant decision-making capacity.[19]

Despite the similarities in the situation in the non-northern parts of Sudan, and the grievances of these populations toward the ruling elites, the civil wars in the South and the West were motivated by different factors. More specifically, these differences are connected to the reactions of various ethno-religious groups to the racial–religious hegemonic discourse that had emerged in Khartoum since independence. The Jellaba, the class of wealthy merchants and officials whose origins can be traced to the Nile Valley, were a thriving sector at the time of the Turco-Egyptian conquest in the nineteenth century, and they continued to prosper under British colonial rule. Through the British colonial system, the Jellaba created networks of political and economic alliances with British officials and traditional rulers, resulting in the spread of this elite group into the southern, eastern, and western districts of the colony. As a result, the Jellaba were better prepared to inherit political and state power in 1956. Their dominant discourse, characterized by Nilo-centrism and Arabism, including the group's use of Arabic as the language of instruction in schools and Islamism as the state ideology, changed little after independence. African exclusionism was illustrated in the emerging hegemonic discourse on the origins of Islam in Sudan, emphasizing its eastward origins (from the Arab peninsula and the Nile Valley), ignoring the earlier West African penetration of Islam to some parts of Sudan (such as the western part of the country), and minimizing the contribution of non-northern parts of the country to the Islamic renaissance in other periods (such as the nineteenth century Mahadiyya movement).[20]

While the inhabitants of Sudan's predominately Christian and traditionalist South expressed their rejection of the hegemonic Nilo-Islamist discourse through ideological argumentation and guerilla warfare, this discourse was not challenged by Darfurians. Though local "African" ethnic groups in Darfur, such as the Fur, Masalit, and Zaghawa, were permanently deprived of political representation, it seemed that the Darfurian interests and hopes of better integration within Sudan focused more on the socio-economic rather than ethno-racial arena. This assumption was basically valid until the mid-1980s, when ecological and political factors gradually changed the ethno-racial balance in Darfur. Climatic changes, such as desertification and drought, had affected the Sahara belt, including Darfur, since the 1970s, and these effects intensified in the 1980s. The drought in 1983–4, for example, triggered a wave of migration from south of al-Fasher to Bahr al Arab, greater in scale and permanence compared to the migrations of the 1970s.

Although deteriorating ecological conditions aggravated the competition over natural resources, traditional mechanisms of arbitration and reconciliation apparently prevailed, enabling continued coexistence in Darfur's multi-ethnic and racial society. Darfurian scholar Ali Ali Dinar argued that

> land ownership, and ethnic boundaries have been respected amicably by different ethnic groups in Darfur [...] disputes were resolved in traditional conferences (*ajaweed/mutamarat al sulh*) whose rulings were always respected and honored. Even at times when the government was involved, it served as a facilitator and not as an enforcer. Government neutrality

> contained ethnic conflicts not only in Darfur but also in Kordofan and in the south.[21]

In the 1990s, however, the situation in Darfur escalated when traditional dispute resolution mechanisms were overshadowed by regional and national factors. The implications of the adverse climatic changes on ethnic relations were described in the report of Crisis Group Africa:

> In late 2000, nomadic communities, mostly from the far north of Darfur, with some participation by cattle and camel herders from different parts of the region used force to access protected grazing land and water in the rich farming lands around Jebel Marra, Darfur's most ecologically stable zone. This aggravated a sensitive situation stemming from numerous clashes and disputes over the years between pastoralists and sedentary communities related to natural resources. As part of its Arabisation and Islamisation project, the present regime has manipulated the concept of the hakoura (tribal homeland), in the process arming some Arab groups from Darfur and neighboring countries and rewarding them with money and administrative power. Their occupation of large areas has changed the demographic nature of the hakoura, disempowering the non-Arab landowners.[22]

The regional factors that contributed to the escalation of the situation were related to the intervention of Chad and Libya in Darfur. The formalization of Sudan's borders in the colonial period had created a tangled web of interests involving the region of Darfur and the colony of Chad, establishing new political entities and dividing ancient ethnic identities, such as the Zaghawa and Bideyat, across the colonies of Sudan and Chad. The Chadian civil war, instigated by northern Muslims in 1965, was strongly connected to the region of Darfur. The Chadian rebel movement FROLINAT was established in 1966 in Nyala, South Darfur, and the ethnic affiliation between groups such as the Zaghawa on both sides of the border ensured the spillover of the Chadian civil war into Darfur, through actions such as hosting the rebels, transferring stores and ammunition, etc. The relations between Chad and Darfur were no longer concealed after Idriss Déby monopolized power in Chad in 1991. His extended network of associates, members of the Bideyat clan of the Zaghawa, became key leaders in the events in Darfur, as discussed below.[23]

The spillover of the Chadian civil war into Darfur also led to increased Libyan intervention in Sudan in general, and in Darfur in particular. While the GoS supported Hissène Habaré, his opponent Goukouni Oueddei was supported by Libya, under the leadership of Colonel Muammar al-Qaddafi. Habaré was also the West's preferred candidate to control the capital, and the rivalry between Habaré and Oueddei became a proxy war between Libya and the West. In that period, al-Qaddafi established the Islamic Legion as the vanguard of his military aspirations to establish a Saharan Empire. Proceeding to invade Chad and destabilize Sudan,[24] al-Qaddafi recruited soldiers for his incursions into Chad among the Arab groups of Darfur (although some African groups such as the Zaghawa also joined).[25]

Al-Qaddafi's intervention in Sudan and Chad in the 1970s and the 1980s had important consequences for ethno-racial relations in Darfur; a comprehensive review of his actions in this region is, however, beyond the scope of this book. Al-Qaddafi's rhetoric not only reflected Arab supremacism, but was blatantly racist, categorizing people of African origin as *zurqa* (blues), as opposed to *akhmar* (reds), people of Arab origin. Libya's ideological influence, combined with its supply of arms to Darfur, soon resulted in violent clashes between the Fur and local Arab groups. Al-Qaddafi actively supported the Arab supremacist organization known as the *Tajamu al-Arabi* (variously translated as the "Arab Gathering", "Arab Alliance", "Arab Congregation", and "Arab Congress"), led by Moussa Hilal, the future Janjaweed leader. Arguably, al-Qaddafi's rhetoric and policies contributed more to the intensifying of ethno-religious conflicts in Darfur at that time than did intra-Sudanese influences.

The GoS was unable to overcome the effects of Darfur's chronic marginalization and underdevelopment, and its attempts to relieve the famine crisis of its Western region in the 1980s were ineffective.

The government in Khartoum preferred to ignore the local government's warnings about the impending famine, focusing instead on the campaign "We eat what we grow". The waves of famine in 1984–5 took their toll, leaving in approximately 95,000 dead.[26] The acute competition over water and land resources heightened ethno-racial differences, and fueled mechanisms of hatred and demonization of the "other". The second half of the 1980s also marked the emergence of organized armed groups that would subsequently play a role in the contemporary conflict in Darfur. By 1990, the armed militia of Fur, which operated against Chadian militias, supported by local Darfurians of Arab and Zaghawa origin, was 12,000 strong. Some groups of Arab Darfurians, on their part, reinforced their Janjaweed ties. *Janjaweed* literally means "a man with a gun on a horse", and the term traditionally referred to outlaws and highwaymen from Chad, whose origins could be traced to the local clans, mainly the camel-herding Abbala Rizeigat in the 1920s. These Janjaweed outlaws were a sporadic and fluid group, even when fighting against the local Fur militias throughout the 1980s in clashes that portended the contemporary conflict, including its tactics of mass killings and village burning.[27]

The waves of violence and the growing divisions in Darfurian society were not merely a reaction to the heightened competition over access to dwindling natural resources, but also a response to the attitudes of the Islamist revolutionary regime toward Darfur after 1989. With the Islamic revolution of 1989, it seemed that the new agenda would bind together the Muslims of Darfur under a new national order. This feeling was strengthened when Hassan al-Turabi, the ideological leader of the Islamist revolution, claimed that all Darfurians, including the Fur, Zaghawa, and the *fallata*, are equal citizens of the Sudanese *umma*.[28] Well aware of the need to instill a new mode of belonging among Darfurians, he appointed a Darfurian, Ali al Haj Mohamed, as his deputy, and attempted to establish a popular base for the revolutionary regime by convincing Darfurians that colour-blind Islamism would eventually trump Arabism, and that Islamic faith would be the basis for the genuine integration of Darfur in the Sudanese state. Al-Turabi's intentions were, however, proven wrong by a rebellion initiated by Fur activist Daud Yahya Bolad in the early 1990s. This event illustrates many features of the ethnic and racial divisions that developed in Darfur since 2003, and therefore a more detailed explanation of the roots and development of the rebellion is warranted.

Waves of drought and famine in the early 1990s, combined with new Arab supremacist ideology, encouraged Fur politicians to believe that the time had come for a more decisive protest against their deprivation and marginalization. Bolad, the first non-northern National Islamic Front candidate for president of the Khartoum University Students Union and a close ally of the Front's leader, Hassan al-Turabi, was considered to be on the fast track to national political leadership. Bolad, however, criticized al-Turabi's silence at Libyan-backed attempts to instigate violence in Darfur. When Bolad came to view al-Turabi as merely one of many northern supremacists, he turned to find other allies. After he was unsuccessful in gaining the support of Chadian President Hissène Habré, Bolad met with SPLA leader John Garang in Ethiopia and, in 1990, Bolad decided to join the Sudan People's Liberation Army (SPLA). He received military training from the SPLA in South Kordofan, and was appointed the political commissar of an SPLA military expedition into Darfur that was launched in November 1991.

From a military perspective, the results of the expedition were disastrous. Facing a Beni Halba Arab militia, the expedition was immediately defeated, Bolad was killed, and dozens of Fur villages were burned. The long-term results of that expedition were even more disastrous for the Fur. Journalist and Sudan expert Julie Flint claimed that from this moment the Fur became the main enemy of the National Islamic Front (NIF), which later became the country's ruling party: The organization increased its support to the Arab militias around Jebel Marra, and especially to the young leader Moussa Hilal, who would later play a critical role in Darfur developments after 2003. Bolad's failed expedition had another crucial result for future developments in Darfur: It alerted Abdel Wahid Mohamed al-Nur,[29] future leader of the SLM/A, to what might be done in Darfur.[30]

Abdel Wahid was born in Zalingei to a deep-rooted Jebel Marra Fur family. As a law student in Khartoum University, he was influenced by John Garang's vision of "New Sudan", although he rejected its ideological dimension, claiming that citizenship is more important than ideology. With the memories of the first Arab–Fur war and Bolad's failed expedition still fresh in the minds of the Fur, Abdel Wahid and several of his university friends organized a clandestine organization with financial contributions from Fur in Sudan and the Diaspora, and recruited and operated networks of Fur military and traditional leaders. As Abdel Wahid subsequently admitted, the organization's message of Fur self-defence was deliberately blurred in order to attract as much support as possible.[31] The conditions after 1995 were especially ripe for such a message, since the government had divided Darfur into three voting districts in a move that was perceived by locals, especially Furs, as a deliberate effort to forestall their chances to achieve political dominance in Darfur.[32] Abdel Wahid's real intentions, however, extended beyond a self-defence organization for the Fur: His aim was to create a pan-Darfurian organization that would demand a much more central role for Darfur at the Sudanese state level.

One of the lessons of Bolad's failed rebellion attempt was the necessity to integrate Arabs into the organization. "If we move without the Arabs, the government will move the Arabs against us", Abdel Wahid claimed.[33] The split between Arabs and Africans was, however, not the only challenge to a united front of the different Darfurian groups. Among the four founders of Abdel Wahid's organization, three were Fur and the other Arab (Hafiz Yousif, a Darfurian of Arab origin who specialized in *shari'a* law); none was a Zaghawa. The Fur and the Zaghawa had extensive grounds for cooperation, as the lands of both groups were threatened by armed nomads who denied them access to water and pasture. Furthermore, the Zaghawa could share their experience in anti-governmental fighting, which they had gained in their extensive involvement in the Chadian civil war, in support of their co-ethnics in Chad. Abdel Wahid managed to create a limited alliance, and Fur and Zaghawa activists met in July 2001 and swore on the Quran to work together to foil Arab supremacy. Nonetheless, the Zaghawa were the source of the two major challenges, one from within the movement and the other from without, which threatened Abdel Wahid's dominance. The internal divisions that threatened SLA unity are discussed in detail below.

The external threats were related to the internal competition to dominate the ruling party, especially the rivalry between Omar al-Bashir and al-Turabi. Since the establishment of the National Islamic Front (NIF) in 1993, al-Bashir's dominance in the revolutionary regime was evident: Under his leadership the NIF adhered to its traditional agenda of promoting Northern–Islamic hegemony, a tradition that became the target of attack in *The Black Book: Imbalance of Power and Wealth in Sudan*, published and circulated in May 2000. Demanding "justice and equality", the authors of the book tracked Northern dominance in all government agencies and powers including the police and military hierarchy, the judiciary, provincial administration, banks, and development administrations. "Every president had come from this region. Most senior ministers and generals too", the authors claimed. The authors argued that most of the Sudanese wealth and political power had been controlled by three northern tribes since independence, and criticized the NIF for its "inability to depart from established patterns of injustice".[34] The surprising popularity of the book and its impact were mentioned in William Wallis' *Financial Times* column:

> One Friday after prayers in May 2000, as many as 1,000 copies of an unremarkable A4 manuscript appeared mysteriously in mosques and other public places in Khartoum, the capital of Sudan. And not just in public places. Omar Hassan el-Bashir, the president of Sudan, found one on his desk when he returned from his devotions. Thereafter, the document, in its Arabic original, was in and out of photocopying machines across Sudan. One Sudanese academic who was involved in its translation claims that as many as 50,000 copies were eventually circulating – reaching remote and undeveloped parts of the country, where the Internet was as yet science fiction.[35]

One of the book's authors, Idris Mahmoud Logma, was interviewed by Wallis. Logma described the motives behind the decision of 15 young Muslims, most of whom were graduates of Khartoum University, to risk their lives by publishing the subversive document. Their message, he says, was designed to appeal to all marginalized Sudanese – whether of Arab, Afro-Arab, or African identity, Christian, or Muslim. This publication in fact had special significance for future developments in Darfur. Logma himself became one of the representatives of the Justice and Equality Movement (JEM), which was founded by a group of Darfurians involved in the publication. Although they were members of the Islamist party, they were becoming disenchanted with its leaders, including al-Turabi, and the NIF's failure to create a more equitable division of wealth and power. More fundamentally, they feared being singled out by the ruling party as a rebellious element in the NIF. Their fears were not groundless, as revealed in a decree issued by al-Turabi at the height of his power in the NIF party:

> The Islamists of Negro tribes became hostile to the Islamic Movement. The Islamic Front aims to support the Arab tribes by these steps: forced displacement of the Fur from Jebel Merra to Wadi Salih, followed by complete disarming of the Fur people, for good; they are to be replaced with the Mehairiya, Itaifat, and Irayqat (Arab tribes). Arms must never return to the Zaghawa, who must be moved from Kutum to Um Rwaba (North Kordofan State); the Arab tribes should be armed and financed to act as the nucleus of the Islamic Arab Alliance.[36]

This group of Darfurians began to meet secretly and establish the foundations for a new organization. A prominent figure among group members was Dr Khalil Ibrahim, a Zaghawa from the Koba clan, a former enthusiastic supporter of the NIF and al-Turabi, who even served as state minister for education in Darfur between 1991 and 1994. In early 2001, Dr Ibrahim was appointed spokesperson of the new organization, the Justice and Equality Movement (JEM), which had transformed into a military movement by the end of its first year of operations. JEM's initial close cooperation with the SLA led to several impressive Darfurian military victories against the Sudanese armed forces. Over time, however, friction and divisions between (and within) the two movements, sparked by ethnic affiliations, ideological leanings, and personal rivalries, made it almost impossible to develop united action or a united voice against Khartoum. The friction and divisions are elaborated below, with reference to the challenges they posed for AU's diplomatic efforts in the region.

The events of 11 September 2001 mark another milestone in the relations between the Sudanese state and its western province, and had a direct effect on the struggle for power in the NIF, Sudan's ruling party. In Western eyes, and especially in the view of the Americans, al-Bashir was considered pro-Western and moderate in comparison to al-Turabi, who was known for his pro al-Qaeda sympathies. In his efforts to reinforce his image in the West, and to secure the revenues from the country's fledgling oil industry, al-Bashir initiated intensive negotiations toward a peace accord between the South and the North. The Naivasha peace talks between the SPLM/A and the GoS between 2003 and 2005 culminated in the Comprehensive Peace Agreement (CPA) in 2005, ending the longest and most brutal of all African post-colonial wars. As argued above, the "feel-good factor" that accompanied this peace accord eased the GoS's dismissal of the initial rumours of violent clashes in Darfur.

In fact, the government in Khartoum was already well aware of the escalating tensions in Darfur in 2002, when a government official visited there and promised "a hundred kilometers of good roads". This declaration highlights the depth of Khartoum's misunderstanding of the region's grievances, and its perception of Darfurians as ignorant farmers. The clashes between the GoS and the two local Darfurian groups – the SLA and the JEM – continued with increasing frequency. The first attack by the two rebel groups targeted the small town of Golu on 26 February 2003, and resulted in the deaths of 200 Sudanese army soldiers. The local forces proceeded to gain other victories in other parts of Darfur later that year, including the conquest of al-Fasher airport on 25 April and the city of Kotum.

Initially, the SLA's military victories triggered direct GoS responses (in the form of air raids on Darfurian villages), and indirect responses, through GoS involvement in the activities of the quasi-governmental Janjaweed militias. Fearing rebel mobilization among the Darfur tribes, the GoS launched a security crackdown on the Fur, Massalit, and Zaghawa populations. Educated young men and people connected to the rebels by kinship or residence were detained, intimidated, tortured, and, in some cases killed. Indeed, the GoS's reaction to the rebellious forces in Darfur appeared to be motivated by panic. The panic was not merely a reaction to the rebels' military victories, or fear of an international response, whose media had begun to report the violent acts in Darfur,[37] but something deeper. Historian Gérard Prunier diagnosed the situation as follows:

> The North–South conflict has been in many of its aspects a colonial conflict, while the Darfur uprising was from the beginning much closer to a genuine civil war. And civil wars are often the most relentless forms of conflict because they involve relatives. In Khartoum, the government panicked because it suddenly felt that the Muslim family was splintering, potentially with enormous consequences.[38]

Another explanation for the severity of the GoS's response to the insurgence in Darfur was the central government's fear that the escalating situation would eclipse the peace process in southern Sudan. Interestingly enough, SPLM/A leader John Garang expressed explicit interest in extending the peace process between the North and the South to include Darfur, proposing a deployment of 10,000 SPLA troops in Darfur as part of the AU peacekeeping force.[39] However, the government's hasty rejection of his proposal was proof of its reluctance to expand the peace process to other parts of Sudan that also yearned for a more equal participation in the state. Its aversion is connected to the Turbulent State paradigm, which is discussed below.

The government in Khartoum claimed that its actions in Darfur were a local counter-insurgency response,[40] but there were many indications that the relations between the nomadic and settled populations had undergone a material change: The sedentary farmers, mostly African, came under the dual pressure of drought and competition over scarce resources with nomadic tribes, mostly Arabs, who acted with the government's indirect support, or at least the latter's blind eye. One typical incident was reported by a UNHCR team that visited Darfur in 2004:

> Another problem frequently reported is the destruction of crops by grazing cattle belonging to Arab nomadic tribes. It is currently harvest season in Darfur, but villagers in several locations were unable to bring in their crops before they were destroyed. In previous years, there has been a customary understanding for coexistence for grazing cattle and agricultural crops, but these agreements do not seem to be respected anymore [. . .]. Sheiks in Bangadid also reported crop destruction in the area, saying that in the past two years, some of the Arab tribesmen have started to appear in military uniforms and carrying weapons, arriving with their cattle in groups of four or five and threatening villagers who might protest the destruction of the crops. Since their crops were destroyed, the primary means of subsistence in this village has been collecting firewood to make charcoal for sale in El Geneina. The problem of crop destruction was also reported to UNHCR in Masteri.[41]

The GoS's violent campaign against the rebel groups in Darfur involved aerial bombarding of villages and fighter camps. In his best-seller *The Devil Came on a Horseback*, Brian Steidle, a former US Marine captain, who in September 2004 accepted an assignment as one of three US military observers for the African Union in Darfur, mentioned the frequency and intensity of the aerial bombarding he witnessed when he was stationed in al-Fasher in October 2004: "I began to notice helicopters flying around every day; GoS Mi-24 Hind attack helicopters. They went out fully loaded with weapons and returned, hours later, with empty missile pods."[42]

Another fundamental factor that contributed to the rising levels of violence against local Darfurians of African origin was Khartoum's steady (yet covert) support and arming of the local Janjaweed militias. One particularly striking example from this period was an attack on Tawila in North Darfur on 27 February 2007. Contrary to other attacks, the attack on Tawila became known internationally due to its documentation by UN officials who arrived in the area only several days after the attack, and interviewed survivors. According to the officials' report, of the town's original 14,000 residents and 9,000 refugees, they were able to locate merely 2,000–3,000 individuals, whose testimonies included horrors such as raping daughters in front of their fathers and gang rapes. They concluded by pointing an accusing finger at the government-backed Janjaweed:

> It should be finally be noted that those we speak to in Tawila town stated that government helicopters were providing ammunition to the Janjaweed during the attack which if true would be a pattern reported following other Janjaweed attacks in Darfur area. They also claimed that the Janjaweed were using Land cruisers provided by the government, and in any case it is no secret that the government has armed and trained the Janjaweed for use in the war against the SLA (even local GoS officials will admit this in private).[43]

According to Richard Cockett, Africa editor of the *Economist* and a senior lecturer of politics and history at the University of London, this report served as a tipping point for international policy makers in the UN and beyond, proving that the "arguments for keeping Khartoum happy to save the CPA, or to get more intelligence on al-Qaeda" were no longer viable.[44] Responding to changing international reactions to its deeds, Khartoum defended itself by arguing that the Janjaweed were the authentic expression of the Arab people of Darfur. The fact was that the GoS had, for several years, intensely manipulated the situation on the ground, and it had sponsored the Janjaweed militia since 2003, when Moussa Hilal, mentioned earlier, established a militia base in Misteriha in north Darfur, from where he spread his supremacist ideology and launched the attacks against African villagers, aiming to "change the demography of Darfur and empty it of African tribes".[45]

Hilal also initiated a massive recruitment of north Darfurian Arab Rizeigat tribes and Abbala (camel herders) into the Janjaweed. As both groups had no traditional land rights in Darfur, government promises of land ownership dramatically changed the traditional structure of Darfurian society, and threatened the livelihood of the local African tribes. Moreover:

> This extensive recruitment of Arab groups was complemented by support for an Arab supremacist organisation, the "Arab Gathering", which was given arms communications equipment, light artillery and military advisers. The government allowed, and often encouraged, its regular soldiers and auxiliary forces to ignore the laws of war, resulting in widespread crimes against humanity and war crimes.[46]

In the context of the emerging Darfur conflict, the claim for Arab supremacy calls for further elaboration. There is extensive evidence of the use of racist terminology in Darfur since 2003. In testimonies gathered from Darfurian women staying in refugee camps in Chad, many recounted that, while being raped, their rapists boasted that they were "sowing tomatoes". In the racist terminology of Darfur, the meaning of this phrase is that they were creating a new generation of Arabs, known in the local terminology as *akhmar* (reds), in contrast to the *zurqa* (blues, i.e., the Africans). Reports by Documenting Atrocities in Darfur, an organization that collected testimonies from over 11,000 Darfurian refugees in Chad, contained extensive evidence of a rhetoric of ethnic cleansing by the attackers of the African villages, who routinely used slogans such as "Cleaning Darfur of an African presence", and the term *'abid*.[47]

The terminology of slavery has particular significance in the context of Darfur. The historical memory related to this reference is tied to the deep-rooted relations between Arabs and Africans during different phases of the region's Islamic conquest and domination. More recently, this terminology was adopted by and assimilated into the attitudes of Khartoum's Nilo-centric elites and re-adopted by the Arabs of Darfur who sought to identify with these elites and acquire a sense of belonging to the centre of the Sudanese state, rather than to the country's backward periphery. Nonetheless, despite repeated calls for creating solidarity among the Arabs there, it is important to note that not all Arab groups were involved in the present conflict.[48]

For the African groups of Darfur, issues of identity and belonging were much more complex. Since the beginning of the conflict, it seems that African fighter groups were more strongly influenced by ethno-religious identities than by their assumed "African" identity. Ethno-religious motivations were already evident in March 2003, when Khalil Ibrahim's announcement of the establishment of the JEM was received with scorn by SLA leaders and fighters. Even the joint interests of these groups did not erase their ethno-religious differences: While the JEM recruited its supporters among the Koba clan of the Zaghawa and represented an Islamist orientation,[49] SLA supporters and fighters were mainly Fur, yet included Zaghawa and Masalit, and its orientation was more secular and more closely tied to the southern SPLM/A. These differences prevented the development of a unified front in the various efforts to resolve the conflict, as will be elaborated later.

Notwithstanding these divisions, a discourse on the African identity of the Darfurians appears to be emerging at the cultural level, which is influenced by the southern discourse on this theme, and serves as a "marker of difference" of the African inhabitants of Darfur.

Reviewing the historical roots of the ethno-racial conflict in Darfur today, it seems that there is evidence to support Alex de Waal's argument that, while the ethno-racial dichotomy did not play an essential role in historically determining the relations between the different groups in this region, it had a tremendous effect in fueling the present conflict. For many centuries, Darfurian society was hybrid in the sense that the delicate fabric of collaboration and stability continuously incorporated local and immigrant groups, notwithstanding many periods of competition over resources and domination. This pattern was gradually interrupted by Darfur's inclusion within the colony of Sudan, and subsequently within the independent state that pursued the colonial heritage regarding the North's supremacy over Sudan's other areas. The ongoing marginalization and deprivation of Darfur, and the increasing struggle over resources, combined with assimilation of racist terminology, were responsible for the escalation of the situation in Darfur "from resource-based conflicts to crimes against humanity".[50] Although the terminology of genocide does not appear in any official AU document, the AU recognized the scale and intensity of the conflict in Darfur, as well as its potential national and regional implications, which triggered an almost immediate response by the AU.

The events in the Darfur region in Sudan can be classified under the evolving category of conflicts known as the "new wars". This term typically refers to the post-Cold War wars since the 1990s, especially in Africa, characterized by changing relations between the sovereign state and the multiple internal and external actors and stakeholders, all struggling to define their position within the state. Following Phillip Cerny, Mark Duffield summarized the features of "new wars" as

> the trend toward competing institutions and overlapping jurisdictions of state and non-state interest groups; a greater fluidity of territorial boundaries both within and across states, the growing importance of identity and single issue politics; increasingly contested legal statutes, property rights and conventions; the spread of geographical and social "no go areas" where the rule of law no longer extends, and so on.

All these features, which tend to create a situation of "durable disorder",[51] appear to exist in the case of Darfur: The multiplicity of non-state actors, such as the various groups and organizations opposing the dominance of the state in this region, undermined efforts to reach an agreed solution to end the conflict. The proliferation of light weapons, another characteristic of the new wars, increased levels of violence, as did the number of actors demanding their share in the potential benefits of any future agreement.

"New wars" tend to spill over beyond their native region to other regions of the state and beyond state boundaries. "Weak states", a term that is applicable in varying degrees to most African states, have, by definition, limited ability to control their territory and maintain stable borders. In weak states, borders are permeable and frequently penetrated by goods, people, and arms. Moreover, the arbitrary borders of African states frequently divide ethnic groups, creating cross-border alliances based on co-ethnicity, economic interests (such as smuggling or access to water and food resources), or security motives, escalating in some cases to attacks against security forces and civilians across borders.[52] As mentioned, the conflict in Darfur was closely interwoven with the situation in neighbouring Chad, through the fleeing refugees from Darfur and the extension of fighting into Chad, for example. As early as the fifth meeting of the PSC in April 2004, the AU acknowledged the risk that the Darfur conflict would spill over into neighboring Chad:

> The Darfur crisis also has adverse effects on the stability of neighboring Chad, which shares a 10,000 km long border with Sudan. More that [*sic*] 110,000 refugees have fled to Chad and a number of ethnic groups affected by the conflict saddle on both side of the border.[53]

Alex de Waal opposes the classification of Darfur as a "new war", and argues that many of the characteristics of the conflict in Darfur are merely a continuation of traditional patterns of action employed by the Sudanese government to control its rebellious peripheries. Instead, de Waal proposes the Turbulent State paradigm, claiming that most Sudanese leaders, independent of their ideological or religious affiliation, or even to their mode of rule,

> have converged on the same mixture of presiding over an unstable regime that endorsed extreme violence. We should not have much confidence that simply changing the man in charge will alter this tendency. This is not to excuse criminality, but rather to ask, what it is about ruling Sudan that causes its

> leaders to behave in such a way? Part of the answer must lie in the structure of the Sudanese polity. Another part lies in the fact that the Sudanese political conditions selectively permit those with certain skills and proclivities to rise to the top.[54]

Whether we classify the conflict in Darfur as an example of a "new war" or contend that it is merely one in a series of violent eruptions on the continuum of Sudan's brutal history, the conflict's timing calls for special attention from an African perspective. Changes in African positions on intervention in intrastate conflicts prompted extensive AU intervention efforts, both on the ground and in the diplomatic sphere, to resolve the region's crisis. The next chapter describes the roots and the initial phases of this intervention.

CHAPTER 3

INTERVENTION FROM THEORY TO PRACTICE: THE AFRICAN UNION MISSION IN SUDAN (AMIS)

The desire to establish an effective African force to support multifaceted conflict resolution missions in Africa was already implied in the 2002 protocol of the Peace and Security Council (PSC) of the African Union:

> Desirous of establishing an operational structure or the effective implementation of the decision taken in the areas of conflict prevention, peace-making, peace support operations and intervention, as well as peace-building and post-conflict reconstruction, in accordance with the authority conferred in that regard by Article 5(2) of the Constitutive Act of the African Union.[1]

Article 7 empowers the PSC commissioner to submit recommendations to the AU Assembly regarding necessary interventions, including the deployment of peacekeeping missions in member states, when acts of genocide and other crimes against humanity are committed.

The new organization's desire to establish an effective conflict resolution mechanism was part of the broader process of learning the lessons from the OAU's earlier failures and ineptitude. In nearly a decade since its establishment in 1993, the PCS's predecessor, the OAU's Central Organ of the Mechanism for Conflict Prevention, Management, and Resolution, had deployed only small military observer missions to Rwanda, Burundi, and the Comoros, typically with fewer than 100 personnel per mission. These small missions suffered from many logistical and financial flaws, and had little practical effect. The Central Organ also suffered from an ungainly decision-making mechanism and lack of commitment of its members to pay their dues. As a result, even the limited budgets of these small-scale missions were mostly funded by external donors.[2]

The AU aspired to establish its PSC as a more effective mechanism for conflict resolution. Its membership was based on four criteria: peacekeeping experience, capacity to pay, financial contributions to the AU's Peace Fund, and constitutional governance commitment. Rather than the OAU's insistence on consensus in voting on substantive issues, the PSC required a two-thirds majority, and also allowed the representation of sub-regional and civil society organizations.[3] The chairperson of the AU Commission also plays an important role in this mechanism, by bringing to the attention of the PSC any threat to the internal peace and security of any member state, and taking "all initiatives deemed appropriate to prevent, manage and resolve conflicts".[4] The chairperson is also allowed to appoint special envoys from among members of various regional economic communities as well as from the five-member Panel of the Wise, another conflict resolution mechanism that was modeled after a similar ECOWAS organ.

The African Standby Force (ASF) was yet another mechanism designed by the AU to deal with African conflicts that were emerging with increasing frequency and intensity. The ASF was planned as five "regional" brigades with a total of close to 20,000 troops. Its prospective missions were peacekeeping, disarmament programmes, and humanitarian relief, and it was scheduled to commence operations by 2010, in two phases.[5] The supposed contribution of this and future peacekeeping forces in Africa was defined as early as the ninth meeting of the PSC, held on 25 May 2004:

> The importance of the establishment of the African Standby Force for effective of conflict resolution in Africa cannot be overemphasized. In a number of conflicts, often prevailing on suspicion among the parties and the complexity of the issues at stake, make the presence of a third party on the ground imperative, often in the form of a peacekeeping operation.[6]

Despite the complex efforts and long duration invested in its establishment, the ASF was unable to offer any effective assistance, military or otherwise, throughout most of the period of the Darfur conflict. In contrast, the foundation and operation of the Continental Early Warning System (CEWS) was accomplished with ease and speed. Article 5(2) of the Constitutive Act of the African Union identified the CEWS as one of the five key bodies assisting the PSC, with planning elements stationed in each of the five African regions, and a situation room located at the Conflict Management Directorate of the Union. The necessity of an early warning system of this kind was one of the preliminary lessons learned from the Rwandan tragedy, and the concept was one of the OAU's relatively beneficial legacies. The importance of an effective situation room was mentioned in the PSC resolution of 25 May 2004:

> The Situation Room, located at the Conflict Management Directorate of the Union, and responsible for (a) data collection and analysis on the basis of an appropriate early warning indicators module and (b) observation and monitoring units of the Regional Mechanisms to be linked directly through appropriate means of communications to the Situation Room, and which shall collect and process data at their level and transmit the same to the Situation Room.[7]

The decision to establish an early warning system in general and an efficient situation room in particular, to collect, analyze, and convey information on indicators of emerging conflicts was also based on the experience of regional organizations such as ECOWAS and IGAD in dealing with intrastate conflicts.[8] In the case of Darfur, it seems that previous experience facilitated efficient and immediate data collection and analysis, and allowed UN observers to collect and document personal testimonies from the local people as early as 2004. Many observers claimed that the early warning system's rapid response helped to dispel the initial obscurity surrounding events in Darfur.[9] The CEWS's numerous shortcomings were, however, revealed as the conflict persisted. As a result of a lack of expertise and skills in political analysis, raw data collected from governments or international media sources were conveyed by the CEWS without further elaboration or analysis, and over-reliance on governmental information sources, rather than civil society organizations and NGOs, led to reports based on partial and insufficient information in several cases.[10] The initial hopes and subsequent disappointment with the CEWS's performance to some extent resemble the hopes that accompanied the establishment of AMIS, as well as the subsequent disappointment.

The escalation of the armed conflict in Darfur and the gravity of the humanitarian violations there were acknowledged by the PSC in April 2004, as evident from the communiqué of its fifth meeting:

> Since the beginning of hostilities in Darfur, over a year ago, the humanitarian situation has dramatically deteriorated according to UN agencies, human rights groups attacks against civilians have increased both in scale and brutality. It is reported that over 10,000 civilians have been killed since February 2003; more than 750,000 people are estimated to have been displaced, while another 110,000 people are reported to have fled into neighboring Chad. The intensity of the conflict has also resulted in the destruction of social infrastructure, thereby exacerbating the humanitarian crisis.[11]

Prompted by the PSC's declarations, the Government of Sudan (GoS), the Sudan Liberation Army (SLA), and the Justice and Equality Movement (JEM) signed a ceasefire accord in N'Djamena, the capital of Chad, in April 2004. The negotiations and their implication for future diplomatic efforts are discussed in the next chapter.[12] Alleged violations of the ceasefire terms led to the Addis Ababa agreement of 28 May 2004, which introduced additional safeguards for the ceasefire: A decision was made to establish a Ceasefire Commission (CFC) and send a small monitoring group to the area. In June, the AU Commissioner for Peace and Security announced the deployment of the African Mission in Sudan (AMIS) in Darfur;[13] and in early July that year, the PSC announced that the number of AU Military Observers (MILBOS) would be increased to 60, with 300 soldiers to protect them.

The first AMIS contingent to arrive in Darfur included 456 personnel from ten African countries. From an African perspective it is interesting to note that Rwanda was one of the first countries that agreed to send its troops to AMIS. Barely ten years after the genocide in his country, Rwandan President Paul Kagame noted that their mandate would also include the use of force, if necessary, to protect civilians, "Our forces will not stand by and watch innocent civilians being hacked to death like the case here in 1994."[14] Memories of the Rwandan experience clearly highlighted AMIS's limited mandate, and the troops in Darfur, as well as others in the AU, were aware of the serious limitations imposed by the force's ability to respond to the events on the ground. As Kagame stated before the Rwandan soldiers left on their mission in Darfur, "It makes no sense to protect the peace monitors while the population is ignored and left to die."[15] As one Rwandese soldier stationed in al-Fasher, was quoted as saying, "Every night you go to sleep thinking 'I could do more'. We could do more with a better mandate."[16]

To reinforce the mission, on 20 October 2004, the PCS extended AMIS's mission, in what came to be known as AMIS II. The strengthened force included 3,632 personnel: 2,341 military personnel, 450 MILBOS, 815 civilian police, and 26 international civilian staff/CFC members. The force's assignments were to ensure compliance with the N'Djamena Humanitarian Ceasefire Agreement, contribute to the delivery of humanitarian aid, improve security in Darfur, and guarantee the safe return of refugees and IDPs to their homes.[17]

Although AMIS was initially established as a ceasefire monitoring force, it is important to note that in October 2004, with its transition to AMIS II, the PSC announced its intention to turn the force into a full peacekeeping mission. At the 17th meeting of the PSC, an announcement was made of the AU's intention to develop

> a comprehensive plan on how best to enhance the African Mission in the Sudan (AMIS), *including the possibility of transforming the said Mission into a full-fledged peacekeeping mission*, with the requisite mandate and size, to ensure the effective implementation of the Humanitarian Ceasefire Agreement of 8 April 2004. [italics added][18]

In the field, however, the new force soon realized that its efforts to fulfill even the minimal assignments of a ceasefire monitoring force would be hampered by several geographical and humanitarian factors.

Geographically, the region of Darfur presents a very hostile environment. Its huge size (equal to the size of France) and mostly desert terrain, combined with the almost complete absence of infrastructure, including accessible roads, created complex challenges for any peacekeeping mission, the more so for the pioneer AMIS force. The lack of accurate geographical knowledge or adequate equipment, and the small number of AMIS troops stood in sharp contrast to the well-equipped local government and rebel forces, who navigated their native landscape with no special difficulty.[19] The inexperience of the new force soon became evident. According to a November 2004 article published in the *Economist*:

> The AU's new interest in peacekeeping bodes well for future conflicts. But what difference will it make to Darfur, a remote stretch in Africa's biggest country? The AU has only few vehicles to transport its men overland and almost no aircraft to hand. It has too few tents to shelter even its men now on the ground. And the valuable computer equipment it has been given for communication came with software and instructions written only in German, which no African there understands.[20]

In the humanitarian sphere, it was clear from the very inception of the mission that the IDP situation would present one of the major challenges to AMIS' activities in Darfur for two main reasons relating to the general definition of the IDPs' status, and specifically to their status in Darfur. First, there was no clear legal foundation for any potential action to address the IDP challenge, even from an international perspective. Although the UN had attempted to firmly define the rights of IDPs, it nonetheless presumes that the primary responsibility for their security and defence lies with local governmental authorities.[21] Second, since the arrival of the first AMIS troops to Darfur, it was immediately clear that the multi-faceted IDP issue would claim much of AMIS's attention. As early as November 2004, it was estimated that 1.5 million people had fled from their homes,[22] and by 2005, two million people were crowded into several dozen camps scattered throughout Darfur.[23] All eight AMIS headquarter locations (al-Fashir, Nyala, Geneina, Kebkabiyah, Tine, Kutum, Zalingei, and el-Daʿein) were chosen based on their proximity to IDP concentrations, and the force's entire operational framework was focused on the IDP population; yet AMIS was not permitted to provide physical security to the IDPs camps. This task was considered to be the responsibility of the Sudanese police, which agreed only to the presence of AMIS's unarmed Civilian Police (CIVPOL), and even in this case imposed many restrictions on its operations,[24] including for example, a 6 pm to 6 am curfew, a "temporary fuel shortage", and severe restrictions on aviation movements. The broader context of the GoS's policy toward AMIS presence is elaborated below.

Despite these restrictions, from late 2004 to mid-2005, AMIS had some success in addressing various IDP-related issues, as reported by Chin and Morgenstein:

> Earlier in the year, AMIS had been able to provide some security and deterrence. Displaced persons were congregating near AMIS bases; the UN World Food Program started parking its vehicles near AMIS sites, AMIS escorted humanitarian convoys, and helped victims of attacks to get to hospitals.

> The round the clock presence of civilian police in some IDPs camps [*sic*] has provided a greater sense of security to a population that is distrustful of the Sudanese police. AMIS forces have helped to restore order and provide security during the very difficult IDPs re-registration process.[25]

In late 2004, for example, a local AMIS commander decided to deploy his troops in the town of Labado, South Darfur, and nearby villages after numerous attacks in this area. The decision, which was implemented despite the potential risks for the troops, allowed the local people to gradually return to their homes and rebuild their lives.[26] Another example of a successful AMIS action was reported from Kebkabiyah:

> Following months of daytime violence in Kebkabiyah (North Darfur), AMIS established a permanent mission in late 2004, with the result that the *Janjaweed* no longer terrorize residents and IDPSs inside the town, markets have re-opened, and humanitarian NGOs operate in a more secure environment.[27]

AMIS also assumed additional IDP-related tasks, such as temporary accompaniment of local people, usually to destinations outside IDP camps; patrolling in areas suspected as being potential crisis locations; and mediating between local groups, and between them and various aid groups and workers.[28]

The UN's July 2005 report noted that

> violence in Darfur has diminished greatly since the period from early 2003 to mid-2004, which was prior to Security Council decisions and the deployment of AMIS. There can be little doubt that the situation in Darfur is less dangerous for civilians than it was a year ago. Attacks on civilians have declined significantly over the past 12 months, and humanitarian relief workers have access to far more people in need than they had at the time the joint communiqué was signed, in July 2004. These developments should be welcomed by the international community.[29]

The deployment of AMIS II proceeded in a satisfactory manner. On 28 April 2005, AMIS was further expanded to a total force of 6,171 (of which the Civilian Police accounted for one quarter of the force, or 1,560), and in some cases its presence checked the violence and human rights violations of human rights in different areas of Darfur. Satisfaction with AMIS's accomplishments was reflected in an AU press release:

> The first of the six Troops [*Sic.*] contributing countries (TCCs), Nigeria, had successfully completed the deployment of one battalion of 680 troops on Wednesday 13 July 2005; Nigeria will further deploy two more battalions to the enhancement. The deployment was completed a day earlier than scheduled. Two Rwandese Battalions are expected to follow suit and they would be airlifted by the US using C130 aircraft from Kigali to El Fasher. This is expected to take place between 16 July and 9 August 2005. The other Troops from contributing Countries: South Africa, Senegal, the Gambia, and Kenya would deploy troops according to schedules prepared by the DITF and the International Partners. The deployments would bring the AMIS II to a full strength of more than seven thousand troops. The enhancement of AMIS II is expected to be completed by 30 September 2005.[30]

Other prominent scholars on Darfur concur that AMIS's presence helped reduce the violence and establish some degree of stability in the first year of its deployment. Mahmood Mamdani claimed that that the AU was "able to reduce deaths from political violence", and, combined with NGO activities, it also reduced the number of drought-related deaths.[31] Alex de Waal added, "In the twelve months after the initial deployment in July–August 2004, AMIS helped bring increased stability in most areas of Darfur."[32] These evaluations confirm that the roles played by AMIS during its first year of deployment extended beyond traditional ceasefire monitoring.

One of the more innovative roles assumed by AMIS was protection of women in the camps against sexual abuse during the conflict period. A huge number of women and girls had been raped or sexually abused since the outbreak of the conflict in Darfur.[33] As incidents of gender-based violence typically occurred when girls and women left their camps to gather firewood and water, many AMIS troops felt obligated to escort women outside the camps and ensure their personal safety, in what came to be known as "firewood patrols". In an interview, Baba Gana Kingibe, head of AMIS in July 2005, claimed that he viewed the protection of women against acts of sexual violence as one of the force's major commitments:

> I think from a realization that in and around the IDPs camps there is a lot of gender-based violence – the kind that only the police would be better placed to deal with than the military. We had women incorporated into our police component since they could talk to the women and child victims of rape and other assaults. It becomes evident that the times of the day when these attacks occur are when the women leave the camps to get the usual likes of life sustenance, like firewood and so on – whatever they need to get from outside the camp. That's when they are attacked, so the best way to extend protection is to accompany them when they are on the road.[34]

This interview sheds light on the ambivalent nature of AMIS's operations in Darfur. The realization that prevention of gender-based war crimes is one of the important tasks of a peacekeeping mission was a novel concept compared to previous pan-continental interventions. Nonetheless, most AMIS personnel were not qualified to deal with the sensitive issues relating to gender-based violence, and the number of women members of AMIS forces, especially those who spoke local languages and were able to interview local women, was negligible.[35] As a result, AMIS's ability to prevent gender-based violence and related crimes was limited, and could be considered a drop in the ocean in view of the large scope and frequency of such crimes throughout the period of the conflict. Still, AMIS's attempts to address various aspects of gendered crimes had implications for further peacekeeping missions; These will be discussed below. In the short term, AMIS's limited accomplishments in this area are merely one more example of the force's ineffectiveness as a peacekeeping mission.

From the onset, it was quite clear that the restrictions imposed on AMIS would affect its ability to effectively protect the people of Darfur. AMIS's mandate was to observe and monitor the Humanitarian Ceasefire Agreement signed by the Sudanese parties to the conflict, and to report alleged violations to the CFC. AMIS personnel were not permitted to intervene between the parties on the ground, whatever their actions, and were only able to fire in self-defence if directly threatened.[36]

By July and August 2005, AMIS's prospects of dealing effectively with the situation in Darfur appeared to be improving, notwithstanding its limited mandate and lack of peacekeeping experience, and confident predictions were voiced by AU's then chairman[37] and by international observers, such as Refugees International.[38] In September–October, it was already clear that the forecasts had been overly optimistic. John Garang's death on 30 July 2005, only several weeks after he was nominated as Sudan's first vice-president, and the failure of another round of negotiations in Abuja triggered a national climate of uncertainty and fuelled renewed waves of violence in Darfur.[39] Numerous reports of the escalating violence included Janjaweed attacks in the town of el-Geneina on 21 September, and attacks on the Aru Sharow IDP camp on 29 September, in which 29 civilians were killed and about 4,000 IDPs were forced to flee to the desert.

During this period, reports of AMIS casualties also increased in frequency. The first incident in which six AMIS troops were killed and three wounded (presumably in an SLA ambush) was reported from the vicinity of Kourabishi, South Darfur, on 8 October 2005.[40] These threats added to the difficulties of the ill-prepared force, which had operated under severe financial, logistical, and operational constraints since its establishment.

AMIS's budget was not a reflection of the AU's little regard for the mission's tasks. The AU was itself struggling with an inadequate operating budget, caused by delays in member countries' payments, and gaps between income and expenses. Inefficient financial management of the budget exacerbated the budgetary shortage. As a result, some of AMIS's expenses were shifted to several, but not all, member states, imposing a heavy burden on their economies.[41]

Most of AMIS's financial support was received from the European Union through the African Peace Facility (APF), which was established at the AU's request.[42] Between June 2004 and December 2007, the EU committed a total of over €300 million to the APF in support of AMIS, and EU member states additionally made substantial bilateral financial and in-kind contributions, including expertise, equipment, food rations, and airlifts. In total, the EU's contribution to AMIS reached some €500 million in this period.[43] From June 2004 to September 2006, the US government also provided about US$1 billion to Darfur. Of this sum, US$280 million was allocated primarily to build and maintain the 32 camps for AMIS troops throughout Darfur.[44]

Still, these funds failed to satisfy the expensive maintenance needs of such a complex mission, especially in view of the constant discrepancies between promised donations and actual transfers to the AU. In 2005, for example, only US$79 million was effectively received by the AU of a total of US$252 million that had been pledged to the peacekeeping mission that year.[45] This failure to comply with the financing assurance was mentioned in a report of the chairperson of the Commission to the PSC in January 2006:

> The exclusive dependency on funding based on voluntary contributions and ad hoc arrangements has exposed a further vulnerability in the AU's peace support operation in Darfur. This is clearly highlighted by the current state of affairs whereby the continuing funding of AMIS is not guaranteed beyond the next few weeks.[46]

A change in the financial situation of AMIS operations in Darfur was noticeable only after the UN approved two support packages to Darfur and the establishment of a hybrid AU–UN force, which will be elaborated below.

Another major difficulty facing AMIS was the slow pace of the troops' deployment, and, more generally, the insufficient number of troops for the tasks at hand. This problem had already been noted by Susan Rice, then a senior fellow at the Brookings Institution, who analyzed the situation in August 2005:

> More than one year after it took on the Darfur mission, the African Union has deployed only roughly 3,000 troops to cover an area the size of Texas. The A.U. has committed itself to increasing its force to 7,700 by late September, but U.S. officials doubt it will meet that target. Even if the A.U. force reaches full strength on time, it will still be too small to protect many of the displaced persons scattered across more than 100 camps and insecure areas. The A.U. is considering further increasing its force to 12,000 by the second quarter of 2006 but has made no firm decision to do so. The additional troops are not yet identified, much less available.[47]

Based on the recommendations of International Crisis Group (ICG), an independent nongovernmental organization and a leading authority on Darfur, Rice estimated that an additional 12,000 to 15,000 NATO troops, with a new enforcement mandate, would be needed to adequately protect civilians at risk in Darfur. She mentioned the ICG's recommendation to deploy NATO troops as a "bridging force" of one or two brigades to bolster the AU mission that would remain until African governments would be able to deploy at least 12,000 capable, well-equipped troops.[48] However, neither the international, African, or Sudanese climates were ready to accept a deployment of non-African forces in Darfur, even as a transitional measure.

AMIS's budgetary shortage had an obvious impact on its resources on the ground. The lack of transport capability was a major obstacle to effective AMIS operations in Darfur. From the outset, the critical shortage of armoured vehicles limited AMIS's ability cover the long distances in Darfur, and to protect its soldiers in transit. In July 2005, for example, AMIS had merely ten armored personnel carriers, some with heavy machine guns and a limited number of light armoured vehicles at its disposal. Adding to the lack of efficient transport and combat vehicles were the difficulties of transportation on unpaved roads and the troops' inexperience in off-road driving and recovery skills.[49]

The shortage of transportation and mobility of resources was confounded by a lack of strategic knowledge and intelligence to support the operation. This critical lack of knowledge was reported by Brian Steidle who accompanied the first phase of AMIS's organization in the field:

> Simple geography and logistics were problems. In the Marine Corps, the very first thing we would acquire was a map. But the AU had no maps. Instead, we had to rely on the knowledge of our SLA and JEM representatives to guide us, and when all else failed, we asked a local where to go. When we inquired exactly how long it will take to get to our destination, it was never clear whether the estimate corresponded to a journey by foot, donkey or a truck.[50]

The AMIS force in Darfur was further compromised by its lack of aviation forces, which limited its reconnaissance, transportation, and military potential. Compared to the GoS, which has purchased many airplanes and helicopters, and used them to bombard villages and rebel camps from the air, AMIS forces had a limited number of transport airplanes and helicopters at their disposal, as reported by the International Crisis Group in July 2005:

> AMIS uses eighteen Mi-8 helicopters for most air operations. These are contracted, unarmed civilian aircrafts without forward looking infra-red (FLIR), tactical communications or night capability. AMIS ground facilities cannot communicate with or direct them in flight. The mission thus cannot send forces into hostile environment or conduct sustained day or night-time patrols, including along likely avenues of approach to target attackers may use or aid agency transportation routes. Nor can it do extended reconnaissance or tactical lift. Its aircraft perform limited patrols but not to the degree necessary to establish a presence throughout Darfur.[51]

Helicopter patrols were further curtailed by the shortage of fuel, and were consequently cut from 60 hours per month to an average of 30 per month.[52] On 14 September 2006, *Washington Post* reporter Craig Timber reported, "This week, the government seized a tanker full of African Union jet fuel in El Fasher and used it to fill its own military aircraft, African Union sources said, speaking on condition their names not be published."[53]

The GoS also imposed various restrictions on AMIS aviation operations, including restrictions on oil suppliers and the demand that all pilots must be civilians. AMIS's relative aviation inferiority could easily have been solved through an international resolution to declare Darfur a no-fly zone, as the AU had repeatedly requested.[54] The international community's failure to do so is related to the wider context of the relations between the regional and international organizations at the time. This context is elaborated below, in the discussion on the transition from AMIS to UNAMID.

AMIS was also plagued by problems that were not directly tied to its budgetary constraints. For example, a wide gap existed between the intelligence capabilities of the force's headquarters and the intelligence resources of the different sectors, including insufficient knowledge of the rival groups, their networks, locations, and operations. As a result, the force faced major problems in predicting future attacks and preparing its moves accordingly.[55]

Finally, one of the most interesting challenges facing AMIS was the issue of the language. This issue was particularly important for peacekeeping missions that encountered the linguistic diversity of Africa, in terms of both the diversity of the *lingua franca* and the local languages. AMIS lacked foresight in determining in advance how language should be used as a channel of communication between AMIS personnel, and as a means of communications with the local population. Catherine Guicherd summarized the language issue in her report, "The AU in Sudan: Lessons for the African Standby Force":

> AMIS has encountered difficulties on both fronts. Within the mission, problems have arisen especially within the police

> component – this was amply reflected at the seminar – as Francophone officers had difficulty finding their place in a majority English-speaking environment, and they felt their personal skills were not being recognized. Vis-à-vis external actors, the difficulty resided in the lack of qualified interpreters in sufficiently large number to allow for communication with the locals, although a budget for them existed. However, this communication is essential to ensure that the mandate of the mission is well-understood; it is particularly important for police work (for investigation purposes, but also if like in AMIS, the CIVPOL component has important training and mentoring tasks of the local police); and it is also vital for Humanitarian Officers and for CIMIC whose role it is to liaise with local actors and NGOs. In addition, without the right language capability, the mission deprives itself of a key information gathering tool.[56]

The issue of language was indeed crucial not only on the ground, but also in the diplomatic sphere, as one of the causes of the diplomatic failures in Darfur was the lack of linguistic accessibility to the written text of the agreements. This issue and others that relate to the AU efforts to end the conflict by diplomatic means are discussed in the next chapter.

CHAPTER 4

FROM ABÊCHÊ TO ABUJA: THE AFRICAN UNION MEDIATION EFFORTS

Article Four of the Constitutive Act of the African Union proclaimed "the right of the Union to intervene in a Member State pursuant to a decision of the Assembly in respect of grave circumstances, namely: war crimes, genocide and crimes against humanity."[1] While the decision to establish the African Union Mission in Sudan (AMIS) and its continuing presence in Darfur signify a turning point in the policies of this pan-continental organization on intervention in intrastate conflicts in Africa, the AU's failure to enforce its resolutions on the Government of Sudan (GoS) raised doubts about the intervention's efficacy and the organization's genuine intentions to carry out its decisions. Many critics of the AU intervention in Darfur claimed that the GoS, acting under the banner of "African solutions to African problems", cynically manipulated AMIS's presence in order to squash other, potentially more effective international interventions that were accused of being part of a Western, imperialist conspiracy. As this chapter shows, the AU was in fact committed to a diplomatic solution of the conflict, and invested constant efforts to this end. This chapter analyzes the AU's diplomatic efforts to resolve the crisis in Darfur, and reviews the organization's successes and failures.

The AU's first efforts to mediate between the GoS and the SLM/A took place as early as September 2003. Under the auspices of Chadian President Idriss Déby, the parties met in Abéché, Chad, signed a ceasefire agreement, and agreed to cease hostilities for 45 days and commence comprehensive political talks. Violations of the ceasefire agreement, primarily by Janjaweed militias against civilians, led to another round of talks in N'Djamena in April 2004, culminating in the signing of the Humanitarian Ceasefire Agreement.

From the outset, the GoS agreed to AU's presence in its negotiations with the Darfur rebels, to help end the conflict in its embryonic stage,[2] and, at the same time, rejected the presence of the international community in the talks and refused to participate in face-to-face negotiations with the rebel groups. Both the agreement of the GoS to AU presence in the early phase of the negotiations and its rejection of broader international participation were related to the government's priority to end the conflict in the south before addressing the conflict emerging in the country's western region. At the time, the Naivasha talks between the North and the South were progressing rapidly, and the GoS was eager to bring them to a successful conclusion. The GoS had been forced to accept international intervention in the negotiations between the North and the South, yet it certainly did not want to expand the international intervention to the conflict in its western region. Still, AU mediation would help the GoS prevent a second civil war within Sudan that would attract more international criticism regarding its violence toward its citizens.

The AU shared this opposition to international intervention in Darfur. In an effort to organize a summit of five heads of states in Sirte, Libya, the Nigerian minister of foreign affairs asserted that it was important that the crisis in Darfur be resolved by African elements, especially under the authority of the AU, without interference by foreign elements. It is important, he added, that the PSC be fully committed to constructing a solution to the crisis, and to proving that Africa is capable of handling its own problems.[3] At the Sirte Summit, held in October 2004, the heads of state of Egypt, Sudan, Nigeria, Chad, and Libya communicated to the international community that

Africa could handle its own crisis, and rejected international intervention in general and military intervention in particular, as detrimental to the continent's sovereignty. At least until mid-2005, the AU and the GoS shared this desire to prevent international intervention in Darfur, as discussed extensively in the following chapter.[4]

Within a mere two months of its signing, the Humanitarian Ceasefire Agreement became fully operational, and the first AMIS contingents were deployed. The violence on ground, however, continued to escalate, as both sides accused each other of ceasefire violations. The SLM/A and the JEM also claimed that the civilian population was being continuously bombarded by Antonov airplanes and helicopters, and that the GoS was supporting attacks on the ground by Janjaweed militias. The international community's concern about the widening conflict in Darfur increased, and the word "genocide" began to appear in the media and political discourse (discussed further below). UN Secretary-General Kofi Annan demanded a specific timeline for action, and even warned that "the Sudanese Government doesn't have forever" to meet the ceasefire obligations.[5] The AU accepted the challenge, and AU Chairman Olusegun Obasanjo organized direct negotiations between the GoS, the SLA/M, and the JEM.

In August 2004, the parties' representatives met under AU auspices in Abuja and declared their intention to reach agreement on the principles that would lay the foundation for a political accord.[6] This was the second of seven rounds of Abuja peace talks (the first was held in Addis Ababa one month earlier) that preceded the signing of Darfur Peace Agreement in May 2006. The AU seemed to be determined to achieve a diplomatic solution to the crisis in Sudan, and ensure that a final agreement was signed. Although the 2006 agreement did not achieve peace, and in certain respects even heightened the conflict, it was the product of the AU's first intensive diplomatic efforts to resolve an African conflict through diplomacy (accompanied by efforts on the ground). As the first AU intervention of this kind, the nature of these AU mediation efforts and their effect on the situation in Darfur served as crucial lessons for subsequent mediation efforts, and therefore warrant further elaboration.

Indeed, even in the initial rounds of the Abuja talks, it was quite evident that the AU's role in the Darfur conflict was viewed as a test case for African ability in general, and the ability of the AU in particular, to handle Africa's own affairs. In the first round of the Abuja talks, the parties comprehensively discussed measures to improve the humanitarian situation, including unrestricted movement and access of humanitarian workers, assistance and protection of civilians, respect for the rights of the IDPs and refugees to return to their areas of origin, and other measures. The parties also agreed on the need to strengthen AMIS's presence on the ground. To grant the force effective monitoring authority, it was agreed to establish a Joint Humanitarian Facilitation and Monitoring Unit based in al-Fasher to ensure enforcement of the monitoring terms.[7]

Since the first round of the negotiations in August 2004, all parties noticeably devoted extensive attention to security issues and humanitarian relief, while avoiding any profound discussion of the roots of the conflict. Although the PSC recognized that "the core of the conflict in Darfur is political and socio-economic in nature and that the Abuja Peace Talks provide the most viable mechanism to achieve a negotiated and lasting solution",[8] it seemed that the AU mediators in Abuja acquiesced to the GoS's agenda to stress security and humanitarian issues at the expense of a debate on a broader political agenda. The UN also apparently supported the AU's aversion to addressing the roots of the conflict in Darfur. In December 2004, UN Envoy to Sudan Jan Pronk argued that the crisis in Darfur was considered a specific conflict rather than an intrinsic element in the Sudanese political equation.[9] The AU supported the need to focus on the root causes of the conflict, yet instructions to its negotiators remained ambiguous, as evident from the detailed report by the chairperson to the 17th meeting of the PSC:

> In preparation for the resumption of the Talks in Abuja, I have directed my Special Envoy to undertake consultations with the Parties and other stakeholders. Those consultations would help determine how best to organise the discussions on the remaining items on the agenda of the Talks. Over the past

> weeks, two views have emerged in this respect. Some are of the view that the next round should complete the discussions on the Draft Protocol on Security Issues, as an agreement on this Protocol would enhance confidence among the Parties, thus enhancing the prospect of reaching a consensus on the political issues. Others are of the view that the next round should proceed directly to the consideration of the political issues, as most of the issues in the draft Security Protocol are being addressed in other fora, including the Joint Commission.[10]

This ambiguity was also manifest at the opening meeting of the third round of talks, in October 2004, where the AU mediators expressed ambivalent attitudes on which issues should be considered first. As the negotiations progressed, representatives of the both the SLM/A and the JEM pushed toward a political discussion, and, for the first time, presented their vision of a comprehensive political settlement that included claims for a more equitable distribution of power and wealth and an end to the deprivation of Darfur, accompanied by their reaffirmed commitment to Sudan's unity and sovereignty. GoS representatives, on their part, persisted in focusing on security and concentrated on issues such as the demand to replace use of the term "*Janjaweed*" with "armed militias". The rebel representatives understood that a resolution of major security issues, such as GoS consent to impose a no-fly zone over Darfur, was required before negotiations could proceed to more fundamental issues, and, in a dramatic move in the evening of 4 November, the movements' representatives agreed to accept the draft of the security protocol, even though they considered it less than satisfactory. With equally surprising swiftness, the GoS representatives announced their acceptance of the draft the following day.[11] When the GoS rejected last-minute additions proposed by the rebels, the euphoric climate dissipated with equal swiftness. In retrospect, this round of talks was the closest the parties came to a viable agreement, as the subsequent mediation efforts were overshadowed by internal splits within the rebel movements.

In the fourth round of the Abuja talks, conducted 11–21 December 2004, the leadership of the SLM/A failed to appear. It was an alarming omen. The fifth round of the Abuja talks took place several months later, 5–10 July 2005, after various SLM/A factions repeatedly requested to postpone the talks to allow them to organize a general congress of the organization, which ultimately never took place.[12] Since the previous December, the attention of most parties seemed to be drawn to the rebel movements' growing fragmentation and the rebels' inability to present a unified front against the GoS. Commenting on the rebels' missed opportunity to introduce their own political agenda, Alex de Waal noted, "By focusing on issues that are secondary to the outbreak of the war, the rebels are failing to develop a political agenda that can be the basis for the settlement."[13] He and Julie Flint also attributed this fragmentation to the awkward composition of the rebel movements:

> Darfur's rebels are an awkward coalition of *Fur* and *Masalit* villagers, *Zaghawa* Bedouins out of patience with Khartoum, a handful of professionals who dared to take the leadership, and disillusioned Islamist intellectuals. Unlike the first generation of SPLA fighters, who emerged from army mutiny, few of Darfur's guerrillas had military experience or discipline before they took up arms. The two main rebel groups are united by deep resentment to the marginalization of Darfur, but are not natural bedfellows and could easily be split apart. Theirs is not an insurgency born of revolutionary ideals, but rather a last-ditch response to the escalating violence of the *Janjaweed* and its patrons in Khartoum.[14]

In the period following December 2004, media coverage tended to paint the rebel movements as the main culprits behind the lack of progress in the negotiations. In many news items published in this period, rebel movement representatives were accused of imposing tough pre-conditions. Agence France-Presse reported, "The rebel groups, however, insist that they want the African Union to pressure Khartoum into granting Darfur and other regions greater autonomy and a better share of the national income. They are also refusing to disarm."[15] Other articles blamed the movements' representatives for damaging the prospects for an agreement on humanitarian and security issues, and commented on the rebels' frequent departure from the meeting rooms.[16] Indeed, these observations accurately illuminated the splits and divisions that the negotiation process triggered, both within the movements and between them.

In her sharp analysis of the composition of Darfur's armed movements, Julie Flint explains the fact that eventually most of the significant participants did not sign the Darfur Peace Agreement (DPA).[17] The main split within the SLM/A was the result of a power struggle between Abdel Wahid and Minni Arko Minnawi. In contrast to Abdel Wahid, who came from a respected Fur family and was a practising lawyer who had been educated at Khartoum University Law School, Minnawi was the son of a humble Zaghawa clan and a secondary school graduate who worked as a school teacher. The circumstances of his rise to power are not altogether clear: Despite his lack of political or military experience, he became secretary to the first SLA chief of staff, Abdalla Abaker, and, after Abaker was killed in January 2004, Minnawi appointed himself "secretary general" of the organization. To Houreld, a South African journalist who interviewed him in late 2004, Minnawi introduced himself as the military leader of the SLA. The journalist was very impressed by his modesty and moderation.[18]

Actually, Minnawi's rise to power may be explained by the very personal traits that Abdel Wahid lacked. Although respected for his vision and integrity, Abdel Wahid lacked crucial leadership skills. Flint noted his lack of basic organizational skills, his "almost pathological" distrust of everyone, and his inability to cooperate with others.[19] Minnawi possessed many of these leadership traits, and, contrary to Houreld's impression, he was neither modest nor moderate. With the narrow support of his own Zaghawa clan, he brutally climbed his way to the top of the SLA pyramid, terrorizing and killing his opponents, alienating many other Zaghawa and other ethnic groups in Darfur. Nonetheless, it was Minnawi, rather than Abdel Wahid, who was appointed senior assistant to the president of Sudan in August 2007, officially the fourth highest-ranking executive position in the country.[20]

The nomination is partly explained by Minnawi's internal and external reputation as the SLM/A leader, which he had built for himself in 2005 and 2006. In November 2005, Minnawi convened a conference in the small town of Haskanita in eastern Darfur, where he was elected chairman of the SLM/A by the attendees, most of whom were members of his Zaghawa clan. The conference and the subsequent elections were held against the advice of AU mediators in Abuja to Minnawi. Abdel Wahid initially approved the conference, and, although he later withdrew his support, the conference continued until Minnawi was elected. Flint claims, "The Haskanita conference did not resolve the legitimacy question. Rather, it confirmed the split."[21] AU mediators in Abuja were now forced to conduct separate negotiations with the two factions – Minnawi's SLA and Wahid's SLA. Moreover, as the seventh and final round of the Abuja talks approached, discord intensified not merely between the two factions of the SLM/A, but also within each faction. A splinter group of 19 prominent dissenters from Abdel Wahid's faction set itself up in northern Darfur under the name SLA-Unity. Animosity also emerged between the SLM/A and the JEM. Minnawi was consequently the only leader who was willing to sign the final draft of the agreement.

The final round of the Abuja peace talks commenced on 29 November 2005 and ended more than five months later, on 5 May 2006. This period of "long, difficult, and frustrating negotiations" included talks on many points of disagreement, including the future status of the region within Sudan, political representation in Darfur and in national organs, and payment of funds to the Darfur Reconstruction and Development Fund.[22] Nevertheless, as researcher Laurie Nathan, a member of the AU mediation team in Abuja, claims, the "deadline diplomacy" that was used in the seventh round of the Abuja talks resulted in an unsatisfactory agreement.[23] His analysis was based on the multiple deadlines issued by different actors involved in the talks, such as the UN, the AU, the EU, and the donor governments. One of the most critical of these was the deadline of 30 April 2005, related to the pressure put on the parties to sign the final agreement. In practice, the parties were given less than one week to read, comprehend, deliberate upon, and endorse an 86-page

English-language document describing a set of complicated security, political, economic, and administrative arrangements designed to achieve a ceasefire and resolve the causes of the civil war.[24]

Beyond the deadline factor, another important issue that hampered mediation efforts was the linguistic factor: The translation of the agreement into Arabic, the language of choice for most parties, was completed mere days before the signing date, and contained some significant mistranslations and ambiguities. Abaker Abuelbasher offers an example of the problems created by the imprecise translation:

> It had been agreed that all documents should be originated in the English language and that Arabic and French copies had to be translated from it. However, the Arabic version was not correctly translated in many parts, e.g., the Wealth Sharing Commission indicates that IDPs and Refugees have no rights for compensation; also the word Commission was translated to give the meaning of committee and in that sense Compensation Committee shall be established rather than Compensation Commission, which is precisely what was meant by the negotiating Parties.[25]

Finally, in his commentary on the Abuja talks, Nathan employed William Zartman's concept of "ripeness for resolution". Zartman claims that conflicts are resolvable at certain moments but not at others. In the context of extremely violent conflicts such as Darfur, the psycho-political dynamics requires trust-building steps before an agreement to resolve the conflict can been achieved. The mediator's role is to build parties' confidence in each other and in the prospects of the negotiation process. This, Nathan claimed, did not happen in Abuja, where mistrust and suspicion was one of the primary constraints to progress in the talks, as many mediators admitted. As noted earlier, mistrust and suspicion prevailed both between the movements and within each group. Many observers noted that, in the final month of the talks, the representatives of the splinter rebel groups were no longer making any attempt to negotiate or find common ground between them. The failure to create a united front of all the armed movements was described in a slightly cynical tone by *Speigel Online* reporters, Thilo Thielke and Volkhard Windfuhr:

> The scene had something of the quality of a B movie. One by one, the leaders of the various factions were summoned into a room by representatives of the African Union. "Will you sign?" a man from the African Union would say. "No," Abd al-Wahid al-Nur responded, on behalf of the Fur, saying that he would first have to consult with his advisors. Chamis Abdullah Abakr, the Massalit leader, also refused to sign. And Khalil Ibrahim, the man from the JEM, said that the agreement was unacceptable because it represented "Khartoum's position." Minni Arkou Minawi was the only rebel leader to sign the document. In return, he was apparently promised that his name would be removed from the list of war criminals.[26]

Mistrust and suspicion were even more intense between the rebel movements and the GoS, where the imbalance of political, economic, and military power palpably affected the atmosphere of negotiations. Arguably, one of the main obstacles to the mediation efforts in Abuja was the non-recognition of the unequal terms that the parties brought to the discussion table.

> Throughout the entire process of negotiations at Abuja, the African Union Mediation was constrained by several important factors. An elementary reality, that sometimes appears to be lost on some commentators, is that the Movements did not win a military victory and were therefore not in a position to impose their terms on the Government of Sudan. Any deal reached involved the SLM/A and JEM making compromises on dearly-held political objectives. The fact that they failed to achieve all their goals at the negotiating table is not, however, tantamount to capitulation to the Government of Sudan. The DPA represents a compromise, and gives the Movements the opportunity of achieving all their stated objectives through peaceful democratic processes.[27]

In addition to deadline diplomacy tactics, language issues, gross power imbalances, and disunity in the rebel camps, two additional important issues undermined the AU mediation talks. First, the AU mediation team had decided to divide the negotiation process into three areas, each of which would be headed by a commission: power sharing, wealth sharing, and security arrangements. Although land was one of the root causes of the contemporary conflict and a significant issue for the Darfurians, who greatly valued land as a proxy for political power and a source of wealth-generation, none of the three commissions addressed the land issue. As a result, one of the crucial elements that might have made a considerable contribution to a genuine solution was ignored.

Second, on a personal level, it seems that the failure of the DPA can be attributed to AU mediators' attitude toward Abdel Wahid in the final phases of the negotiations. Even before the DPA was signed, the PSC's decisions carried a threatening tone toward the SLM/A:

> [The PSC] *reminds* the leaders of the SLM/A of their heavy responsibility not to prolong the suffering of their people in Darfur and, in this respect, *strongly demands* that they put aside their differences and personal ambitions and focus on the negotiations to end the conflict. [italics added]

In another decision, the PSC threatened sanctions "against any party that will undermine or constitute an obstacle to the peace process in Darfur".[28] Although he was not explicitly mentioned, it was clear that this declaration referred to Abdel Wahid. This was the also view of several AU team members to the Abuja talks. Nathan claims that Abdel Wahid was perceived by the AU as one of the main spoilers of the negotiations, and was described by several mediators as "erratic and indecisive, projecting confusion and backtracking on signing of the final draft."

Abdel Wahid participated in the negotiations until their final phase, and, while the agreement remained open until its scheduled signing date, Wahid introduced some minor demands involving the three core issues of the DPA: security arrangements, wealth sharing, and political sharing. Even these relatively modest demands were rejected, leaving the leader who represented the largest and most influential ethnic group in Darfur outside the negotiations and the subsequent agreement. According to Abdourahman A. Ibrahim, acting head of AMIS in Khartoum at the time, despite the deadline strategy, many of the representatives of the armed groups remained in Abuja many months after the DPA was signed, mainly due to personal reasons. In their absence, alternative local leaders emerged and acquired power, and, in some cases, even diluted the authority of the original Darfurian leaders, exacerbating the fragmentation of Darfur's rebel groups further.[29]

On 5 May 2006, the Darfur Peace Agreement was signed by Dr Majzoub al Khalifa on behalf of the GoS, and by the SLM/A-Minawi faction.[30] The agreement established the Transitional Darfur Regional Authority (TDRA), a new entity mandated to administer Darfur, and provided seats for the SLM in the regional and national parliament, as well as several top positions, including the chairmanship of the TDRA and senior presidential assistant. Yet, for all the reasons mentioned above, and particularly the exclusion of the most genuine representatives of the Darfurian society, the DPA failed to gain popular support in Darfur.

The DPA lacked many major elements of a comprehensive resolution, including a mechanism for justice and accountability, but provided for the creation of the Darfur–Darfur Dialogue and Consultation (DDDC), which was intended to be a grassroots reconciliation process involving the rivaling local parties and interest groups in the region, as mentioned in the following statement:

> The Darfur–Darfur Dialogue and Consultation [DDDC] is constituted under Chapter 4 of the DPA as a means of informing the people of Darfur about the DPA, and obtaining popular support and buy-in amongst all Darfur stakeholders. The Dialogue process aims to bring the grass-roots population together, to deal with those issues not directly dealt with under the DPA, including the root causes of the conflict. The process is intended to lead to peace and reconciliation in Darfur.[31]

It seems that every round of negotiations ignited a new wave of violence in Darfur. In September 2005, for example, Abdel Wahid claimed that 20 people killed in attacks in the village of Sheng al-Tobei were victims of GoS attempts to derail the peace talks that were underway in Abuja at that time.[32] On 19 April 2006, several days after the failure of another round of talks in Abuja, 30,000 people, newly displaced as a result of violence, were reported in the Jebel Marra mountain range.[33]

The exclusion of most of Darfur's genuine representatives in the DPA triggered unprecedented violence, especially between the armed movements. The *Irish Star* reported:

> The non-Arab militias – portrayed in some western media accounts as the "good guys" – have also been breaking international law. In July the Sudanese Liberation Army/Minnawi faction undertook what international observers have described as offensives in the Korma area involving many unacceptable acts against the civilian population including murder, rape and village expulsions amounting to ethnic cleansing. This 14-day campaign "cleansed" 20 villages and created 10,000 new refugees. Minnawi's fighters have also been guilty of racketeering and intimidation, robbery and assault of humanitarian workers and obstructing African Union troops. The other main faction of the Sudanese Liberation Army – the non-signatory Wahid/Shaafi faction – is charged with similar violations of international law over the past three months. They are strongly suspected to have been involved in the deaths of up to 12 local non-governmental organisation (NGO) workers: some were apparently lynched on the basis of tribal identity.[34]

In view of this spiral of failed diplomatic efforts and increasing violence in Darfur, Salim Ahmed Salim, AU special envoy and chief mediator for the Sudanese peace talks, stated,

> The international community is growing deeply skeptical of the agreements signed and the words of peace spoken. What

> we see is a list of ceasefire agreements and humanitarian protocols, which are violated every day. We cannot continue like this. We must hold ourselves to higher standards of respect to our words.[35]

After the signing of the DPA, the AU appeared to adopt a double standard toward the different armed groups. Publicly, at its 51st meeting, the PSC resolved to

> **Undertake[s]** to review regularly, in close coordination and consultation with the UN Security Council, the implementation of the DPA and to take strong and effective measures against any individual or group in Darfur that violate the Ceasefire Agreement and those who may attempt to block the implementation of the DPA, including a request to the United Nations Security Council to impose a travel ban and assets freeze, as provided for in Resolution 1591 (2005).[36]

Yet in practice, instead of "strong and effective measures", the AU used its payrolls to finance extortion fees to various armed forces located in Darfur, including the Sudanese army and the different armed movements, in exchange for freedom of movement in the region for its troops. According to the DPA, all local groups sent official representatives to each of the AU's eight sector headquarters to help monitor and investigate ceasefire violations, but AMIS officials were forced to pay these representatives for running convoys between two of its bases, and were further forced to secure the permission of each of the groups that controlled territory along the route. If one of the groups refused to give its permission for the convoy, AMIS forces were paralyzed.

In addition to the financial significance of these payments for the cash-strapped organization, which was frequently unable to pay salaries to its own staff, the consequences to the security of the citizens of Darfur were much more severe. "It is very frustrating. The peace agreement states that we have freedom of movement", said Colonel Richard Lourens, a South African officer, "It is totally against the agreement that we don't. We cannot monitor freely, we can only monitor in consultation."[37]

Acts of violence by the armed movements were not only directed against each other or against the Janjaweed or the Sudanese army and police, but also toward AMIS troops, as well as other humanitarian agencies. In December 2006, for example, AMIS troops were attacked by SLM/A soldiers.[38] In contrast to subsequent attacks, this specific incident ended without casualties to AMIS troops. Involvement in violence was not the exclusive purvey of the rebel movements. According to Prunier:

> The Islamic government of Khartoum justifies frequent raids by claiming their victims are rebels who refused to sign the Abuja "peace" treaty in Nigeria on 5 May 2006. In reality, the Sudanese government is trying to prevent the fighters from holding a congress that will unify the movement and enable them to start negotiations with the support of the international community.[39]

Summarizing the nature of the mediation efforts between the parties in the Abuja talks, Alex de Waal claims:

> Darfur's peace talks were conducted while fighting continued and the humanitarian crisis remained unresolved. The negotiations were often intermittent and always appeared agonizingly slow. Darfur burned while Sudanese leaders talked, or talked about talking, or refused to talk. Darfurians died while the negotiations remained stuck on agreeing on the movements' representation or adopting an agenda for the security arrangements track, the urgency of concern manifested by humanitarian workers and activities did not seem matched by the slow pace of talks [...][40]

A comparison of the AU's mediation efforts in Darfur and its mediating role in the conflict between the North and the South of Sudan generates some interesting insights. The AU produced most of the diplomatic initiatives pertaining to the Darfur conflict, while the diplomatic initiatives of the OAU (and later, the AU) in North–South negotiations were rather negligible. The Darfur peace talks were not the first time that a call for "an African solution" was voiced: Shortly after the National Islamic Front (NIF) seized power in Sudan, negotiations commenced between the new ruling party and the SPLM/A. The then Nigerian president and OAU chairman, Ibrahim Babaginda, initiated two rounds of talks in Abuja, in 1992 and 1993, which failed, for various reasons that are beyond the scope of this discussion.[41] It is, however, interesting to note that already in this early phase of al-Bashir's rule, he argued against "imperialist and neo-colonialist" intervention in his state's affairs, and for the need to establish a broad foundation for "African solutions". Al-Bashir also favoured cooperation with Muslim President Babaginda against what he perceived as a Western conspiracy against the Muslims in his country. He re-emphasized this rhetoric in the case of Darfur. In transitioning from the OAU to the AU, the continental organization assumed a more active role to ensure that African problems would indeed be resolved by Africans.

Much of the success of the North–South dialogue could be attributed to massive diplomatic efforts of the regional Intergovernmental Authority on Development (IGAD).[42] After the collapse of the 1992–3 Abuja peace talks, the NIF had approached the regional body of the Inter-Government Authority on Drought and Development (IGADD) in its summit meeting of 1993,[43] requesting its leaders to mediate in the Sudanese conflict. In response, an IGAD sub-committee on conflict resolution in the IGAD sub-region was formed, whose members were the presidents of Kenya, Uganda, Eritrea, and Ethiopia. It was the first political mediation effort of IGAD, which until then had mainly concentrated on ecological disaster relief efforts.

The GoS had agreed to IGAD's diplomatic initiative, especially since its Islamist policy had come under strong international diplomatic and financial pressure after the Islamist revolution of 1989. Despite its concerns about IGAD's disposition toward the GoS, the SPLM/A had several reasons for joining the process, including its growing difficulties to manage a successful combat operation at the time. Eventually, the North–South mediation process continued for more than a decade, followed by ups and downs triggered by intra-Sudanese factors as well as external factors, such as the split within IGAD following the Ethiopia–Eritrea War between 1998 and 2000.

IGAD's persistent efforts in the peace process between the North and the South were acknowledged in the PSC meeting of August 2007: "[The PSC] welcomes the appointment by the Chairperson of IGAD of former President Daniel Arap Moi as Special Envoy for the CPA, in order to sustain and enhance efforts towards the full and timely implementation of the Agreement."[44]

The case of IGAD's intervention in the conflict between North and South illustrated how proactive intervention and mediation efforts by a regional organization can contribute to relatively successful conflict resolution. Other examples of regional mediation successes include ECOWAS's involvement in the conflicts of Liberia and Sierra Leone, and its more recent involvement in the elections crisis in Côte d'Ivoire (discussed in Chapter 8). That no regional organization had a direct motivation to intervene in Darfur may have reduced the prospects for successful resolution of this conflict.[45] In the following chapter, we proceed to analyze the GoS's ideological and practical position on AMIS's presence in Darfur.

CHAPTER 5

THE GOVERNMENT OF SUDAN RESPONDS TO AFRICAN UNION INTERVENTION

Even before AMIS's initial deployment, the AU clearly tended to accept the GoS's restrictions on the force's official authority. After AMIS forces were in place, the GoS consistently rejected proposals to increase the number of AMIS personnel or extend its mandate, and repeatedly restricted AMIS ceasefire monitoring activities to limited areas.[1] In July 2004, African leaders met to define the force's mandate. Mali President and African Union Commission Chairman Alpha Oumar Konaré declared that he would not stand idly by when civilians were being killed, even though the force's official mandate was limited to the protection of observers and humanitarian workers. He added that the force could be enlarged without changing its defined role. Although Chadian Minister of Foreign Affairs and African Integration Nacoum Yamassoum confirmed that the leaders agreed that the force would thereafter also protect civilians, this claim was rejected by the Sudanese minister of foreign affairs.[2]

One month later, the GoS minister of agriculture refused the AU's request to enlarge its force in Darfur, claiming that his government was perfectly capable of dealing with the security situation in Darfur. The same month, GoS minister of humanitarian affairs reiterated his government's position, calling upon the AU to focus exclusively on mediating between the parties and monitoring the ceasefire agreement, instead of dealing with humanitarian issues.[3] Stronger opposition to intervention was expressed by Dr Mustafa Uthman Ismail, Sudanese minister of foreign affairs, who declared that Sudan rejected the transformation of the current force into a peacekeeping force. The GoS, he said, welcomed the presence of the 315 AMIS troops, yet would not allow its transformation into a full-fledged armed force that intervened between the rebel groups, or between them and the Janjaweed. He clarified that Sudan did not view the African forces as an occupation force, since Sudan was a member of the AU, which authorized their presence.[4] Sudanese opposition had its effect: In August 2004, AU Spokesperson Adama Thiam announced that the AU would postpone sending an additional 300 soldiers to Darfur, due to Sudan's opposition.[5]

Based on their declarations, GoS officials were concerned not only with the AU force's size and mandate, but also with its composition, and their criticism sought to ensure that the troops would arrive from friendlier and less critical African countries. For example, the Sudanese minister of affairs admonished the Rwandan president for commenting on the restrictions imposed on AMIS's scope and mandate by the Sudanese government.[6] In one case, Rwandan soldiers were even blamed of being HIV carriers. Al-Tayb Mustafa, a member of the NIF's National Council, blamed the Rwandan troops for participating in the massacres and ethnic cleansing in their country. He also blamed the AU for sending them to Sudan, and the GoS for not conducting the required HIV tests with their arrival.[7]

Despite the GoS's adamant opposition to attempts to enlarge both the scope and the authority of the new force, the communication channels between the AU and the Sudanese government remained open. In October 2004, negotiations were held between AU and GoS representatives in Addis Ababa.[8] As mentioned, these talks paved the way for the enlargement of AMIS, which later became known as AMIS II. At one point, the GoS even announced that it might allow AMIS to handle the disarmament of the local armed groups,[9] yet, GoS support for AMIS proved to be inconsistent. Shortly afterward, Sudanese Vice Minister of Interior Ahmad Mohammad Harun declared that the Sudanese police rather than AMIS (which had meanwhile increased by an additional 3,500 troops and 800 CIVPOL) would maintain responsibility for the security situation in Darfur, and the Sudanese police proceeded to deploy 10,250 police officers and policemen in the region to restore security and peace. Harun also mentioned that the role of AMIS observers should be limited to supervision of the Sudanese police in the IDP camps, to help restore trust between the police and the camps residents.[10] The GoS continued to object to the new definition of the AU force as "peacekeepers" on numerous occasions.[11]

GoS objections to AU intervention in Darfur can be divided into two main categories. The first category of arguments referred to an objection to AMIS's instrumental role in reinforcing Western intervention. In the context of the discourse on Africa unity and the sovereignty of its states, the GoS argued that international intervention in general, and military intervention in particular, violated not only Sudan's sovereignty, but the sovereignty of the entire continent.[12] In fact, al-Bashir had used the neo-colonial and "African solutions" arguments since the early 1990s. Justifying his consent to IGAD's mediation between the North and the South, he stated on one occasion, "Africans have become mature enough to resolve their own problems [...] and are [no] longer in a need of a foreign guardian." On another occasion he suggested that IGAD's mediation would be neutral and transparent, "without loopholes through which colonialism could penetrate on the pretext of humanitarianism".[13]

In the beginning of the twenty-first century, following the Western invasions of Iraq and Afghanistan, the GoS augmented this argument by objecting to Western (and, as such, Christian) intervention within the boundaries of the Muslim world. Thus, when Britain declared that it was willing to send 5,000 soldiers to Darfur (if so requested by the GoS), al-Bashir threatened to withdraw the Sudanese army from Darfur, leaving the region to its fate, and accused the international community of over-involvement in Sudan's affairs, motivated by their wish to weaken the Islamic state of Sudan rather than by genuine concern for Darfur.[14] Referring to US involvement in Iraq and Afghanistan, Sudanese Foreign Minister Mustafa Uthman Ismail cautioned the United States against unjustified intervention in the affairs of another Muslim state.[15]

A statement in a similar vein was made in response to Security Council Resolution 1593 and the referral of the situation in Darfur to the ICC to enforce warrants of arrest against Ahmad Muhammad Harun and alleged Janjaweed leader, Ali Kushayb, for crimes against humanity and war crimes. Referring to Sudan's colonial past, Majdhub al-Khalifah, Sudanese minister of agriculture, protested, "We totally reject the resolution, as it presents a harsh violation of the Sudanese sovereignty [. . .] we declare a comprehensive recruitment of the Sudanese people to defend its estates, as it protected its independence in the past."[16] GoS officials also accused the rebel organizations of trying to forge alliances with other international organizations to delegitimize the GoS and interfere with the country's sovereignty.[17]

The second category of arguments, understandably interwoven with the first, concerned Sudan's colonial history, and, as such, these arguments were part of the prevalent discourse of ex-colonized states. Thomas Weiss claims:

> Contemporary politics in developing countries is deeply conditioned by the legacy of colonialism. [. . .] What may appear as narrow legalism in the North – for instance, that Security Council authorization is a prerequisite for humanitarian as for other type of intervention – often appears in the South as a necessary buttress against new forms of arrogance and imperialism.[18]

Indeed, in their statements, Sudanese officials clearly represented international intervention as neo-colonialist interventionism, while African intervention was considered legitimate, internal involvement. "The era of colonialism is over, and you should leave the place if you do not provide clarifications in regard to your threatening declarations about imposing sanctions on Sudan", pronounced Sudanese Foreign Minister Ismail to a European Union delegation visiting Khartoum in October 2004.[19] Using anti-colonial rhetoric, Abd al-Basit Sabdrat, Sudanese minister of information and communication, insisted that the solution to the Darfur problem lay in an internal solution, and declared that Sudan would only accept African forces on its soil.[20] One fantastic example of an alleged international (specifically, Norwegian, Jewish, and Zionist) conspiracy against the GoS appeared in a book, *The Absent Truth*, published by the Sudanese Media Center:

> It is strange for such a small country [i.e., Norway] to have such unusual influence in the world. However, the source of surprise disappears if one looked deeper into the international politics of Jews in dealing with Islamic countries through being an unquestioned intermediary [this is far from clear, but seems here to refer to Norway] by the Islamic countries that was allowed to engineer the Oslo agreement between Israel and the Palestinians.[21]

In 2004 and most of 2005, the AU also used the neo-colonial argument against international intervention in Darfur. The common memories of European colonial occupation and successive foreign interventions in the internal affairs of African states seemed to create a feeling of unity among AU members and a strong desire to prevent a renewal of international intervention in Darfur. As a result, the majority of the AU member states did not reject, and in some cases even defended, GoS policy. In 2004, for example, the African bloc in the UN Human Rights Commission rejected international criticism of GoS atrocities in Darfur.[22] Following US attempts to define the conflict in Darfur as genocide, an anonymous senior AU official stated that the organization was averse to definitions of this kind. The AU's first priority, he claimed, was to put an end to the suffering of the inhabitants in Darfur, and it was therefore unnecessary to conduct empty debates on "genocide".[23]

In January 2005, Itai Madamombe of *Africa Renewal* reported,

> The European Union (EU) proposed a resolution to condemn the atrocities in Darfur in the UN General Assembly's Third

> Committee, which deals with social, humanitarian and cultural issues. Led by African representatives, a majority of delegates voted to take "no action" on the resolution. The African group of delegates explained that while there is no denying the human rights violations, it did not agree with the "double standards" by which only certain countries are condemned. Moreover, it pointed out, the EU had failed to consult with the AU mediators, thereby detracting from the principle of African political leadership in resolving the crisis.[24]

Interestingly, this last claim that African states were being excluded from handling their own conflicts was also voiced in the course of the Libyan crisis of 2011, as elaborated below.

In May 2005, seven African leaders meeting in Libya rejected any intervention in Darfur by a non-African nation.[25] The AU even supported the GoS's rejection of Security Council Resolution 1593, mentioned above, claiming that the humanitarian situation in Darfur was an "African–Sudanese" issue.[26] During his visit to the United States in June 2005, South Africa President Thabo Mbeki told President Bush,

> It's critically important that the African continent should deal with these conflict situations on the continent, and that includes Darfur. [. . .] We have not asked for anybody outside of the African continent to deploy troops in Darfur. It's an African responsibility, and we can do it.[27]

On the ground, the AMIS troops themselves apparently experienced a sense of pride in their ability to perform an exclusive African task. This feeling is evident from the personal testimony of Brian Steidle, supposedly to be deployed as a US monitor on ground (the United States being the mission's primary financial supporter). His request for deployment was denied repeatedly until

> My colleagues explained that the AU was afraid that the West would take over its mission. Darfur represented the first time

> the AU had ever conducted a full scale operation, and its leaders felt strongly that they had to demonstrate their own success without the UN, NATO, EU, or US interference or, even worse, dominance.[28]

Expressions of pride regarding Africa's ability to handle its own crisis without foreign intervention were common among AMIS commanders and troops until mid-2005,[29] when the general deterioration in conditions in Darfur forced AMIS to recognize its own limitations and caused a blow to their confidence.

The AU was not the sole defender of the GoS's position against international intervention. The League of Arab States (LAS) was an even more ardent champion of the Sudanese position, and had been so since 2004.[30] In this regard, it is very important to note that nine of the 22 members of the LAS are also members of the AU, and these overlapping memberships played a decisive role in shaping both organizations' policies on Darfur. Egypt, for example, was considered a leading member in both organizations. Its policy on Darfur was shaped by its own geo-political interests and its historical partnership with Sudan since the latter's colonial era, described in Chapter 2. Egypt's special concern for the Nile River water sources and the need to closely cooperate with the Sudanese government on this issue satisfactorily explain the aligned positions of both governments on Darfur and their influential support for GoS claims both in the AU and the LAS.[31] It is important to note, however, that Egyptian public opinion was not as supportive of the GoS. Coverage of the conflict by *al-Ahram* correspondent Gamal Nkrumah, for example, was critical of the GoS and introduced a more balanced view of the parties' arguments at different phases of the conflict.[32]

The LAS delegation that arrived in Darfur in July 2004 to investigate alleged human rights violations pledged the organization's support to AU efforts to resolve the conflict, and rejected the idea of an internationalized force.[33] In practical terms, however, LAS support of the AMIS was negligible. According to *Al Hayat* reporter Nadim Habani, at the March 2006 Khartoum summit the LAS responded to harsh criticism against its lack of practical support for

AMIS by pledging US$150 million to the force; yet one year later, less than 10 percent of the sum had been received. In view of the tremendous wealth of several LAS member states, Habani argued, there was no justification for the fact that most of the force's budget was received from the West, or that fewer than 76 of the 7,000 troops deployed at the time were from Arab countries.[34]

In contrast to its lassitude in financing AMIS, the LAS was much more resolute in its diplomatic efforts to defend the GoS's position on Darfur in the UN. Since 2004, the two non-voting Arab members of the Security Council, Algeria and Qatar, either abstained from or managed to tone down resolutions that were unfavourable to Khartoum's Darfur policy. Their speeches consistently defended Sudanese sovereignty and opposed intervention in Sudan's internal affairs. Recalling the AU reaction to Resolution 1593, LAS Secretary-General Amr Musa stated that, while his organization did not challenge the Security Council, the resolution should be implemented with special attention to the rights of all the parties, first and foremost with regard to Sudan sovereignty.[35] Idris Ibrahim Rizq, official JEM spokesman, criticized Egypt and the LAS for their support of the GoS's stance. The LAS also concurred with the GoS position on the transition to a hybrid force and the ICC's rulings, elaborated below.

If until September 2005, the AU, the LAS, and the GoS were united in their opposition to international intervention, the AU's position changed noticeably after this date. In the autumn of 2005, with violence in Darfur escalating, the previously united front revealed several cracks, specifically on the issue of the GoS's responsibility for handling the situation. The transition from AU rejection to acceptance of international forces to Darfur was, however, neither immediate nor unanimous. The South African president championed opposition to a hybrid force, and promoted the idea of an anti-hybrid force, while Senegalese Foreign Minister Cheikh Tidiane Gadio suggested to American Secretary of State Condoleezza Rice that the international community should intervene more actively in the conflict, including on the ground. The situation in Darfur was "totally unacceptable", he claimed, because "Those militias, they're still very active [. . .] killing people, burning villages, raping women."[36]

In September 2005, Jan Pronk, UN special envoy to Sudan, analyzed AMIS's failure to control the escalating situation in Darfur. Referring to its limited manpower strength, Pronk stated:

> Their numbers are not satisfying at all, because the militias and other powers could fight in places where the AU forces are not available. We need reinforcement, because Darfur is a large region. We like to have larger forces next year, in order to protect the villages.[37]

Baba Gana Kingibe, head of AMIS at the time, accused Sudanese governmental forces of direct involvement in the attacks on North Darfurian villages and collusion with Janjaweed militias. Kingibe stated that this, his first press conference since his arrival in Darfur 18 months earlier, was triggered by these "exceptional circumstances" in Darfur.[38] In response, the GoS called for Kingibe's expulsion, claiming that his presence was beginning to interfere with general Sudanese interests, and that his announcement exceeded understandings that had been previously achieved with the GoS.[39]

As the AU acknowledged its own inadequacy to improve the situation in Darfur, and realized that only an international force could handle the situation effectively, the organization became less supportive of the GoS's resistance to broad international intervention in Darfur. The AU's new understanding of the situation can be partly attributed to growing grievances voiced by Darfurians, both civilians and armed group members, concerning the AMIS's failure to stop the escalating violence. Reporter Craig Timberg offers an example of AU impotence in his *Washington Post* column:

> Investigations of major breaches of the cease-fire, meanwhile, have been stymied. That includes an incident Saturday in which villagers who had been attacked by Janjaweed militiamen two weeks earlier gathered near the ruins of their homes in South Darfur to speak to A.U. investigators set to

> arrive by helicopter. But the helicopter turned back because of severe rain, and the Janjaweed attacked again, killing 18 of the survivors of the earlier assault and dispersing as many as 25,000 into a remote southern region far from humanitarian assistance or military protection, rebel leaders here said. Minnawi complained to top African Union officials about the incident, and the group's cease-fire commission twice scheduled investigative trips to the site of the atrocities, only to cancel them as commission members quarreled over the importance of the journey.[40]

The AU could no longer turn a deaf ear to the intense criticism originating from AMIS personnel. Although AU Chairman Alpha Konaré and Sudanese Foreign Minister Lam Akol published a joint statement in February 2006 on the African nature of the Darfur crisis, and African responsibility for its resolution,[41] in an address to AU headquarters in Khartoum that same month, Baba Kingibe attacked the GoS directly for its failure to disarm the Janjaweed militias and prevent them from committing "wide-scale killings, burnings and rapes".[42] *Sudaneseonline* had exposed a secret agreement between the GoS and the militia leaders, which included a promise of immunity to Janjaweed members, deposition of military powers, and control of the conquered lands.[43]

At the March 2006 PSC meeting, the AU and the GoS were already clearly divided. The AU issued another resolution, stating,

> The Peace and Security Council (PSC) of the African Union (AU), at its 46th meeting, held on 10 March 2006. [. . .] *Decides* to support in principle the transition from AMIS to a UN Operation, within the framework of the partnership between AU and the United Nations in the promotion of peace, security and stability in Africa.[44]

Sudan's representatives to the meeting clung to the country's neo-colonial argument. Several days before the PSC meeting, the Sudanese minister of state for foreign affairs stressed to an AU delegation to Khartoum that the continent, having come out of colonialism, should be able to solve its problems by itself. He argued that it was on this premise that his government had accepted the deployment of AMIS in 2004. He drew attention to the sensitivities in Darfur, which, as an Islamic society with ingrained Islamic values, required caution in any attempt to hand over the Mission to the UN. He also expressed GoS suspicions that the transition was not motivated by financial straits, as claimed, but was a ploy to promote a hidden agenda of several countries. On behalf of the Sudanese government, he offered to help raise the required funds for AMIS to continue its operation, if the transition was indeed genuinely based on the missions' financial difficulties.[45]

At the PSC meeting on 10 March 2006, commissioner for peace and security, Said Djinnit,

> informed the Sudanese delegation that the idea of handing over to the UN was envisaged within the framework of the partnership between the AU and the UN which, in any event, had the primary responsibility for the maintenance of international peace and security. He recalled how the OAU/AU handed over AMIB to the United Nations. Finally, he made it clear that, if the PSC so decides the AU was envisaging handing over AMIS only to the UN and not to any other organization.[46]

The meeting's report also noted that the transition had been requested by most SLM/A and JEM members for a long time: JEM's spokesperson to Abuja stated that the protection of civilians in Darfur was a matter of top priority that should override the government's opposition against the envisaged transition from AMIS to a UN-led operation. The report further mentioned popular demonstrations in IDP camps including al-Fasher, Nyala, and Gradia, demanding the transition.[47] At that point, the AU's position appeared to be much closer to that of the Darfurians than to that of the GoS. Negotiations to establish of a joint AU–UN force gained momentum, and the AU-led peacekeeping mission quickly transformed into a hybrid AU–UN force, despite fierce GoS opposition.

The LAS remained adamant in its refusal to embrace the hybrid force, and continued to support the GoS's stand against international intervention. Samir Husni, head of the LAS's Africa department, criticized rumoured US attempts to prevent the upcoming LAS Summit in Khartoum, in order to put pressure on the organization to accept the transition. This was unacceptable interference in the LAS's inner affairs, he claimed, and emphasized the LAS's leading role in the efforts to bring the conflict to its end.[48]

The GoS's continued opposition to international intervention was, furthermore, a function of the political factor that Alex de Waal described as "instability in the center".[49] In some cases, the fragility of Sudan's political center was apparent from opposition parties' criticism of the ruling party, first for creating the Darfur crisis, and, second, for submitting to foreign pressure. Accusations of this kind were also voiced by Muhammad Uthman al-Mirghani, leader of the powerful opposition Sudanese Democratic Unionist Party (DUP), who protested against international intervention in Darfur in early 2006.[50]

Even more effective was the criticism directed toward the NIF by Sadiq al-Hadi al-Mahdi, leader of the influential Umma Party, and two-time president of Sudan (1966–7; 1986–7). Al-Mahdi, who is also the great-grandson of Muhammad Ahmed al-Mahdi, is also the spiritual leader of *ansar*, a Sufi *tariqa* (brotherhood) with many followers in Sudan.[51] Al-Sadiq blamed the GoS for opening the door to international intervention and to the threat of military intervention by the Western powers. The mistakes that were committed by the GoS, he claimed, were the reason that the problem of Darfur turned into a crisis.[52]

The main challenge to GoS policy on Darfur, however, seemed to come from power struggles between al-Bashir and al-Turabi. Although al-Bashir successfully cultivated remarkable continuity among senior officials, especially the security officials that were closely affiliated with him, his rule was nevertheless constantly challenged by charismatic al-Turabi. The threat to the ruling party's hegemony increased after al-Turabi founded the Popular Congress Party (PCP) and a united Islamist opposition front became a realistic possibility.[53]

While al-Turabi's role in resolution of the conflict in Darfur is described elsewhere in this book, it is important to examine how al-Turabi's statements influenced GoS officials' opposition to foreign intervention in Darfur in general, and especially their position on the transition to the hybrid force. Al-Turabi's policy statements were not consistent: For a while he defended the arrival of an international force in Darfur, claiming that it would be the only cure to Darfur's chaotic situation. Later, however, he criticized the GoS for admitting the international forces into Darfur. In an interview for the BBC in January 2006, al-Turabi argued that the presence of foreign forces in Darfur debilitated Sudan to the point that it could no longer be called a sovereign state.[54] Al-Tuarbi's criticism became particularly scathing after the GoS approved the arrival of attack helicopters. He stated that the foreign presence would act as "a cancer in the nation's body".[55]

In some cases, al-Turabi's frequently repeated opposition to foreign intervention in Darfur and the popularity of his statements were instrumental in radicalizing the GoS's own position. This was particularly relevant after the JEM's armed attack on Khartoum and Omdurman on 10 May 2008. This armed attack came as a complete surprise both to the GoS and to the residents of these two cities. This attack brought the war home after Khartoum had enjoyed the reputation of one of the safest cities in Africa despite decades of violent history throughout the country.[56] Although the motives for this almost-suicidal attack were not entirely clear, the GoS suspected that both al-Turabi, who was known for his ties with the JEM, and the Chadian government, which was ethnically identified with the movement, were involved. As a result, al-Turabi was arrested once again, and the GoS toughened its opposition to outside intervention in general, and to UNAMID in particular.

For the GoS, the sense of internal instability in view of growing criticism directed toward its policies was aggravated by events in the African arena. The tension between the Sudanese government and the AU was revealed when the AU rejected Sudan's bid to chair the organization. In the absence of criteria for AU chairmanship other than the principle of rotation among Africa's sub-regions, it is not inconceivable that Sudan's abysmal human rights record and its responsibility for massive crimes in Darfur were the reasons behind the AU's decision. The AU's role in mediating peace negotiations in Darfur was probably another critical factor: Many observers mentioned the potential conflict of interests if one of the warring parties in Darfur were to hold the AU chair.[57]

In his daily column in *al-Ray al-a'm*, Rashid Abd al-Rahim summarized the criticism against the AU for surrendering to international pressure:

> The Sudanese people have the right to feel bitterness because Sudan didn't get the AU Presidency. The bitterness isn't caused by the fact that Sudan failed in obtaining this important position, or from the discovery that its strength is deficient. This bitterness isn't directed toward the African people, but it stems from the fact that the [African] continent is still in captivity. If Sudan would have lost the position because of African will, this would have elicited a different response, but the fact is that Sudan has to battle against the United States on an African matter. [The United States] is standing behind [African] leaders who cannot accept decisions that result from their responsibility toward the continent.[58]

The AU's refusal to approve al-Bashir as chairperson of the organization seemed to signify the AU's commitment to a new path of greater concern for human rights, and reduced commitment to indiscriminate protection of ruling elites. By adopting greater alignment with the interests of civilians, the AU appeared to distance itself from its predecessor, which had also been known as the "dictators' club". It is nonetheless impossible to ignore the fact that the substitute chairperson was Denis Sassou Nguesso, president of the Republic of Congo, hardly a model defender of human rights.

The rejection of the Sudanese bid may also have been related to the bid's timing, at the climax of the Abuja talks, which made Sudan's leadership of the organization all the more inappropriate. Sudan's bid for the organization's chairpersonship in the following year was also rejected. This time the chair was handed to the Ghanaian president, who had a more favourable human rights record.[59]

Despite the AU's rejection of Sudan's bid to chair the organization, several Arab countries continued to support Khartoum's position, and expressed sympathy with the perceived threat to Sudanese sovereignty. Qatar, one of the non-permanent members on the Security Council at the time, abstained from voting on Resolution 1706, the transition to a hybrid force. This abstention is interesting in light of the future role that Qatar would play in the mediation efforts in Darfur. The GoS's responses to the deployment of the hybrid force in Darfur, and the complex international setting in which the hybrid force operated are discussed in the next chapter.

CHAPTER 6

THE TRANSITION TO UNAMID – A HYBRID FORCE EXPERIMENT

Based on evidence collected in refugee camps on the Chad-Darfur border in August and September 2004 by the Coalition for International Justice, at the behest of the US State Department, US Secretary of State Colin Powell defined the events in Darfur as "genocide". "We concluded that genocide has been committed in Darfur and that the Government of Sudan and the Janjaweed bear responsibility and genocide may still be occurring", he declared in September that year. The testimonies collected in the camps, he said, showed a pattern of violence that was coordinated, not random.[1]

The UN was slower to adopt the term "genocide", although Secretary-General Kofi Annan had already declared in April 2004 that "outside military action may be needed in western Sudan to halt 'ethnic cleansing' in the strife-torn Darfur region",[2] and the UN International Commission of Inquiry on Darfur report delivered in January 2005 found evidence of war crimes and crimes against humanity in Darfur. The Commission, led by Antonio Cassese, prepared a secret list of 51 suspected criminals, including Ahmed Harun and al-Kushayb, and recommended that the ICC investigate the Darfur atrocities.[3] The fate of this recommendation is discussed in Chapter 7.

Despite overwhelming evidence of the scope of the humanitarian crisis in Darfur, which frustrated AMIS's limited resources and rendered the mission ineffective, it was not until July 2007 that the Security Council adopted Resolution 1769, demanding the establishment of a hybrid UN–AMIS force (UNAMID) in Darfur. Three years of hesitation and failure to offer an effective solution to the conflict in Darfur resulted in the estimated loss of 250,000–400,000 lives and more than 2.5 million refugees and IDPs.[4] What were the reasons for the international community's reluctance to replace weak continental intervention with a strong international intervention force despite growing evidence of the deteriorating humanitarian situation in Darfur?

One way to answer this question is to turn to an analysis of international relations and their effect on the international response to the situation in Darfur. One explanation for the international community's hesitancy is the decline in the prestige and role of the West, especially the United States and Britain, in humanitarian intervention after the invasions of Iraq and Afghanistan. James Kurth claims that after these invasions, the United States (and in some respects, Europe) lost its legitimacy for intervening, especially in the internal affairs of Muslim states, as Westerners came to be perceived by many Muslims around the world as their enemy.[5]

Nick Grono attributed the inaction of the West to interests rather than inability. "Darfur does not matter enough, and Sudan matters too much", he stated, and blamed the US for its priorities in the war on terror, which resulted in greater intimacy in the relations between Washington and Khartoum, at the expense of the interests of the Darfurians.[6] Susan Rice strongly objected to the use of Western intervention in other Muslim state affairs as an excuse for non-intervention, arguing:

> Western military intervention in another Muslim country could create a new front for jihadist attacks. However, it is hard to see how allowing this fear to deter us from saving Muslim lives would salve anti-American hostility in the Muslim world.[7]

Mathew Lippman claimed that the failure of the international community in general, and the UN in particular, to impose effective sanctions on Sudan was a symptom of "genocide denial syndrome":

> The question arises why the international community has insisted that Darfur is not a witness of genocide. The simple answer is that Darfur has fallen victim to a toxic mix of the politics of oil, multinational investment and arms sales and that events in the Middle East and Africa have made the international community reluctant to intervene in the affairs of a fundamentalist Islamic regime.[8]

Alex Bellamy's analysis of the less than successful attempts of the United States and Britain to pass resolutions in the Security Council between 2003 and 2005 also highlights the rising power of China and Russia in Africa in this period.[9] China's longstanding relations with Sudan became stronger in the early twenty-first century as Chinese interests in Sudanese oil increased, prompting repeated Chinese efforts to undermine Security Council resolutions concerning Darfur. According to human rights groups and other observers, the Chinese government became the principal supplier of weapons to the GoS, in violation of a UN weapons embargo on Sudan. In 2005, China reportedly sold Sudan US$24 million in arms and ammunition and US$57 million worth of spare parts for aircraft and helicopters.[10] Russia, another member of the Security Council, also developed important economic and military interests in Sudan, especially through arms sales to the GoS. As a result of the changing balance of power in the UN Security Council, many of the Security Council draft resolutions were adopted in their mildest version or were not passed.

One example of diffused resolution making was the US effort to impose an oil embargo on Sudan in February 2005. Both China and Russia opposed the initiative, and Resolution 1591, adopted on 29 March that year, was limited to travel bans on suspected war criminals.[11] Repeated efforts to declare Darfur a no-fly zone, described earlier, constitute yet another example of such failed efforts.

The need to declare Darfur a no-fly zone was noted in the text of the 17th meeting of the PSC in October 2004, which stated that "[. . .] the Movements [SLM/A and JEM] requested the establishment of a no-fly-zone for military aircrafts and civilian aircrafts used for military purposes over the Darfur region."[12] Nonetheless, the UN Security Council repeatedly failed to pass a resolution to this effect. As a result, military activities continued in Darfur's airspace: In June 2008, the BBC acquired satellite photographs of two Fantan fighter planes at Nyala airport in South Darfur[13] and, in July 2008, BBC Television reported evidence of Chinese army trucks and several A5 Fantan fighter planes in Darfur, which had been used the previous February to bomb the town of Beybey in Darfur in which a number of civilians were reportedly killed.

The lack of international intervention in Darfur can also be traced to the UN and US failure in Somalia between 1992 and 1995. Therefore, an explanation of the background to operations in Somalia and the implications of this failed initiative are warranted. In its efforts to broaden the scope and intensity of peacekeeping operations in the immediate post-Cold War period, the UN launched large-scale operations in Cambodia (1991–3) and Somalia (1992–5) in response to severe deterioration of the humanitarian situation in both states. In Somalia, the explosion of violence and anarchy following the expulsion of Siad Barre's dictatorial regime in January 1991 resulted in rapidly deteriorating living conditions for most Somalis. In early August 1992 it was estimated that one-quarter of the country's population were in danger of death by starvation, and the remainder were at a high risk of starvation. Somalia's problems – an estimated 800,000 refugees – soon spilled beyond state borders into its neighbouring countries.[14]

Following the growing violence of Somalia's civil war, intensive diplomatic efforts by both the UN and the OAU culminated in a ceasefire agreement signed by the country's two key factions in March 1992. With the understanding that some kind of peacekeeping force would be required to sustain the agreement and ensure humanitarian relief efforts, the Security Council adopted Resolution 751, which led to the establishment of United Nations Operation in Somalia

(UNOSOM), a monitoring force. Significantly, UN Secretary-General Boutros Boutros-Ghali believed that the situation warranted implementation of Chapter VII of the Charter of the UN, which recommends "action by air, sea or land forces as may be necessary to maintain or restore international peace and security."[15] This Resolution, the first time the UN ever endorsed such an intervention, might have had very important implications for future humanitarian interventions had its implementation on the ground not encountered several serious problems.

In view of the parties' general contempt for the ceasefire agreement, provisions were made to increase the initial force of 50 troops to 3,000 troops. Most UNOSOM troops, however, were never deployed. In view of the deteriorating humanitarian conditions,[16] the US government decided to lead, under UN auspices, a Unified Task Force (UNITAF) for a five-month period, which became known as Operation Restore Hope. The new force (later transformed into UNOSOM II by Security Council Recommendation 837 of March 1993) was assigned to create a model for task-sharing between the UN and the US government, as was described by the UN secretary-general:

> The United States has undertaken to take the lead in creating the secure environment which is an inescapable condition for the United Nations to provide humanitarian relief and promote national reconciliation and economic reconstruction, objectives which have from the outset been included in the various Security Council resolutions on Somalia.[17]

UNOSOM II's deployment was accompanied with the overtly optimistic expectation that it would establish a new model for peacekeeping and reconstruction of a "collapsed state". With 28,000 personnel from 26 countries, and an annual budget of US$1.6 billion, UNOSOM II was expected to establish a new transitional government, supervise the disarmament of the forces, reconstruct the infrastructures, and resettle refugees. Although the new force induced Somali leaders from 15 different factions to sign the Addis Ababa Agreement in March 1993, few of its objectives were ever achieved.[18] A discussion of the reasons for the mission's failure is beyond the scope of this chapter, yet, for the purpose of our discussion, the events of July–October 1993 were crucial in the sense that they determined not only the fate of Operation Restore Hope, but also the fate of future international interventions in intrastate African conflicts.

In June 1993, 24 Pakistani UNOSOM troops were killed in an ambush by a Somali militia allegedly belonging to one of the powerful warlords, General Mohamed Farah Aidid. Following this incident, most UNOSOM efforts were redirected to defeating Aidid's forces and personally capturing him. These efforts included a combined aerial and ground attack on 12 July on a house that was believed to host a meeting of members of his movement, whom the Americans suspected were planning additional attacks against US and UN forces. The growing tensions between Aidid's factions and the international force led to the Battle of Mogadishu on 3–4 October, where two US Black Hawk helicopters were shot down, 18 American soldiers killed, and 73 wounded. Although the Somali casualties significantly outnumbered American casualties, the images of the failed American operation, and especially the images of the bodies of two US soldiers being dragged through the streets, had a tremendous impact on American and Western public opinion regarding intervention in risky areas overseas.[19] The incident recalled the circumstances of UNAMIR's withdrawal from Rwanda after the killing of ten Belgian peacekeepers by Hutu extremists on 7 April 1994, described earlier. When the US government decided to withdraw its forces from Somalia shortly thereafter, other nations followed suit, and UNOSOM was finally disbanded in March 1995.[20] The "body-bag syndrome" and increased reluctance of the international community to intervene in intrastate conflicts that place peacekeeping forces in life-threatening situations, remains one of the driving forces behind the call for "African solutions to African problems" in present conflicts in Africa, including in present-day Somalia, as elaborated below.

In contrast to Operation Restore Hope, an exclusively international force in which the continental organization played no role, foreign intervention in Darfur was initially African, and only later became international. Following the Security Council's failure to impose effective sanctions on Sudan in 2004–5 and the continuing diplomatic failure to end the conflict, the UN sought to collaborate more strongly with the AU in peacekeeping missions. In fact, UN interest in greater collaboration with Africa's regional (including continental) organizations was not a novel concept in the peacekeeping history of the UN operations in Africa. Chapter 5 of the UN Charter refers to "pacific settlement of local disputes through such regional arrangements or by such regional agencies either on the initiative of the states concerned or by reference from the Security Council". By the early twenty-first century, the number of peacekeeping operations had grown considerably, and the international climate was more favourably inclined to support increasing involvement of regional organizations in intrastate conflicts, both collaboratively with the UN or independently of it, as was the case with NATO-led missions in Afghanistan.[21] The conflict in Darfur seemed to offer optimal conditions to implement UN–AU cooperation.[22]

A pattern of cooperation between the UN and the AU had already been implemented when a hybrid force was established in Burundi. In February 2003, the PSC authorized the deployment of 3,500 personnel in the AU's first peace mission, the African Union Mission in Burundi (AMIB). Within a year, UN forces effectively controlled the political climate in Burundi, and, by June 2007, after steady progress in the peace process, the UN withdrew from the country, leaving the AU to support further advancement.[23] Although the mission in Burundi was limited in scope, focused mainly on the political sphere, and was free of many of the complications of a multi-task peacekeeping operation such as in the case of Darfur, there was one lesson from Burundi that was subsequently applied to Sudan. At the 46th meeting of the PSC, based on previous experience in transitioning to a hybrid force, members explicitly acknowledged the need to consider African governments' sensitivity to external intervention:

> In light of the sensitivities to the presence of non-African troops in Darfur, and should the PSC agree to a transfer, the

> Commission emphasized the need for the UN to absorb and, if need be, to augment the existing African troops in the Mission, as well as retain the African leadership of the force, as was the case when the African Union Mission in Burundi (AMIB) was transformed into the United Nations Operations in Burundi (ONUB). Although the UN delegation expressed understanding to this proposal, it however stated that the UN would, as usual, avail the African TCCs of the UN conditions and allow them to declare their interest as to whether to contribute troops to the UN Mission or not.[24]

In May 2006, the Security Council adopted Resolution 1679, which called for the UN and the AU to strengthen their cooperation to provide better security conditions for the people of Darfur.[25] This resolution, however, had little impact on the actual conditions in Darfur: Its primary commitment was to the sovereignty of the Sudanese state and its purpose was to secure the consent of all parties to external intervention, especially one that included military intervention. Although Resolution 1679 contained a threat of sanctions against Sudan, the Security Council fell short in its ability to implement these threats, especially due to Chinese and Russian opposition.[26] In August that year, the UN Security Council adopted Resolution 1706, which called for the expansion to Darfur of the United Nations Mission in Sudan (UNMIS), which had been deployed in South Sudan since 2005 and which was in practice already collaborating with AMIS on issues such as protection of civilians.[27] The GoS was ambivalent about the decision to extend UNMIS to Darfur. While this could prevent the deployment of a second international force within its territory, UNMIS was mandated to play a crucial role in the future referendum, especially in buffer zones, including the controversial Abyei zone. As a result, the GoS did not express official support for Resolution 1706.[28]

Resolution 1706, adopted on 31 August 2006, outlined a three-phase plan for dealing with the humanitarian crisis in Darfur, including two phased support packages and the subsequent establishment of a hybrid AU–UN force. The "light" package comprised US$21 million worth of technical and personnel support, and the "heavy" package provided for personnel and equipment at an estimated cost of US$300 million to be delivered over the first six months of operations.[29] The decision to implement these packages, which greatly improved AMIS's financial and human resource capabilities, was perceived as "new hope for Darfur".[30]

In a detailed article, however, Eric Reeves proved that the two packages would be ineffective without the deployment of the hybrid force:

> For the first time since 2004, the malnutrition rate, a gauge of the population's overall distress, has crossed what United Nations officials consider to be the emergency threshold. Just as important, the increase has occurred despite the efforts of more than 12,000 relief workers in Darfur, drawing from an annual aid budget of about a billion dollars. Aid officials said that they were concerned that even with all these resources, the people in Darfur seemed to be getting worse.[31]

In a second article he wrote, "given the paucity of available AU troops, this ensures that insecurity will remain at intolerable levels throughout Darfur and Eastern Chad".[32]

Despite these and similar warnings, implementation of the third phase of Resolution 1706, which entailed the deployment of the hybrid force, was repeatedly obstructed by the GoS, whose officials strongly opposed this move, even threatening that Sudan would secede from the AU.[33] In June 2006, Sudanese President al-Bashir explained his objection to a hybrid force by comparing the situation in Sudan to that in Iraq, vowing that he would not allow foreign occupation of his country.[34] Gradually, however, the international pressure brought to bear on the GoS bore fruit, and in December 2006 al-Bashir announced his approval of the deployment of the international force.[35] The change in the GoS's position may also have stemmed from internal divisions within the National Congress Party (NCP) on this very issue: Vice President Taha hinted that a UN peacekeeping force could be deployed in Darfur if negotiations in Abuja produced an agreement with the rebel groups.[36]

Another explanation for the GoS's change in position is related to Beijing's policy line in the Security Council. China, one of the five permanent members of the Security Council, had threatened to use its veto powers in many Darfur-related resolutions, yet surrendered on the deployment of a hybrid force in Darfur under the threat of a boycott of the approaching Beijing Olympics of August 2008.[37] An intense media campaign was launched against China's legitimacy as a host of the Olympic Games due to the country's indirect involvement in the conflict in Darfur and its policy in the Security Council. The campaign, initiated by various NGOs, and headed by the Save Darfur Coalition,[38] which used terms such as "the genocide Olympics" and featured prominent actors such as Mia Farrow and George Clooney, attracted strong international attention. Protest against the Olympics was not confined to Western humanitarian and activist groups. In Africa, various nascent organizations such as Nigerians Against Darfur Genocide (NADG) pressured their governments to boycott the forthcoming Olympics unless the host nation changed its policies toward Darfur. "Just like Tibet, China is responsible for the genocide in Darfur and their cultural annihilation", stated an NADG spokesperson.[39] These voices of protest and their threat to collect one million signatures originating from Nigeria, one of China's important oil suppliers, persuaded Chinese policymakers to reconsider their policy on Sudan and Darfur. Concerned over a potential cancellation of the Olympics, and to distract attention from the evolving revolt in Tibet, the Chinese abandoned their long-touted policy of non-interference in the internal affairs of their allies, and made a proactive attempt to persuade the Sudanese government to withdraw its objection to the deployment of the hybrid force. *Washington Quarterly* reporter J. Stephen Morrison described the Chinese involvement in this process:

> As the debate over an AU–UN peace operation accelerated in the second half of 2006, senior Chinese officials intervened at key moments in the UN Security Council, the AU summits, and Khartoum directly to press Khartoum first to accept the Annan plan devised in 2006 and subsequently for Resolution 1769, authorizing the UNAMID deployment. In May 2007,

> Ambassador Liu Guijin was appointed as the Chinese special envoy for Africa, expressly charged with handling Darfur. In that post, he and others such as Assistant Minister Zhai Jin and the Chinese ambassadors to the UN and Washington became highly active, consulting widely with Western powers, other African officials, and the AU and UN. Liu and others traveled throughout Darfur and showed an unprecedented receptivity to extensive engagement with activist critics.[40]

Chinese involvement continued in late 2007 and early 2008. The Chinese were involved in practical arrangements, such as pressing Khartoum to resolve delays over visas and customs clearances, and in more general diplomatic efforts, such as threatening the GoS with sanctions if it continued to deliberately retard UNAMID deployment plans.[41] The Chinese government even announced that it would send a small force of soldiers and engineers to UNAMID (an announcement received with resentment by many Darfurians). It was not certain, however, whether the Chinese were willing to commit to a resolution of the conflict beyond the efforts required to protect their immediate interests related to the Olympics, if such a commitment compelled them to compromise on more fundamental issues, such as weapon supplies to the GoS.

Despite GoS reservations, joint UN–AU teams had arrived in Darfur by June 2006 to prepare the ground for the actual deployment of the hybrid force, which was established on 31 July 2007, with the adoption of Security Council Resolution 1769. The force was deployed to replace AMIS several months later, in 2008. The decision to establish UNAMID is precedential in many respects, as noted by Andrews and Holt:

> This operation will consist of up to 19,555 military troops and 6,432 civilian police, predominantly from African countries. The mission is to have a unified command and control structure, with a single chain of command. Under Chapter VII of the UN Charter, the resolution grants uniformed personnel with UNAMID the authority to use force. The resolution also

> mandates the mission to implement the Darfur Peace Agreement; secure freedom of movement for mission staff and humanitarian personnel; provide protection to civilians; and monitor the presence of arms materiel in Darfur. UNAMID is expected to deploy by 31 December 2007 and to cost upwards of $2 billion annually. *This agreement on a hybrid force represents a major political achievement for the UN and AU and ushers in a new phase in their relationship. Deployment of the force with joint command and control structures will be the most complex collaboration the UN has ever undertaken with a regional organization.*[42]

Ahmed Ibrahim Diraige, governor of Darfur from 1980 to 1983 and chairman of the Sudan Federal Democratic Alliance, addressed the Sudan Peace Forum of the United States Institute of Peace in November 2007. He claimed that UNAMID was the best chance for restoring security in Darfur. Commenting on GoS attempts to delay or impede UNAMID's deployment, he predicted that the GoS would persist in "such games" until the international community imposes sanctions that force the GoS to modify its behaviour. He emphasized the importance of the international community's role in enforcing UN mandates and holding UN member states – including Sudan – to the obligations set forth in the UN charter.[43]

In developing a model for UNAMID, the new hybrid force, efforts were made to learn from the previous failures of AMIS in Darfur. The comprehensive 31-page joint report of the co-chairperson of the AU Commission and UN secretary general on the hybrid operation in Darfur, which was presented to the November 2007 PSC meeting, offered a detailed analysis of the failures and weaknesses of AMIS operations and the implementation of the DPA.[44] The report also offered very important insights on the changing AU attitudes toward the Sudanese government. The tone of this report tended to be highly critical, especially toward the GoS, and noted that "since its signing on 5 May 2006 in Abuja, the Darfur Peace Agreement has run into considerable difficulties". Even worse, almost no progress was made to implement any of the issues agreed upon in the DPA, including the issue of wealth sharing:

> No significant progress has been made in the implementation of the wealth sharing provisions of the Darfur Peace Agreement and compensation provisions remain outstanding. The Darfur Joint Assessment Mission, which was required to assess development and reconstruction needs in Darfur, has had to suspend its work because of security concerns. Consequently, the donors' pledging conference that was to be held in 2006 was postponed on account of the fact that the Joint Assessment Mission process was not concluded.[45]

According to the report, the GoS had marginalized other fundamental issues of the DPA, such as political sharing or disarmament of the Janjaweed militias, and had dragged its feet on implementation more than one year after signing the agreement. Interestingly, the report referred to the non-signatory parties of the DPA. It mentioned that the Joint Commission, established after the signing of the agreement, approved the establishment of two separate chambers for signatories and non-signatories, but the second chamber was never utilized, as no consensus on its operation was ever achieved. This time, the accusing finger was directed to the armed movements, especially the JEM, and their increasing fragmentation.[46] Still, the very understanding that a viable solution to the conflict required the inclusion of the non-signatory parties was valuable.

The report also mentioned the "high cost of providing a large number of representatives with allowances". Indeed, the need to pay "allowances" to the different rebel splinter groups in Darfur was one of the difficulties facing AMIS's operation, especially in view of its chronic budget deficiencies. The report recommended "to reduce the scale of party representation and amount of mission subsistence allowance paid to party representatives at the Ceasefire Commission level, and review the status and privileges of party representatives to the Ceasefire Commission".[47]

Rodolphe Adada of the Republic of Congo was appointed the UN–AU joint special representative for Darfur.[48] When he later visited al-Fasher headquarters on the first day of UNAMID operations, Adada expressed his hope that the deployment of the new force would be "one more step closer to embark on our peace keeping mandate for the people of Darfur".[49] General Martin Luther Agwai of Nigeria, former deputy force commander of the UN Mission in Sierra Leone (UNAMSIL),[50] was designated commander of the hybrid force.

The hybrid force was also expected to dispel international and African concerns that the Darfur conflict would spill over into neighbouring countries, and specifically to Chad and the Central African Republic. Darfur played a central role in the complex relations between Sudan and Chad (discussed briefly in Chapter 2) and the growing tension between the two states in 2006–7 and the danger of spillover of the Darfur conflict into Sudan's neighbours was acknowledged by the UN Security Council.[51]

Attempts to intervene in Chad and the Central African Republic were strongly criticized by the AU PSC, which stopped short of explicitly mentioning Sudan's role:

> [The PSC] **condemns strongly** the attacks perpetrated by armed groups against Chad and the Central African Republic, which constitute an unacceptable attempt to take over power by force, in violation of the Lomé Declaration on Unconstitutional Changes of Government. Council **demands** that these armed groups immediately put an end to their attacks and seek a peaceful solution for their grievances. [...] **Reaffirms** its commitment to the sovereignty, unity and territorial integrity of all the States of the region, as well as to the respect for the principles governing the relations of good neighborliness between Member States, as enshrined in the Constitutive Act of the AU.[52]

In this regard, it could be claimed that, as the continental body representing African states, the concern of the AU regarding the sovereignty, unity, and territorial integrity of its states sometimes overshadowed its concerns regarding the deterioration of the humanitarian situation within the particular state. In any case, the above PSC communiqué stressed the need to speed up the deployment of the force as part of the effort to find a solution at the regional level.[53]

Hopes for an immediate change both in the humanitarian and security situations in Darfur, and for progress in the peace talks between the rival parties, dissipated soon after UNAMID deployment. The disappointment was not completely unanticipated. Problems with the arrangements of the newly established peacekeeping force were predicted by General Martin Luther Agwai, as early as October 2007. In response to a question about his concerns over the insufficient pace of change, he stated,

> Definitely. I am very concerned. I accepted the job because I wanted to give it my best, and I can only give it my best and be judged by the world depending on the resources available to me. And the resources are not forthcoming. They are not giving me 20,000 [troops], not to mention the equipment the troops will use, not to mention the other staff we will need in the mission. Nothing. So I am really, really concerned. Plus, there's no peace deal yet. How can you be expected to provide security when there's no peace deal? Lack of peace on the ground is definitely another big challenge because we are here *as peacekeepers*, and our job would be easier and smoother if there were a peace deal brokered for us. Unfortunately, right now, there is no peace to keep. So it has become another Herculean task to see that people are protected. We hope the talks in Libya [scheduled to start 27 October] result in an acceptable, comprehensive peace agreement for us and for every party involved.[54]

An analysis of the transition from AMIS to UNAMID from a historical perspective may yet be premature, but it soon became clear that UNAMID inherited some of the faulty and ineffective procedures of its predecessor AMIS, although improvements were also evident. The remainder of this chapter reviews the primary features of UNAMID and its accomplishments and shortcomings, as well as continuity and change as AMIS transitioned into UNAMID.

The collaboration involving international and continental organizations in UNAMID appeared to be an important experiment in task-sharing and bridging two different organizational cultures. From the initial negotiations between the organizations, the partners agreed that the new mission would retain an "African character", in the sense that the head of the mission, the commanders of the army, the police, and the majority of the deployed forces would be African.[55] On the task-sharing level, it was agreed that the UN Department of Peacekeeping Operations would provide logistical support for the mission in conjunction with the AU Peace and Security Council.[56]

Many incidents demonstrate that UNAMID replicated almost the identical pattern of surrender to GoS interests employed by its predecessor AMIS. This gave Khartoum many opportunities to interfere with the deployment of both AMIS and UNAMID, and limit their operational capabilities. For example, the GoS demanded that the new force be comprised almost entirely of African contingents, and refused to approve deployment of troops from Nepal and Thailand.[57] Even after the deployment of the hybrid force, the GoS continued to use the slogan "African solutions to African problems" as a mantra to rebuff demands for more international intervention in Darfur. In October 2007 al-Bashir argued that the GoS was fully committed to cooperation with the hybrid force in order to conclude the peace process in Darfur,[58] yet in May 2008, after UNAMID forces had already been deployed in Darfur, he notified the AU chairman that the Darfur problem should be considered an African problem.[59]

The GoS was effective in deliberately retarding the pace of UMANID deployment, as it had been with respect to AMIS: By April 2008, only 9,000 of the 26,000 peacekeepers and police officers scheduled for deployment by 2009 were in place. As those troops effectively replaced the 7,000 AMIS troops, only 2,000 troops were actually added to the force.[60] Reports from February 2009, for example, indicated that UNAMID was not executing its mandate, and only 64 percent of its authorized personnel were actually deployed in Darfur.[61] This situation persists to this very day: In 2011, Alison Giffen, deputy director of the Henry L. Stimson Centre's Future of Peace Operation programme, noted that the Sudanese government still imposes arbitrary restrictions on the movement of UNAMID personnel, delays supply shipments, and creates other obstacles. "The government has been good at playing the UN and the AU off of one another", she reported.[62]

Another weakness that UNAMID seemed to have inherited from AMIS was its deficiency in operational resources and equipment. Notwithstanding the force's annual US$2.5 billion budget, Rodolphe Adada stated that UNAMID lacked five critical elements to become fully operational: attack helicopters, surveillance aircraft, transport helicopters, military engineers, and logistical support. Shortages in personnel and military equipment were mentioned in the UN Secretary General's report dated 9 June 2009 (covering the period from April 2008 to May 2009):

> The continued lack of key military enabling units, such as the medium transport units, an aerial reconnaissance unit, 18 medium utility helicopters and a Level-II hospital in al-Fasher, continuous to be a source of concern, as well as the adequate maintenance of contingent-owned armoured personnel carriers. In addition, the withdrawal of Canadian-owned armoured personnel carriers by June 30, 2009 could create a temporary decrease in operational capacity for up to three months while units await the arrival of their new equipment.[63]

This report attributed the slow deployment of UNAMID troops to restrictions imposed by the Sudanese government, as well as to insufficient willingness of the international community to fulfill its financial commitments toward the force.

Cage Banseka, a Cameroonian-born Briton who arrived in Darfur as a political officer in 2006, had witnessed the negotiations between the AU and the League of Arab States (LAS) on financing for the AMIS. When the LAS postponed remittance of its promised US$150 million contribution for many months and ultimately donated a mere fraction of the promised sum, Banseka concluded that they were just "playing games".[64] Western promises for financial and logistical support were not as illusory, yet in the case of both missions, contributions were insufficient to meet even basic needs. According to Richard Cockett, the gaps between promised and actual funds were one of the main causes of the slow deployment of UNAMID forces. Cockett claimed that in early 2010 there was still a shortage of 6,000 soldiers and policemen in the mandated force.[65] According to a 2011 report, the mission never achieved its full mandated strength:

> UNAMID military and police components which have now reached 18,002 and 2,751, that is 92 percent and 73 percent, respectively, of the total authorized strength, as well as the civilian component, which has reached 4,466, representing 81 percent of the authorized strength.[66]

Old patterns of inefficiency persisted in other areas as well. For example, after more than 100 people were killed in clashes in February 2008, it was decided to set up a 600-soldier base in the region of Sileia. The base was never constructed because the UN forgot to send a security patrol to protect the advance team, which prevented the engineers from making accurate sketches of the area for the design team.[67]

The peacekeepers of the new force faced the same problems as the old force: insufficient manpower had challenged AMIS and continued to frustrate UNAMID attempts to negotiate the difficult topographical and human terrain of Darfur. The general atmosphere of anarchy and lack of security not only hampered the effectiveness of the peacekeeping mission, but also endangered the lives of the peacekeepers themselves. Brigadier-General Balla Keita, UNAMID sector commander in West Darfur, described an incident, in which the night patrol was unable to reach his team after its trucks became stuck in the sand:

> I had a tense 30-minute wait in the pitch black just kilometers from the border of Chad at a time when tensions between the two countries are running high. It was one incident, but the chaos on the ground, the lack of communications and the lack of leadership that night was a worrying eye-opener about the huge challenges that lie ahead.[68]

In May 2008, a Ugandan UNAMID officer was killed in al-Fasher, the first of the new force of peacekeepers to be killed in Darfur,[69] but not the last. In a report entitled "Pessimism Hangs over Darfur," Simon Haselock recounted,

> and in July, seven peacekeepers from the joint African Union and United Nations Mission in Darfur (UNAMID) were killed and 22 wounded as they returned from a patrol to investigate rebel claims that two of their fighters had been killed in North Darfur. This attack, the worst suffered by the Mission so far, was highly organized and carried out by 200 gunmen equipped with heavy caliber weapons against which the lightly equipped peacekeepers had little protection.[70]

The frequency of violent incidents increased steadily throughout 2009 and 2010.[71] Attacks on UNAMID patrols resulted in the killing of three Rwandan peacekeepers on 5 December 2009 (and two others seriously wounded), and the killing of two Egyptian military peacekeepers on 7 May 2010, to mention only two of many similar incidents.[72] Abduction of UNAMID troops and workers of humanitarian organizations and NGOs were common, although in many cases the hostages were released after a period of captivity.[73] With elementary human needs unsatisfied, deplorable poverty, hunger, and despair led to an increasing incidence rate of armed robbery and banditry. Ibrahim Gambari, the AU–UN joint special representative for Darfur, recently acknowledged that violence and instability are again on the rise in Darfur.[74]

In spite of the deterioration of the humanitarian and security conditions in Darfur in the two first years of UNAMID's deployment, the transition from the continental to the hybrid force created improvements in four areas: the force's mandate, its international support, its accomplishments in the conditions of the IDPs, and the protection of women from gender-based crimes.

The first noticeable improvement was the extended scope of UNAMID's mandate. In contrast to the AMIS, which was subject to a limited mandate during most of its stay in Darfur, as described in

Chapter 3, Resolution 1769 authorized UNAMID to implement the Darfur Peace Agreement, secure freedom of movement for mission staff and humanitarian personnel, and monitor the presence of arms in Darfur.[75] Any violation of the Resolution, especially by the GoS, was considered an explicit violation of an international agreement. This was probably one of the factors that motivated the ICC's decision to issue an arrest warrant for al-Bashir, discussed below.

Second, AMIS and UNAMID operated under different levels of international commitment: International responsibility to protect Darfur appeared to be much stronger after the deployment of the hybrid force. This solid commitment was evident in the financial sphere, for example. UNAMID's approved budget for the period between 1 July 2010 and 30 June 2011 was US$1.8 billion.[76] Before the deployment of UNAMID, US financial assistance to Darfur was channeled mainly to humanitarian relief projects,[77] but since 2008, a greater proportion of US contributions is used to fund the UNAMID mission, including a US$450 million grant to construct and maintain 34 bases in Darfur for peacekeepers and US$100 million designed to bolster African nations' willingness to provide troops for the force.[78] The EU, on the other hand, announced that its support came to an end with the establishment of UNAMID.

Broad international commitment is also reflected in the composition of the new delegation, which includes troops from countries that were not directly involved in the previous mission: African countries account for 22 of the 38 contributors of military personnel, and 19 of the 41 contributors to the police personnel. Other forces come from countries including Bolivia, Germany, Guatemala, Italy, Nepal, and China, which contributed to both military and police personnel.[79] Dr Mahmoud Suleiman, deputy chairman of the General Congress for JEM, explained the mistrust that many Darfurians felt for the presence of Chinese peacekeepers in UNAMID:

> Recently, the two main Darfur Rebel groups, JEM and the Sudan Liberation Movement/Army (SLM/A) have demanded China to withdraw its troops, which include (135) engineers from Darfur with immediate effect. They said that China is not

> one of the states, which have worked to alleviate the suffering of the internally displaced persons (IDPs) and the refugees in Darfur. Furthermore, the rebels accused China of impartiality toward the crisis in Darfur, and worst, Beijing has been accused of working hard to disrupt and impede the international resolutions in the UN Security Council. The movements added in their opposition to the presence of the Chinese troops that Beijing government has been funding the government of Sudan in its war against the people of Darfur. They also pointed out that China represents the major source of arms and military hardware that the National Congress Party (NCP) government uses to fuel its genocidal war against the people of Sudan in Darfur. Furthermore, they indicated that the early arrival, before the deadline, of the Chinese military personnel is part of its complicity with the evil agenda of the ruling National Congress Party (NCP) in Khartoum and the protection of their bilateral interests rather than coming for the sake of protecting the defenceless civilians in Darfur.[80]

Third, the general conditions in IDP camps had improved since the arrival of UNAMID. The 24-hour patrols around several major IDP camps created an improved sense of security inside these camps, as one IDP representative described: "Our feelings of confidence have increased since UNAMID has provided 24/7 presence in the camp. Our women and children can sleep now outside the tents without any fear."[81] Camp infrastructure, including supplies of water and food, similarly improved. UNAMID extended assistance to IDPs in other areas, including assistance in securing the recent release of IDPs from detention by Sudanese national intelligence officers.[82]

In the fourth area, protection of women against gender-based violence, both AMIS and UNAMID unfortunately failed to create a profound change in the scope and intensity of gender-based violence in Darfur, or in the general attitude of the Darfurian society toward these crimes. Gender-based violence is an area in which AMIS played a pioneering role as an African peacekeeping mission, and also an extremely important issue from the perspective of Africa's new commitment to human rights issues and protecting civilians in conflict situations. As such it is an important area for testing the effectiveness of the two peacekeeping missions in the field. A comprehensive evaluation of the failed efforts of both missions in this area is necessary, if effective lessons are to be drawn for future missions. This chapter therefore proceeds to examine two questions: What are the dimensions of continuity and change in AMIS and UNAMID actions to mitigate gender-based violence, and how were these changes reflected in the broader continental thinking on gender-based violence in conflict times?

The declaration of 2010–20 as the African Women's Decade is intended to advance gender equality, with a special focus on issues relating to women in armed conflict situations. A communique of the 223rd meeting of the PSC on 30 March, which focused on the topic of mitigating vulnerabilities of women and children in armed conflicts, mentioned that the situation of women in an armed conflict zone remains very vulnerable despite many achievements regarding women's rights in Africa:

> Far from decreasing, incidents of violence against women and children in armed conflicts continue unabated in many parts of Africa. Recent conflicts in Guinea and Madagascar, as well as internal and/or cross-border conflicts and mass displacement in the Democratic Republic of the Congo (DRC), Somalia, Central African Republic and Sudan's Darfur region, have seen an abuse of women and children.[83]

Gender-based crimes are a particularly sensitive issue in Muslim-dominated Darfurian society, as women often do not admit to being sexually abused due to their fear of social stigmatization; furthermore, women do not trust the authorities to take action. While women's fears and mistrust encumber efforts to collect statistics and testimonies, and frustrate attempts to accurately assess the scope of gender-based crimes, extensive evidence indicates that rape was commonly employed as a practice of rivalry between the different factions. In February 2008, Human Rights Watch reported that:

> Large-scale air and ground attacks by government and government-supported militia on the towns of Sirba, Silea, and Abu Suruj, in northern West Darfur, led to more than 100 civilian deaths, destruction of property, and massive displacements. In a visit to Sirba, witnesses told UN human rights monitors that up to 10 women and girls were either raped or sexually assaulted."

Not all incidents of rape were attributed to the Janjaweed militias. This report also mentioned incidents of rape committed by SLM members of the Minnawi faction, some of whom were even known as "African *Janjaweed*".[84]

While gender-based crimes were committed mainly in the areas surrounding the IDP camps, especially when women and girls left the compounds to collect wood, food, or water, this report also mentioned the spread of violence, including sexual violence, into the camps themselves.[85]

AMIS's commitment to handle gender-based violence was innovative compared to previous African initiatives in this field, but its inadequate resources and inexperience in this field of action explains its very limited accomplishments. In contrast, UNAMID was more effective in handling these types of crimes and addressed the issue on several levels: It developed informative campaigns to encourage women to report the crimes and to empower them by combating the social stigmatization related to their victims; UNAMID also provided care for the victims themselves through assistance in reporting, medical supplies, and psychological support.

On a more general level, UNAMID enhanced the level of security, especially in and around the IDP camps. In March 2009, with Canadian support, UNAMID conducted a special training course for 30 police officers who were deployed with the UNAMID officers and worked in conjunction with the government of Sudan to mitigate sexual and gender-based violence in Darfur.[86] In August that year, UNAMID established a special investigations unit to monitor and report crimes involving sexual and gender-based violence. The new unit was developed to encourage victims of violence to report incidents to local law enforcement authorities, reduce the stigmatization of sexual abuse victims, and help rehabilitate victims. It was also aimed to support local law enforcement agencies in their investigations.[87] A workshop in Nyala on "Strengthening the Protection of Women through Legislation" was yet another UNAMID initiative designed to raise awareness of gender-based crimes. The event, organized in the framework of the Sixteen Days of Activism against Gender-Based Violence and in celebration of Human Rights Day, was attended by 31 parliamentarians of the South Darfur Legislative Council. Topics of discussion included the role of Islam in combating violence against women, women's rights in national and international law, forms of violence against women in times of war, and early marriage.[88]

In an effort to internationalize awareness of the atrocities to which the women of Darfur were subjected, UNAMID cooperated with a delegation of eight women ambassadors from around the world, led by Kenya's Ambassador to Ethiopia and the African Union Dr Monica Juma, who arrived in Darfur to meet with representatives of internally displaced women, female legislators, and community leaders. In their discussions on the ongoing problems facing women from all walks of life in Darfur, they suggested effective methods to address these issues, including gender-based crimes.[89] The event was part of a broader AU vision not only to reduce gender-based violence during conflicts, but also to integrate women as active participants in all stages of conflict-resolution efforts, as participants in the early warning system in the initial stage of a conflict, as potential mediators in negotiations between conflicting parties, and as policymakers in the post-conflict reconstruction stage. A special session held by the United Nations Development Fund for Women (UNIFEM) at PSC headquarters, entitled "Women in Armed Conflict Situations in Africa: Critical Issues", was specifically devoted to these issues:

> Unfortunately, women rarely receive the necessary support or inclusion in leadership positions as efforts are made to establish a secure and functional state. While peace agreements are

> beginning to contain gender terms that highlight the economic and security needs of women, gender provisions are rarely backed by sufficient resources and political will. It has been suggested that gender sensitive and responsive post-conflict reconstruct must support the following three dimensions: (i) women-focused activities, (ii) gender-aware programming, and (iii) strategic attention to transforming gender relations in order to heal trauma, build social capital and avoid further violence.[90]

In spite of the good intentions, however, such declarations highlight the huge gap between the desire to eradicate gender-based violence and the reality in Darfur. Three years after the deployment of UNAMID, evidence of widespread gender-based violence in various areas of Darfur remain today.[91]

From a broader perspective, it is interesting to examine how UNAMID's actions were evaluated by the force's two main partners, the UN and the AU. The "Report of the African Union-United Nations Panel on Modalities for Support to African Union Peacekeeping Operations", presented to the General Assembly of the Security Council on 31 December 2008, offers a partial answer to this question. The report was dedicated to strengthening cooperation between the UN and regional organizations, and referred to Resolution 1809, adopted several months earlier. According to Resolution 1809:

> [The Security Council] Recalling the resolve of Heads of State and Government of the 2005 World Summit to expand, as appropriate, the involvement of regional organizations in the work of the Security Council, and to ensure that regional organizations that have a capacity for the prevention of armed conflict or peacekeeping consider the option of placing such capacity in the framework of the Arrangements System: [The Assembly] [. . .] taking note of lessons learned from practical cooperation between the United Nations and the African Union, in particular the transition from the African Mission in Burundi (AMIB) to the United Nations Operation in Burundi (ONUB)

> and the African Mission in Sudan (AMIS) to the United Nations-African Union Mission in Darfur (UNAMID) [. . .].[92]

The report acknowledged that the special challenges facing contemporary peacekeeping forces were almost overwhelming for any single organization. Summarizing the attempts to translate the theoretical concept of R2P into practice, the report specifically discussed the effect of these principles on UNAMID's operations, approximately one year after its initial deployment:

> In examining the past operations, it is clear that the African Union faces particular challenges. Recent and ongoing conflicts in Africa such as those in Somalia, the Darfur regions of the Sudan, the Democratic Republic of the Congo and in West Africa illustrates the challenge. The complexity, in terms of the range of responses from mediation to intervention, creates demands that are out of all proportion to the availability of resources to address them.[93]

The report referred specifically to DRC, Somalia, and Darfur as conflicts that posed the greatest challenges for peacekeeping missions in Africa, and stressed the need to ensure the proper mandate and resources to allow these missions to perform their tasks effectively.

> It is important to ensure that missions deploy with what they need or they risk being given a mandate that they cannot achieve; the result is an incremental deployment that is more costly in the long run, not only in terms of resources but also in its impact upon the civilian population of the country concerned. The examples of Darfur and the Democratic Republic of the Congo provide ample illustration of the consequences of that lack of capacity.[94]

All in all, the report criticized the current inadequacy of peacekeeping efforts in Africa despite the huge resources invested: African peacekeeping missions engage nearly 75 percent of all UN peacekeepers deployed worldwide (of which 40 percent is from African troop contributors), and in 2008, consumed an annual UN budget of US$5.162 billion. According to the report, the main problem remains the lack of commitment by African countries and by the international community. The slow pace of deployment; reluctance of countries to contribute troops and budget; and inefficient coordination between the subregional, continental, and international organizations are some of the critical factors that fueled the relative ineffectiveness of peacekeeping missions in Africa in general.

Only several months after the Security Council General Assembly addressed the aforementioned report, UNAMID's peacekeeping operations faced a unique challenge. In March 2009, the ICC issued an arrest warrant against Sudanese President al-Bashir, causing a dramatic shift in the GoS's policy in Darfur in general, and its attitude toward outside intervention in particular. These changes had a significant impact on UNAMID, as will be elaborated in Chapter 7.

CHAPTER 7

DARFUR AND SUDAN FROM THE ICC RULING TO SOUTHERN INDEPENDENCE – 2009–11

Signs of overall worsening in the humanitarian situation in Darfur – in part, an expression of the Sudanese response to the International Criminal Court (ICC) arrest warrant issued against al-Bashir – have appeared since mid-2009, yet were overshadowed by several major events, including the 2010 elections in Sudan and the 2010 referendum in the South. These events, which were strongly interwoven in the relations between the Sudanese state and its western province, had a significant impact on the international efforts to end the conflict in Darfur. This chapter proceeds to analyze the influence of these events on peacekeeping efforts in Darfur.

On 4 March 2009, the ICC issued an arrest warrant for Sudanese President Omar al-Bashir. This precedential court ruling, the first arrest warrant ever issued against an incumbent head of state, produced a very contentious discourse.[1] To understand the developments that led to this precedential ruling, it is necessary to review how the evolution of Darfur conflict influenced ICC attitudes on the relationship between state sovereignty and state-instigated atrocities against its citizens. For this purpose, a brief background of the establishment and development of the ICC is required.

In 1998, the UN General Assembly adopted the Rome Statue by a vote of 120 to 7, with 21 countries abstaining. This was the legal foundation for the permanent International Criminal Court, an independent international organization (not part of the UN system), designed to deliver justice to the perpetrators of the most serious crimes of concern to the international community. Initially, ICC activities implied a propensity to submit to state sovereignty and obtain state cooperation in investigations and prosecution. It was the policy of Chief Prosecutor Luis Moreno Ocampo to seek a state's invitation before initiating an investigation of atrocities perpetrated against its civilians, as was the case in Ugandan President Yoweri Museveni's request to investigate the Lord's Resistance Army (LRA), the notorious Ugandan rebel group implicated in atrocities that included the widespread abduction of children and their forced conscription as soldiers. This policy proved to be a mixed blessing for the ICC: While it encouraged leaders to appeal to the ICC, it inhibited the organization's ability to effectively investigate crimes committed by the states themselves. This was apparently the case in the investigation in Uganda, where the ICC tended to turn a blind eye to the atrocities committed by the Ugandan government, and in subsequent investigations in the Democratic Republic of Congo and the Central African Republic.[2]

The gravity of the humanitarian crisis in Darfur prompted the UN Security Council to determine, on 31 March 2005, that the situation constituted "a threat to international peace and security acting under Chapter VII of the United Nations Charter". Through the Security Council's adoption of Resolution 1593, Darfur became the first case referred by the Security Council to the ICC prosecutor for investigation and prosecution, without an invitation from the state.[3] The UN referral possibly fostered the Sudanese leaders' sense of persecution and their reluctance to cooperate with the ICC, even before specific accusations were directed against al-Bashir. In the context of African discourse on state sovereignty and the right to intervene in domestic affairs for the purpose of investigating human rights violations, it is notable that Benin and Tanzania, the ICC's two sub-Saharan African members, voted in favor of Resolution 1593, while the Arab state members of the UN unanimously supported Khartoum and objected to the commission of investigation. Algeria, which represented the Arab countries in the Security Council at the time, obtusely explained that its opposition to Resolution 1593 was "for the sake of effectiveness and in order to address the urgency and gravity of the crisis".[4]

Notwithstanding these objections, the ICC prosecutor initiated an investigation of the situation in Darfur on 1 June 2005, and the International Commission of Inquiry on Darfur proceeded to investigate Ahmad Muhammad Harun, who had served as the Sudanese minister of state for the interior from April 2003 to September 2005, and Ali Kushayb, a former senior Janjaweed commander, and other individuals. In April 2007, the ICC Pre-Trial Chamber issued arrest warrants for Harun and Kushayb.[5] The long delay between submission of the Commission's recommendations and the issue of the arrest warrants, as well as the ICC's repeated requests for GoS consent, both before and after the warrants were issued, attracted heated criticism by various humanitarian organizations and activists. The discourse that developed around this issue, while beyond the scope of our discussion,[6] had important consequences for the ICC's next action — issue of an arrest warrant for al-Bashir himself.

On 14 July 2008, ICC Prosecutor Moreno Ocampo applied for an arrest warrant for al-Bashir on charges of alleged crimes against humanity and war crimes in the Darfur region. Victor Peskin from the School of Global Studies in Arizona State University claims that, "With his request for the arrest warrant, Moreno Ocampo brought the ICC to the center of world attention and rebuffed those who pressed him to subordinate his legal mandate to prosecute those most responsible for massive human rights abuses."[7] After eight months of consideration, Pre-Trial Chamber I of the ICC issued the warrant of arrest against al-Bashir on 4 March 2009, accompanied by the following statement:

> Omar Al Bashir's official capacity as a sitting Head of State does not exclude his criminal responsibility, nor does it grant

him immunity against prosecution before the ICC, according to Pre-Trial Chamber I.

According to the Judges, the above-mentioned crimes were allegedly committed during a five year counter-insurgency campaign by the Government of Sudan against the Sudanese Liberation Movement/Army (SLM/A), the Justice and Equality Movement (JEM) and other armed groups opposing the Government of Sudan in Darfur [. . .] A core component of that campaign was the unlawful attack on that part of the civilian population of Darfur – belonging largely to the Fur, Masalit and Zaghawa groups – perceived to be close to the organised armed groups opposing the Government of Sudan in Darfur. The said civilian population was to be unlawfully attacked by Government of Sudan forces, including the Sudanese Armed Forces and their allied Janjaweed Militia, the Sudanese Police Force, the National Intelligence and Security Service and the Humanitarian Aid Commission.[8]

The Chamber found Omar al Bashir, as the de jure and de facto president of Sudan and commander-in-chief of the Sudanese Armed Forces, suspect of having coordinated the design and implementation of the counter-insurgency campaign. In the alternative, it also found that there were reasonable grounds to believe that he was in control of all branches of the "apparatus" of the State of Sudan and used such control to secure the implementation of the counter-insurgency campaign.[9]

The AU also explicitly supported the Sudanese arguments against the ICC's investigations,[10] and African leaders almost unanimously supported al-Bashir after the warrant was issued. The AU's general tone, reflected in the text of the PSC meeting of March 2009, was that the ICC's decision impeded African efforts to reach a long-lasting peace agreement in Sudan:

[The PSC] **Expresses deep concern** over the decision taken by Pre-Trial Chamber I of the ICC on 4 March 2009, to issue an arrest warrant against the President of the Republic of the

> Sudan, Mr. Omar Hassan Al Bashir, for war crimes and crimes against humanity, and the far reaching consequences of this decision. Council **notes with regret** that this decision comes at a critical juncture in the process to promote lasting peace, reconciliation and democratic governance in the Sudan, and **underlines** that the search for justice should be pursued in a way that does not impede or jeopardize the promotion of peace.[11]

Indeed, in defiance of the ICC warrant, the Sudanese president visited Egypt, Eritrea, Libya, Qatar, Saudi Arabia, and Ethiopia soon after the arrest warrant was issued. Al-Bashir stated, "The ICC decision has become positive for us [...] We have noticed a firm position by regional organizations, namely the Arab League and African Union."[12] Al-Bashir astutely tapped into the objections to the ICC arrest warrant, which triggered among many Africans, including Arabs, a post-colonialist discourse of ex-colonized people against their oppressors, and fanned their sense of solidarity. These sentiments translated into actions such as the PSC's decision to strengthen cooperation with the LAS in order to find a solution to the conflict, primarily through the High Level Panel and the Doha peace talks, described below.[13]

In the following months, however, it emerged that the AU's unequivocal declaration of support for the Sudanese leader was not backed by all African leaders. Thirteen African state leaders, including Botswana, Chad, South Africa, and Uganda, announced their reservations. President Museveni of Uganda stated, "You cannot stand up and say: 'Don't touch Bashir because he is a president. Suppose he made those mistakes. If you take that position, you will be ignoring the right of the victims.'"[14] "We are signatories of the Rome Statute under which the ICC was established and the treaty has been ratified by Parliament of South Africa to not observe its obligation is arguably unconstitutional and against the law. We would not renege on our international legal obligations", said the director general for international relations and cooperation, Ayanda Ntsaluba, referring to the South African government's reversal of its decision to refrain from arresting al-Bashir if he travels to South

Africa.[15] The African voices that publicly affirmed the ICC decision, which they considered an expression of the voice of African victims against their oppressive leaders, emphasized the diversity of African discourse on sovereignty vs. human rights in general, and on the GoS's treatment of the Darfuri people in particular.[16]

The AU sought to squash rather than accept the diversity of African opinion. Five months after the arrest warrant was issued against al-Bashir, the AU repeated its call, at a PSC meeting, to cancel the arrest warrant, this time with an added warning toward all dissenting member states:

> [The PSC] Urges, once again the UN Security Council to heed the AU's call for the deferral of the process initiated by the International Criminal Court (ICC) against President Omar Hassan Al Bashir in the interest of peace, justice and reconciliation. In the meantime, Council reiterates earlier AU decisions on the ICC process, in particular the non-cooperation of AU member States with the arrest and surrender of President Al Bashir. In this respect, Council requests all AU member States to respect decision Assembly/AU/Dec.245 (XIII) adopted by the Assembly of the Union at its 13th ordinary session held in Sirte, Libya, from 1st to 3 July 2009.[17]

Moreover, in an action of symbolic defiance in the domestic arena, al-Bashir appointed Ahmad Harun, another ICC wanted person, to a variety of key positions, including a somewhat cynical appointment as minister of state for humanitarian affairs.[18] This was just one of the numerous GoS acts expressing disdain for the ICC's decision. In official Sudanese media, three distinct groups of arguments were raised against the ICC's decision to prosecute Sudanese government and militia officials for war crimes. The first general argument claimed that the ICC decision was part of a neo-colonial conspiracy against Sudan. Nafi Ali Nafi, presidential assistant and deputy leader of the ruling NCP, attacked the decision even prior to its publication. He firmly criticized the United States, Britain, and France for using the "despised" Western court as a means to re-introduce colonialism into Africa and the Middle East, and named the ICC a "hypocrite and exploiter".[19]

On 4 March 2009, the GoS announced the expulsion of 13 international NGOs from Darfur, including Oxfam, CARE, MSF-Holland, Mercy Corps, Save the Children, the Norwegian Refugee Council, the International Rescue Committee, Action Contré la Faim, Solidarités International, and CHF International, as well as two local NGOs, Khartoum Centre for Development and Environment and Amal Centre for Rehabilitation of Violence Victims, for their alleged involvement in the ICC investigation into the Darfur crimes.[20] The expulsion was rationalized in the pro-governmental media, which accused these organizations of being tools of Western neo-colonial intentions toward Sudan. In an article replete with references to Sudan's colonial history, Ahmad al-Sharif argued:

> The spy Lawrence of Arabia, who created the Sykes–Picot Agreement that brought the colonial armies and laid the foundation for the Zionist state, passed briefly through Khartoum in his travels, and then ran away and vanished. Yet, he planted the seeds of division and the conspiracy that led to the war in the South. This is the strategy of colonialism and its underlying Zionism, which plan far in advance assuming different shapes and forms. The colonial [humanitarian] organizations are nothing but Lawrence with new faces of compassion, concealing their underlying evil. Only few of the voluntary organizations in our country actually engage in humanitarian activities. Under the guise of voluntary and humanitarian activities they spread poison and engage in intelligence activities even more efficiently than Lawrence's traditional methods [...] These organizations create divisions, sow seeds of tension, and ignite the fire of *fitna* [. . .] While Lawrence spent just slightly more than one year in Sudan, the British, American, Dutch and Norwegian organizations have remained in Darfur for several years and have continued what Lawrence started; They act in the service of the Hague court, which is merely a Zionist entity; The mission of the court was

> to ignite a fire in Darfur and create chaos as part of the scheme to re-colonize Sudan.[21]

The second category of arguments against the ICC investigation focused on the West's double standards concerning the perpetration of human rights violations. Numerous references were made to the aggressive Zionist treatment of the Palestinians, or to American torture of Muslim prisoners in Abu Ghraib Prison and the Guantanamo Bay facility. "In light of their deeds [there], it is better that the Americans not demand to impose punishment on others on the charge of violations of human rights", one article propounded.[22] Another columnist, Abd al-Rahman Daud, urged, Israel is committing the most despicable crimes without any arrest warrant having been issued against its leaders on charges of human rights violations, bloodshed, and rape. Israel enjoys the protection of the United States in the Security Council and in the ICC, whose activities are administered and supervised by the United States, although the United State never signed the Rome Statute because it wishes to protect its soldiers from prosecution for all their crimes.[23]

The third category of news items criticizing the ICC decision focused on the affront to Sudan's unity and sovereignty. Numerous articles emphasized the wall-to-wall support by various segments of Sudanese society for their leader and their rejection of the ICC arrest warrant. This editorial by Abd al-Rahman Daud was a typical voice of this group:

> Sudan in entirety, including its districts, cities and villages, protested the Hague Court decision by Ocampo the Liar, which was based on unfounded accusations and false reports written by the spies belonging to the humanitarian organizations [. . .] 99.9 percent of Sudan's residents denounced Ocampo's decision, and expressed their support in al-Bashir, Sudan's leader who is innocence [sic] of these false accusations [. . .] against the Sudan's best sons, including innocent al-Bashir, Ahmed Harun and al-Kushayb. The entire world witnessed the Sudanese response to the ICC, which was a lesson in manners,

> designed to teach Ocampo something about the Sudanese people, its sovereignty, its honor, and its president. The Sudanese people, including all its various tribes, parties, and ideological currents, are all al-Bashir today. Weak Ocampo is afraid to put the real war criminals – such as Bush, Blair and Olmert – on trial, but is not afraid to use despicable lies to convict al-Bashir, the noblest president in the world.[24]

In fact, the GoS initially based its refusal to deal with the ICC on the latter's alleged lack of impartiality and its violations of Sudan's sovereignty. In October, the Justice Ministry of Sudan published a booklet entitled, *Darfur, The Quest for Peace*, advocating legal defences against Security Council Resolution 1593 (2005) and the ICC's proclaimed jurisdiction over Sudanese nationals. The booklet concluded that Resolution 1593 was flawed and incoherent, and contradicted international agreements, including the Vienna Convention on the Law of Treaties (1969). It argued also that since Sudan was not party to the Rome Statute and had entered into no special cooperation agreement with the ICC, the Security Council had no legal right to refer the alleged crimes committed in Sudan to the ICC. The booklet also claimed that the West manipulated the Security Council into adopting successive resolutions without allowing Sudan adequate time to implement them.

The expulsion of the foreign humanitarian organizations led to further deterioration that was evident not only in Darfur, but also in other regions of Sudan. The role played by the international NGOs in Darfur and in other regions of Sudan was recounted in a Crisis Group Africa Report:

> While a strong reaction was expected, the expulsion of many humanitarian organisations took international actors by surprise. According to the UN, these were covering in Darfur alone almost half the food survival needs of 1.1 million people, health care for 1.5 million and access to safe drinking water for more than a million. They also were helping 240,000 in eastern Sudan (Kassala and Red Sea states) and in the transitional areas

> of Abyei, Southern Kordofan and Blue Nile. By 9 March most of their personnel had left the country, and the government had confiscated their offices and equipment, including personal electronics.[25]

Eric Reeves argued that:

> Informed officials recognized the expulsions for what they were: Khartoum's carefully considered exploitation of the opportunity created by the ICC announcement to do what the regime's *génocidaires* had long wished. The expulsion of aid organizations not only severely compromised the health and lives of millions of people in displaced persons camps and throughout Sudan, but also removed troubling international "eyes on the ground", which had served as a better deterrent to attacks on civilians than had the failing UN/African Mission in Darfur (UNAMID).[26]

The expulsion of the humanitarian organizations also revealed the depth of the debate on foreign intervention in Darfur, especially between the JEM and the GoS, which ignited another wave of violence, noted in a communiqué issued by the AU chairperson:

> The Chairperson of the African Union is greatly concerned by military confrontations taking place in and around the area of Muhajeria in South Darfur. He calls on both the Government of Sudan and the Justice and Equality Movement (JEM) to cease all their military activities in the area with immediate effect.[27]

The AU was particularly concerned over the fate of the Goodwill and Confidence-Building Agreement, signed in Doha, Qatar, on 17 February 2009 by the GoS and the JEM, under the patronage of the State of Qatar and AU–UN Joint Chief Mediator for Darfur Djibril Bassolé.[28] The JEM, for example, refused to participate in the next round of the Doha negotiations in protest of the expulsion of aid groups that provided vital humanitarian services in the area. While

Khartoum continued to accuse the foreign NGOs of colluding with the ICC, the JEM claimed that the eviction of the aid groups was a violation of the Doha agreement, which established that the parties would facilitate humanitarian action in the region.[29]

In an act of intimidation, the GoS published the names of three JEM members who allegedly collaborated with the ICC by transmitting information to an NGO operating in the IDP camp in Kalama.[30] Hassan al-Turabi, who had close ties with JEM leader Khalil Ibrahim, was also accused of indirectly supporting the ICC decision. An editorial in *Al Watan Sudan*, following al-Turabi's release from one of his many detentions, hinted that al-Turabi's refusal to join the denunciation of the ICC decision and his pretentious aspiration to resolve the situation in Darfur through swift, effective action, were hampering the efforts to create stability and consolidation, "not for al-Bashir and his party, not for any sort of regime, but for the sake of the homeland".[31]

A broader national reconciliation process in Sudan that would include a resolution to the Darfur conflict was urgently needed, and the African Union High Level Implementation Panel (AUHIP), headed by former South African President Thabo Mbeki, invested energetic diplomatic efforts to this end. In an attempt to reconcile the tensions created by the ICC arrest warrant against al-Bashir, the Panel's initial proposals included establishment of a Sudanese court to deal effectively with the multiple unresolved legal issues stemming from the situation in Darfur. The Panel's first comprehensive report to a PSC meeting did not openly criticize the ICC arrest warrant against al-Bashir, claiming only that "even at full capacity, the ICC could only deal with handful of individuals, thereby effecting leaving the burden of justice to the national system."[32]

The Panel recommended to include foreign judges in the Sudanese court, and also proposed a national reconciliation mechanism, probably influenced by the experiences of post-apartheid South Africa. The need for a reconciliation mechanism was highlighted by two impending challenges to Sudanese unity – national elections and the Southern referendum.

Fearing that the Darfur conflict would be marginalized by the upcoming elections and referendum, the Panel worked to expedite a diplomatic solution to the ongoing conflict. The parties' concerns were stated explicitly stated in the High Panel's report to the PSC:

> The Council also stresses the need to create inclusive and conducive conditions for the successful holding in Darfur, as well as in the rest of the country, of the April 2010 national elections provided for by the Comprehensive Peace Agreement (CPA), and to ensure that Darfur fully participates in the national debate arising from the 2011 self-determination referendum in Southern Sudan.[33]

The events surrounding Sudan's first democratic local, national, and presidential elections in 24 years highlighted the strong connection between African democratization and state responsibilities for human rights violations. The elections were originally scheduled to be held in 2009, as part of the implementation of the 2005 CPA agreement, but were ultimately held on 16 April 2010. In late March 2010, the SPLM withdrew its candidate, Yasir Arman, from the presidential elections, blaming the continuing conflict in the Darfur region and "electoral irregularities" for his withdrawal. In response, almost all remaining presidential candidates decided to boycott the presidential elections as well as the regional and national elections. However, as Sudanese electoral law requires any withdrawal by candidates to be performed at least 45 days before the election date, the candidates' names remained on the ballots and people reportedly voted for these candidates. This confusion regarding the actual candidates participating in the elections was one of the indications of the problematic nature of the elections described by the Carter Center, one of the groups of monitoring observers:

> Most of the opposition parties joined together to demand the reform of laws and the lifting of restrictions of political freedoms and several major parties ultimately withdrew from the election shortly before election day. Although all candidates

> remained on the ballots, there was little competition in the race for the presidency and reduced competition in other races.[34]

Although the Carter Center's report mentioned many positive aspects of the elections, including the opportunity given to opposition parties and civil society representatives to engage in the political process, and the high percentage of voters, it nonetheless pointed to "important flaws and found that the process fell short of Sudan's obligations and related international standards in a number of respects".[35]

According to official results, al-Bashir received 68.24 percent of the estimated 10.1 million votes. These results suggest that, if several of the opposition candidates had remained in the race, the overall results would have been different.

In the immediate period after election results, the winning party took aggressive action against al-Bashir's opponents. The Freedom House's critical report stated, "Bolstered by his victory, al-Bashir launched a crackdown on civil liberties in the North. Al-Turabi was arrested once more in May and held for two months without charge. Civil society activists, aid workers, and journalists were harassed and obstructed." Still, the overwhelming victory (92.99 percent) of Salva Kiir Mayardit for the post of president of the country's southern region was one of the most significant results of the April elections. The SPLM won 87 percent of the South state assembly seats as well as nine out of ten governorships. In the Southern Sudan Legislative Assembly, the SPLM won all but four seats.[36]

The election results had direct consequences for the referendum in South Sudan held on 9 January 2011, in which the population voted on whether or not to secede from the North and establish an independent state. The connection between the elections and the referendum was noted in the PSC communiqué of its 213th meeting, held on 22 December 2009:

> [The PSC] **notes** the challenges faced by the Sudan in both the implementation of the CPA and the upcoming elections in April 2010, as well as the preparations for the referendum.

> In this respect, Council **decides** to establish an Ad Hoc Committee on Sudan to assist in addressing the challenges. Council **further agrees** to undertake field missions to Sudan in support of the peace processes in that country.[37]

The referendum in Sudan marked a watershed of continental proportions, as the dissolution of Sudan into two sovereign states could be considered the first direct challenge to the sanctity of the sovereignty and territorial integrity of all member states.[38] Notwithstanding the threat to state sovereignty, AU policies and actions almost unanimously supported the Southern Sudanese claim for separation. From an historical perspective, the AU's support of the Southern Sudanese claim to self-determination and even independence marks an almost inconceivable transformation in African perceptions since the OAU turned a blind eye to the desperate cry of the Southern Front in 1965, which had cautioned, "There is a Nazi-type of extermination policy being carried out in the Sudan by the Arab army of occupation on the unarmed and helpless population in the Southern Sudan."[39]

Additional indications of African support for self-determination were expressed, for example, at an international meeting at United Nations Headquarters in New York on 24 September 2010, convened by UN Secretary-General Ban Ki-moon to review the situation in the Sudan before the referendum on self-determination for South Sudan. African attendance at the meeting was impressive, and included the president of Malawi (chairperson of the African Union at that time); the prime minister of Ethiopia (the chairman of IGAD at that time); the presidents of Gabon, Kenya, Nigeria, Rwanda, and Uganda; and representatives of other regional organizations. African Union Commission chairperson Dr Jean Ping urged the leaders and people of Sudan to rise to the historic challenge of organizing a legitimate, credible referendum on the self-determination of South Sudan.[40]

Moreover, less than one month before the referendum, the PSC held a meeting to discuss the AUHIP recommendations on Sudan. The detailed 27-page report is a demonstration of the Panel's decisive efforts to remove all obstacles to the referendum before the CPA expired, and to ensure the smooth administration of the referendum. The Panel even criticized the GoS for the delay in establishing the Southern Sudan Referendum Commission (SSRC), which was working under a very challenging schedule imposed by the Panel. The PSC Communiqué also noted the issues that remained an obstacle to the full implementation of the CPA were mainly divided opinions on oil sharing, debt, citizenship (of ethnic southern Sudanese in the north), and the demarcation of the contested border, especially the Abyei region:

> The issue of Abyei area has proven one of the most difficult and contentious in the implementation of the CPA. The Parties requested the Panel to examine the issue of the eligibility criteria for voters in the Abyei Referendum, this issue being the stumbling block in efforts to establish the Abyei Area Referendum Commission. The Panel visited Abyei and the town of Muglad, the principal centre of the Misiriya, from 6 to 7 July 2011 and met with community leaders and experts on the area. *The importance of ensuring a settlement of the issue, compatible with the livelihoods and historic access to resources, of both the Ngok Dinka and Misiriya, was emphasized by the spokespeople of the two communities. The local leaders also stressed their long history of cooperation and their readiness to achieve an accommodation that would enable them to live as good neighbors.*[41]

This clause has particular importance in the context of the debate on state sovereignty versus citizens' rights. By focusing on the voices of minorities and referring to issues such as "historic access to resources" and "long history of cooperation", African mediation efforts appeared to encompass not merely the sovereign, but also the elements that comprise society and state.

Nonetheless, events following the referendum prove that a profound gap remained between AU declarations on human rights and the realities of unprotected civilian populations facing the atrocities of its government. Ignoring the UN Security Council's resolution to extend the mission's mandate, in June 2011 the GoS unilaterally declared the end of the United Nations Mission in Sudan (UNMIS). Al-Bashir accused the mission of spying for the Sudan People's Liberation Movement (SPLM) after satellite images released by UNMIS reportedly showed crimes committed on 21 May 2011 in SAF-controlled Abyei, which resulted in tens of thousands fleeing from the area.[42] This as yet unresolved dispute between the GoS and the UN may yet have considerable implications for the fate of UNAMID despite the relatively hopeful achievement of the settlement of the conflict in the South.

CHAPTER 8

THE ARAB SPRING, DARFUR, AND BEYOND

Another event with important implications for African attitudes to foreign intervention in intrastate conflicts is the recent wave of protests in the Arab world. Known as the Arab Spring, this cascading surge of popular Arab anti-government demonstrations, which started in the North African states of Tunisia and Egypt in January 2011, and swept rapidly across the Middle East and North Africa, bypassed most Sub-Saharan countries, with the exception of small-scale anti-government protests in Djibouti (nominally, an LAS member).[1] This chapter analyzes the impact of the Arab Spring events on the specific case of AU intervention in Darfur, and offers some broader insights on the differences between the Arab world (mainly the Middle East and North Africa) and Sub-Saharan Africa relevant to this topic. This chapter also examines recent AU peacekeeping experiments, primarily in Somalia, in an attempt to evaluate the lessons learned from the Darfur experience.

One of the salient differences between the Arab world and Sub-Saharan Africa is related to the different pace of democratization in these two regions. One obvious reason for the absence of massive popular protest in Sub-Saharan Africa is the fact that most states in this region gained some experience in establishing democratic regimes in the 1990s, from Benin in 1991 to Nigeria in 1999, albeit with varied degrees of success. In the following decade, germs of successful democratization, such as properly conducted competitive elections and constitutional reforms, developed into relatively promising democratic regimes in Ghana and South Africa, for example. The fact that Sub-Saharan African countries preceded Middle Eastern and North African states in their democratization efforts, and in several cases created viable democracies, is not generally acknowledged. The Sub-Saharan experience contradicts, for example, the common assumption of a country-level correlation between affluence and prospects for achieving and maintaining democracy, especially when we compare the per capita income of rich Arab countries such as Kuwait, Qatar, and Saudi Arabia, with much less affluent African countries such as Ghana and Senegal.

In his illuminating article, "Why Are There No Arab Democracies?", Larry Diamond advances several factors that are fundamental to the Arab Spring protests,[2] including the

> Arab states themselves, who reinforce one another in their authoritarianism and their techniques of monitoring, rigging, and repression, and who over the decades have turned the 22-member Arab League into an unapologetic autocrats' club. Of all the major regional organizations, the Arab League is the most bereft of democratic norms and means for promoting or encouraging them. In fact, its charter, which has not been amended in half a century, lacks any mention of democracy or individual rights.[3]

In contrast to the League of Arab States, the African Union seems more strongly committed to democratization and human rights issues. Also, compared with its predecessor, the OAU, the AU has been much more resolute in condemning unconstitutional governmental action, and has actively intervened to ensure transfers of power based on election results, as it did, for example in Burundi in 2003 and the Comoros in 2008. To be sure, the AU has not been entirely consistent in its policy, which is evident from the organization's benign responses to Zaire's President Robert Mugabe's unwillingness to step down from power after losing the 2008 elections.[4] More recently, following Cotê d'Ivoire's incumbent president Laurent Gbagbo's refusal to recognize the victory of the Northern contender Alassane Ouattara in the country's November 2010 elections, the PSC suspended the Cotê d'Ivoire from all AU activities, and declared its unequivocal support in the Ivorian people's rights to determine their own political future:

> [The] Council expressed AU's total rejection of any attempt to create a *fait accompli* to undermine the electoral process and the will of the people as expressed on 28 November 2010, further complicating an already serious situation, and plunge Côte d'Ivoire into a crisis of incalculable consequences.[5]

Despite the decisive tone of its statement, the PSC in fact sought to find a compromise between the two rivals. It extended the authority of AUHIP beyond Sudan to handle the Ivorian crisis, and authorized its head Thabo Mbeki to conduct "an emergency mission to Côte d'Ivoire in order to find a legitimate and peaceful solution to the crisis, on the basis of relevant AU instruments and decisions".[6]

In contrast to the PSC's conciliatory tone, ECOWAS, the West African bloc led by Nigeria, proved to be much more unflagging in its support for democratic change based on the choice of the Ivorian people,[7] and rejected any compromise between the parties and threatened the use of force if President Gbagbo refused to accept the results announced by the Ivorian electoral commission chief. Ultimately, cooperation between ECOWAS and the AU, combined with international intervention (especially by France, whose military was involved in Gbagbo's capture), led to nomination of the elected president and has so far prevented continuation of the civil war in Cotê d'Ivoire.

While events in Tunisia, Egypt, and Cotê d'Ivoire (the latter are not strictly considered part of the events of the Arab Spring) bear some similarities to the Sudanese case, the case of Libya seems to be most relevant to our study of AU intervention policies for several reasons. First, the events in Libya, like those in Sudan, seemed to be escalating toward civil war rather than civil protest. This was one of the arguments presented by Lisa Anderson, president of the American University in Cairo:

> Whereas demonstrators in Tunis and Cairo successfully ousted their former rulers, Tripoli collapsed into a protracted civil war. Its sustained fighting resulted from Libyan leader Muammar al-Qaddafi's four-decade-long effort to consolidate his power and rule by patronage to kin and clan. Years of artificially induced scarcity in everything from simple consumer goods to basic medical care generated widespread corruption. And the capricious cruelty of Qaddafi's regime produced widespread and deep-seated suspicion. Libyans' trust in their government, and in one another, eroded, and they took refuge in the solace of tribe and family. Libyan society has been fractured, and every national institution, including the military, is divided by the cleavages of kinship and region. As opposed to Tunisia and Egypt, Libya has no system of political alliances, network of economic associations, or national organizations of any kind. Thus, what seemed to begin as nonviolent protests similar to those staged in Tunisia and Egypt soon became an all-out secession – or multiple separate secessions – from a failed state.[8]

The second similarity between Libya and Sudan is related to international and African responses to the developing intrastate conflict. Domestic events in both countries, each considered an important actor in international and African politics, attracted extensive attention outside their borders, although the nature of international and African intervention in these two intrastate conflicts differed fundamentally. As described earlier, the international call for external military intervention in Sudan and a no-fly zone over Darfur were never realized, while in the case of Libya, the UN Security Council declared a no-fly zone almost immediately after bloody clashes between the Libyan government and its protestors began. Paragraphs 6 and 7 of Resolution 1973 of the Security Council clearly stated that the Security Council:

> 6. Decides to establish a ban on all flights in the airspace of the Libyan Arab Jamahiriya in order to help protect civilians; 7. Decides further that the ban imposed by paragraph 6 shall not apply to flights whose sole purpose is humanitarian, such as delivering or facilitating the delivery of assistance, including medical supplies, food, humanitarian workers and related assistance, or evacuating foreign nationals from the Libyan Arab Jamahiriya, nor shall it apply to flights authorised by paragraphs 4 or 8, nor other flights which are deemed necessary by States acting under the authorisation conferred in paragraph 8 to be for the benefit of the Libyan people, and that these flights shall be coordinated with any mechanism established under paragraph 8.[9]

Moreover, with approval of the Security Council, on 31 March 2011, the North Atlantic Treaty Organization assumed sole command of the international air operations over Libya, which had been initially coordinated by the Stuttgart-based US Africa Command (AFRICOM). One possible explanation for the Security Council's speedy decision to launch a military operation was the role of the LAS, which acted as a critical catalyst for the adoption of the Resolution in the case of Libya, but not in the case of Sudan. Paragraph 8 of Resolution 1973 alludes to this, by authorizing

> member States that have notified the Secretary-General and the Secretary-General of the League of Arab States, acting nationally or through regional organizations or arrangements, to take all necessary measures to enforce compliance with the ban on flights imposed by paragraph 6 above, as necessary, and requests the States concerned in cooperation with the League of Arab States to coordinate closely with the Secretary General on the measures they are taking to implement this ban, including by establishing an appropriate mechanism for implementing the provisions of paragraphs 6 and 7 above.[10]

This unusual cooperation between the UN and the Arab states in an act of direct intervention in the domestic affairs of an LAS member state was not merely hypothetical: Jordan, Qatar, and the United Arab Emirates supplied forces to help police the no-fly measure.[11]

In cases of both Libya and Sudan, the AU's response to international intervention reveals the AU's special sensitivity to its perceived ability to solve African problems, and especially when its ability is called into question. The AU as a whole did not embrace the resolution (although three prominent African states, Gabon, Nigeria, and South Africa, voted in favor of Resolution 1973, including the imposition of a no-fly zone). This was not to say that the AU was dilatory in responding to the situation. On the contrary, the AU responded immediately to the Libyan crisis by nominating an *ad hoc* High Level Committee on Libya, comprising heads of state of Mauritania, the Republic of Congo, Mali, South Africa, and Uganda, and the chairperson of the AU Commission. The Committee met in Nouakchott, Mauritania's capital, on 19 March 2011, in an effort to formulate a roadmap to a peaceful solution to the crisis, and "reiterated AU's strong call for an immediate cessation of all hostilities, to ensure the effective protection of civilians and create conditions conducive for a peaceful resolution of the crisis".[12]

In many respects, the AU responded similarly to the Sudanese and Libyan crises. In both cases, the AU affirmed its primary commitment to state unity and territorial integrity, and in both cases the AU first sought the consent of the government in question before intervening. For example, at its 275th meeting on Libya on 26 April 2010, the PSC "welcomes the acceptance by the Libyan government, including Colonel Muammar Qaddafi, of the AU Roadmap, including the specific issue of the ceasefire and deployment of an effective and credible monitoring mechanism".[13] In the earlier case of Sudan, the AU's response was aligned with the international community's reluctance to intervene to stop human rights violations in Darfur. The case of Libya, however, revealed the gap between the AU's more conciliatory position (toward the sovereign) and the international community's activist position and unequivocal support for the Libyan people's demand for a regime change.

An incident discussed at the 275th meeting of the PSC revealed something of the African leaders' sense that their efforts to resolve the situation in Libya, and, more broadly, the organization's role as a mediator in African conflicts, were being marginalized. On the High-Level Ad Hoc Committee's plans to travel to Libya, the communiqué of 20 March 2011 stated:

> To this end, and as required by Resolution 1973 (2011), the Committee, through the commission, sought authorization for the flights carrying its members to Libya, in order to fulfill their mandate. This request was denied. The Committee expressed regret for not being able to travel to Libya as envisaged.[14]

In an interview with the BBC, Jean Ping, chairman of the Standing Commission of the AU, expressed AU officials' frustration over the international rejection of AU proposals to solve the Libyan crisis, and disappointment that they were not consulted about the crisis.[15] In an even more critical tone, South African President Jacob Zuma blamed NATO, and, more broadly, the international community, for causing "regime change, political assassinations and *foreign military occupation*"[16] rather than taking action to protect citizens.

For the second time in two years, the ICC issued a warrant against an incumbent African head of state. Although the AU had not officially changed its policy on the legality of intervention in the domestic affairs of African states, its responses to these arrest warrants illuminates changing African attitudes toward the ICC, and, more broadly, toward intervention in African intrastate affairs. African responses to the warrant of arrest issued against al-Bashir were discussed extensively above. In June 2011, the ICC issued a warrant of arrest for Muammar al-Qaddafi for,

> his alleged criminal responsibility for the commission of murder and persecution of civilians as crimes against humanity from 15 February 2011 onwards throughout Libya in, inter alia, Tripoli, Benghazi, and Misrata, through the Libyan State apparatus and Security Forces, in violation of article 7(l)(a) and (h) of the Statute and as principal to these crimes in accordance with article 25(3)(a) of the Statute.[17]

In 2011, in dissent of the AU's longstanding policy on intervention, a growing number of African states expressed willingness to cooperate with the ICC: In some cases, these African states handed over suspects who were citizens of their own countries to the ICC, and, in other cases, refused to permit the entrance of suspects (as did South Africa and Botswana regarding al-Bashir, described earlier).[18] The Egyptian response exemplifies the changing African attitudes toward ICC decisions. While Egypt under Hosni Mubarak unequivocally supported Sudan in its rejection of the ICC decision, post-revolutionary Egypt announced its desire to join the ICC, as did post-revolutionary Tunisia.[19] Nonetheless, the AU clung to its traditional position, accusing the court of unfairly targeting African countries, and criticizing the arrest warrant issued for al-Qaddafi. The AU preferred to transfer the case to the African Court of Justice and Human Rights, located in Arusha, Uganda, under AU aegis. However, especially in view of the track record of this court, which had never issued a ruling of note, AU declarations appear to be yet another attempt to rebuff international intervention using the hollow "African solutions to African problems" banner.

The AU's relatively marginal role in the intervention in Libya contrasts starkly with its important role in the contemporary Somalia conflict. Comparing AU interventions in Sudan and Somalia offers insights on the features of contemporary intrastate conflicts in Africa and the continental organization's effectiveness in their resolution.

In the scholarly and media discourse Somalia is often defined as a "failed state". One of the reasons for this classification lies in the fact that Somalia is not a single political unit, but actually comprises three political entities, as political scientist Kenneth Menkhaus explains:

> Several regional and transregional authorities have come into existence in Somalia since 1990. Somaliland (a separatist state in the northwest) and Puntland (a nonsecessionist, autonomous state in the arid northeast corner of the country) are the only two such entities that have achieved much functional capacity, but a number of others – the Rahanweyn Resistance Army's

> administration of Bay and Bakool regions in 1998–2002 and the Benadir Regional Authority in 1996 – showed some initial promise. Strictly speaking, most of these regional and transregional polities are or were essentially clan homelands, reflecting a Somali impulse to pursue a "Balkan solution" – or, more appropriate to the Somali context, "clanustans." Puntland's borders, for instance, are explicitly drawn along clan lines, encompassing the territory of the Harti clans in the northeast and contested sections of Somaliland. Even authorities that appear to be based on a prewar regional unit are often thinly disguised clan polities.[20]

In addition to Somalia's internal division, the state also lacks a viable political centre. Menkhaus traces the origins of Somalia's dysfunctional political centre to the pre-1991 period:

> Ample evidence suggests that by the mid-1980s Somalia was already a failed state. With the partial exception of the security sector, most government institutions began to atrophy in the years following the disastrous Ogaden War with Ethiopia in 1977–78. Fierce government repression, heightened clan cleavages and animosities, gross levels of corruption, and low salaries all combined to accelerate the state's decline.[21]

This insight is particularly important to the comparison of the interventions in Somalia and the Sudan, and the fact that intervention was, in both cases, a function of the various degrees of control and functioning of the political centre, as elaborated below.

The roots of African intervention in present-day Somalia can be traced to February 2005, when the country's Transitional Federal Government (TFG) formed in Kenya after two years of IGAD-sponsored peace talks between various Somali clans and factions. In September 2006, the AU endorsed the IGAD Peace Support Mission in Somalia (IGASOM) to support the TFG's relocation from Nairobi, Kenya.[22] After IGASOM failed to lead a process of national reconciliation, control of Mogadishu was seized by the Islamic Courts

Union (ICU) – a coalition of local *shari'a* courts and Islamists – defeating the Alliance for the Restoration of Peace and Counter-Terrorism in June 2006. Although the Islamists' short period of rule in Somalia was considered a period of relative stability, uncommon in Somalia since 1991, the ICU's victory triggered apprehension in and outside Somalia. The ICU-led coalition contained both moderate and extremist factions, but al-Shabab, the best-trained, best-equipped, and most strongly committed faction in the coalition, attracted the most concerns. Ideologically, al-Shabab follows the doctrine of *takfiri*, which allows its members to declare other Muslims unbelievers (*kafir*), resist foreign presence on their land (including peacekeepers, a fact that had major importance for the future AU peacekeeping force), and commit suicide to kill their enemy. Al-Shabab was also suspected of ties with al-Qaeda (its alignment with al-Qaeda was confirmed in February 2010).[23] Neighboring Ethiopia and the West became increasingly alarmed in the face of the growing dominance of radical Islam in Somalia, and, Ethiopian troops, backed by the USA, hastened to invade Somalia in December 2006 in response to the call of Somalia's TFG President Abdullahi Yusuf.

The TFG president's call for outside military intervention turned out to be very unpopular in the eyes of many segments of Somali society, and ignited a new wave of internal violence throughout the country. Although Ethiopia announced that it would not remain in Somalia after the defeat of the ICU, as soon as a peacekeeping operation stabilized the situation sufficiently for its withdrawal. Ethiopian presence aggravated domestic violence even further. Eritrea suspended its membership in IGAD (of which Ethiopia was a key member), which was one of several indications of the declining support for the organization's operations in Somalia.[24] To bolster IGAD's status, the AU was called upon by the UN to intervene in the escalating Somali conflict.

The African Union Mission in Somalia (AMISOM) was created by the PSC on 19 January 2007, with an initial six-month mandate. The following month, Security Council Resolution 1744 approved the mission's mandate,[25] which included support for TFI (Transitional Federal Institutions) efforts to stabilize the country; promotion of dialogue and reconciliation; facilitation of humanitarian assistance; and the creation of favourable conditions for long-term stabilization, reconstruction, and development in Somalia.[26] Although an analysis of the successes and failures of the AU mission in Somalia is both premature and beyond the scope of this book, ANISOM, the AU's mission to Somalia, appears to share many of the features – including the failures and shortcomings – of AMIS and UNAMID. Three points of comparison of the three AU peacekeeping efforts are relevant to our discussion on the AU's changing policy on intervention in intrastate conflicts.

Despite the differences in the status of the political centre in Sudan and in Somalia, both AMISOM in Somalia and AMIS in Darfur were more strongly focused on securing the local government's consent and cooperation and satisfying the demands of the political centre, than on efforts to protect civilians and create a genuine foundation of civilian support for its operations. At the 214th meeting of the PSC on 8 January 2010, the PSC reiterated its strong condemnation of the continued attacks and other acts of terror being perpetrated against the TFG, the Somali people, and AMISOM by armed opposition groups determined to undermine the peace and reconciliation process. The Council further admonished al-Shabab for denying the needy population access to humanitarian aid and services. Conflict resolution expert Paul Williams argues:

> Nominally a peace support operation, AMISOM's main role has become protecting Somalia's Transitional Federal Government (TFG). This has left it in an odd position: it is delivering humanitarian assistance to some residents of Mogadishu while simultaneously trying to counter an insurgency led by *al-Shabab* that is fond of employing terrorist tactics.[27]

In this regard, there is no noticeable difference between AU's strategy in Somalia, the "failed state" with its weak political centre, and in Sudan, with its relatively strong political centre.

Shortage of manpower is a second point of similarity between the AU's previous missions, the African Mission in Burundi (AMIB),

AMIS (and UNAMID), and AMISOM. In their report, "African Union Mission in Somalia (AMISOM) – Exemplifying African Union Peacekeeping Challenges", researchers Cecilia Hull and Emma Svensson summarized manpower strength as follows:

> Whilst Uganda deployed its battalions relatively swiftly, the Burundian battalions long stood ready to be transferred to Somalia but lacked the resources and logistical capacity to sustain a deployment. Similarly, Nigeria and Ghana have offered a total of 1,200 troops but not had the resources to deploy them to Somalia. Even if all the troops pledged would be deployed AMISOM would only amount to slightly more than half the troop size the AU Peace and Security Council estimated it to need to be able to fulfill the mandate. As a result, AMISOM, just like AMIS, has failed to perform most of its tasks. Instead AMISOM's function has been limited to safeguarding infrastructure such as the Mogadishu port, airport and important access routes between them.[28]

In response to the Kampala suicide bombings on 11 July 2010, an attack for which al-Shabab claimed responsibility, the PSC decided to send 2,000 troops as reinforcements for AMISOM. This decision highlighted the fact that only 6,300 AMISOM troops had been deployed (in four Ugandan and three Burundian battalions), despite the initial decision three years earlier to deploy 8,000 troops. Contributing countries (also known as Troops Contributing Counties, or TCCs) were either unable or reluctant to allocate troops to AU missions for a variety of reasons. South Africa, for example, announced that it would be unable to contribute troops to AMISOM due to its commitments to MONUC (the UN mission in the Democratic Republic of Congo) and UNAMID, and to its presence in Burundi. Nigeria announced that it lacked resources and would deploy its forces only if supported by the United States.[29] Africa's smaller, poorer, and weaker states obviously had fewer resources than these two major African countries. Eventually, these tactics slowed the pace of AMISOM deployments, as they had in the case of

UNAMID, and seriously hampered both missions' ability to handle the complex emergencies situations they faced.

The third similarity between UNAMID and AMISOM is interwoven with the previous points, and connected to one of the theoretical questions posed at the beginning of this book, concerning R2P and whether this task was the exclusive responsibility of the AU in Africa. As mentioned earlier, the R2P concept had evolved in parallel with the Darfur conflict, which therefore can be considered as AU's first test case in implementing this concept in practice. The AU's achievements and failures in performing the responsibility to protect the Darfurians were extensively discussed above. At this point, it is interesting to ask whether the AU implemented in Somalia any lessons learned from its R2P experience in Sudan.

According to one view, it is not unjustified to argue that the AU mission in Somalia was a total failure, based on its lack of accomplishments in the humanitarian field. This view was explicitly expressed by analysts Jakkie Cilliers, Henri Boshoff, and Festus B. Aboagye, of the Institute of Security Studies in Pretoria, South Africa:

> According to AMISOM, the political and security situation in Mogadishu and Somalia remain dire, volatile and unpredictable. The realities on the ground in Mogadishu and Somalia present a number of scenarios ranging from civil war to localised insurgencies, in which al-Shabab, Hizbul Islam and other protagonists control portions of the central and southern regions, and large parts of Mogadishu. Somalia's Transitional Federal Government (TFG) and other temporary institutions, weak and lacking in national legitimacy, are actually in control of only a few square kilometres, including the presidential compound and other vital areas. As for the precarious humanitarian situation, Refugees International has indicated that there are "approximately 1.5-million IDPs (internally displaced persons) and over 500,000 Somali refugees in neighbouring countries more than 3.6-million Somalis (40 percent of the population) are dependent on external

> assistance. This situation is expected to worsen given al-Shabab's destruction of relief stocks in recent times."[30]

Such a pronouncement may, however, be overly critical, as recent events demonstrate that AMISOM was objectively ill-equipped to alleviate the deteriorating humanitarian and security situations. With already an estimated one-quarter of Somalia's 7.5 million population internally displaced or living outside the country as refugees, the severe drought afflicting the Horn of Africa in 2011 resulted in new waves of Somalis at risk of starvation and death forced to flee their homes.[31]

In addition to AMISOM's failure to effectively protect the citizens of Somalia, AMISOM personnel were themselves targets of escalating violence. Similarly to AMIS and UNAMID troops in Darfur, AMISOM troops were targets of violent attacks by hostile local groups. The Ugandan contingent suffered such attacks shortly after its arrival, and in May 2007 four Ugandan peacekeepers were killed; the Burundian contingent was attacked soon after its arrival in October 2008.[32] In contrast to the AU mission in Darfur, which suffered from sporadic and coincidental attacks, resistance to AMISOM troops was grounded in an ideological–religious doctrine. The Islamist concept of *takfiri*, embraced by al-Shabab (and to some extent by other groups such as Hizbul Islam), entailed rejection of all manifestations of foreign presence in Somalia, African peacekeepers included. Thus, as Cilliers, Boshoff, and Aboagye claim:

> In the current situation, the AMISOM operation, coupled with U.S., regional, UN and other international support, appears increasingly to serve as a magnet to "internationalise" the conflict, attracting foreign elements to the side of *al-Shabab* and other insurgents and, more pertinently, radicalising such armed groups – and the local population.[33]

The AU evidently acknowledged its own inefficacy in relieving human suffering and improving security conditions in Somalia, obligated by the R2P principle. As in the case in Darfur, the organization's awareness of its own incapability motivated it to endorse a transition from a continental to a hybrid force in Somalia, As early as August 2007, the president of the AU Commission stressed the need for a UN force, stating that "the task at hand goes far beyond the capacity of the African Union" and requires urgent attention by the UN Security Council, "which has the primary responsibility for the maintenance of international peace and security."[34]

In the transition to a hybrid force, there are major differences between the Sudanese and the Somali cases. First, in the case of Sudan, the Security Council's initial objection to deploying a force in Sudan was based mainly on the argument that UNMIS, an earlier mission to Sudan, could be extended beyond South Sudan to include Darfur within its authority. In the case of Somalia, the traumatic legacy of Operation Restore Hope, described above, jelled into firm UN refusal to cooperate in a hybrid force with the AU. Second, the AU (and, to some extent, the UN) were more attentive to GoS objections to the deployment of a hybrid force in Sudan, a fact that delayed the force's establishment and operations. In the case of Somalia, the responses of the country's political centre (if the TFG can be described as such) were of little concern to the African and international communities. Furthermore, the hybrid force did not face organized local resistance in Darfur (other than sporadic cases stemming mainly from economic motives), but in Somalia the presence of a hybrid force is at risk of drawing fire from local fighters who object to any foreign presence on their soil.

While a comparison of the AU's two major peacekeeping efforts, in Sudan and Somalia, points to growing willingness of African states to assume an active role in intrastate conflicts and in complex emergency situations, the results of both missions do not prove that the AU is capable of carrying out R2P, in the sense of providing effective protection for local populations in conflict areas.

CONCLUSION

Concluding his two-day visit to Darfur in late August 2005, Dr Salim Ahmed Salim, AU Special Envoy for the Darfur Talks between 2004 and 2008, commented that the large presence of AMIS troops in Darfur, which was in fact the largest force the African Union had ever mobilized for peacekeeping, was a clear demonstration of Africa's commitment and of the significance that Africa attributed to the Darfur conflict. Dr Salim's statement can be analyzed from two perspectives. From a broader perspective, the role of AMIS and the subsequent role of UNAMID should be evaluated in light of the changes in African perceptions on state sovereignty, the sanctity of state boundaries, and the right of the African people to be protected, which developed over the last two decades. From a more practical perspective, it is important to analyze the achievements and failures of the AU's missions to Darfur, and ask what lessons can and should be drawn from their experience for Africa's peace and security architecture.

In an article entitled "Sovereignty Reconsidered", Letitia Lawson and Donald Rothschild examine developments in African positions on sovereignty in the last two decades. According to Lawson and Rothschild, endorsement of state sovereignty as a prerogative against foreign interference has grown weaker across Africa in recent years. The changing post-Cold War global environment triggered a shift that deflected Africans from their pre-Cold War dream of inviolable African state sovereignty:

> Since the Cold War's end, the development of regional governance and globalization has diminished state authority. Transnational institutions increasingly handle critical problems such as currency control, mineral smuggling, taxation, corporate mergers, communications, defense, border security, broadcasting, and environmental controls. Meanwhile, the electronic and information revolutions have achieved a global reach that is not effectively regulated by states in Africa or elsewhere. And the international movement of migrants, goods, capital, and services continues to undermine borders.[1]

The change, the authors claimed, was forced by a combination of external and internal pressures that affected "the African state, both as an autonomous institutional actor and as a set of patrimonial organizing principles, and created 'insecure states'". External pressures include "an emerging international individual rights regime" that restricts how sovereign states treat their citizens, and "external demands for structural economic adjustment, measures to combat corruption, and democratization as preconditions for continued resource flows". Internal pressures include factors such as "ethnoregional pressures for increased representation, autonomy, or self-determination" and "the proliferation of local international alliances in which local groups seek to affect change within their countries through international mechanisms while international actors seek change within nations by going around states".[2]

While Lawson and Rothschild support their claims with examples from the DRC, the Republic of the Congo, Sierra Leone, Côte d'Ivoire, Eritrea, and Togo, there are two African states that best exemplify the change in African attitudes toward sovereignty and intervention in intrastate conflicts. In Rwanda, the traumatic failure to prevent genocide "contributed significantly to end the African elite pact on state sovereignty". Liberia marked the first case where a sub-regional organization undertook a peacekeeping mission, and in which the UN approved handing over this kind of mission to, and subsequently cooperate with, another organization.[3] Sudan is hardly mentioned in this article, perhaps due to the fact that it was published in 2005, when the AU intervention in Darfur was in its infancy. This book, which focuses on the African Union's intervention in Darfur, shows that, in some respects, this intervention signified a genuine turning point in African propensity for intervention in intrastate conflicts and in the African debate on sovereignty vs intervention, yet in other respects the change proved to be insufficient.

This is certainly true for the period of AMIS's operations in Darfur from June 2004 to December 2007. Despite AMIS's inability to prevent the large-scale atrocities, many observers from the UN and various human rights organizations have argued that AMIS's presence in Darfur helped to reduce the intensity and cruelty of the conflict, especially from the initial deployment of troops in Darfur until mid-2005. As a test case for an African peacekeeping operation, AMIS also proved able to handle various peacekeeping tasks, including in pioneering areas such as gender-based violence. In the case of the Darfur conflict, AU member states proved their readiness to protect civilian population against atrocities committed by the Sudanese government. Moreover, the AU arguably expressed a new African attitude toward the duty of the leaders of African sovereign states to protect their citizens against crimes committed by the states by rejecting Sudan's bids to chair the organization. Yet, as the AU mandate was primarily based on the GoS consent, the actual abilities of AMIS to actively perform in the field were very limited. As a result, it could be claimed that, despite its accomplishments, AMIS forces ultimately failed to stop the armed conflict and the associated murders, rapes, and deportations that created one of the gravest humanitarian crises in the first decade of twenty-first century Africa.

During its stay in Darfur, AMIS's poor performance was not altogether unforeseen. In the words of the participants of a seminar conducted by the International Peace Academy in Accra, Ghana, in October 2006, "AMIS was never planned: it just happened."[4] AMIS was plagued by a long series of shortcomings and problems on practically all levels, including finance, logistics, manpower, and deployment in the field. Furthermore, many critics argued that AMIS served the interests of the Sudanese government. As a result of the

AU's self-assumed dependence on GoS approval, the AU agreed to a very restricted mandate for its mission. Despite the organization's initial intention to enlarge the scale and functions of AMIS to a full-fledged peacekeeping mission, the organization constantly accepted the restrictions imposed on its force by the GoS, on issues such as the size and the national composition of AMIS, and, after its deployment, on issues such as traffic restriction and access to needy populations. It is not inconceivable, therefore, that the AU's failure to take a firm stand against the atrocities perpetrated by the GoS in Darfur was a by-product of its true position of non-intervention at the time.

In its first decade as a new version of a pan-continental organization, the AU's role in Darfur was instrumental in its efforts to develop and consolidate an African Peace and Security Architecture, which encompasses a range of conflict-prevention activities supported by the Panel of the Wise, and the Continental Early Warning System, the five sub-regional response elements that form the African Standby Force. The Peace and Security Council is its primary decision-making body. The case of Darfur illustrates the AU's overlapping theoretical and practical efforts to formulate the keystone of this architecture. One lesson that was quickly implemented in the Darfur crisis itself was the need for an efficient early warning system including key elements such as data collection, strategic analysis, reporting to and engagements with decision-makers, and coordination and collaboration.[5] A lesson for the future that should be learned from AMIS's deployment and functioning was that the increasingly complex demands of peace-keeping in Africa and the expectations of a rapid, reliable response, require a higher standard of performance and credibility in planning the mission's funding, controlling the pace of deployment, and overall organization both before the deployment of the mission and during the operational phase.

Another important observation concerning the factors that influenced the mission's effectiveness is the forces' heterogeneous composition. The resulting diversity reflected the major opinions, positions, and policies that have transformed African states in the last two decades, including on issues such as democratization and citizens' rights to protection against atrocities and violence. Broadly speaking, AU policy was affected by African countries that experienced a genuine transformation in the direction of democratization and pluralism, and has therefore become more attentive to the needs of the people than to the demands of the sovereign. Rwandan involvement in Darfur was an important example of the commitment by a post-genocidal society to another society facing a similar situation. Both Rwandan leaders and AMIS troops from Rwanda advised that the AU's surrender to GoS restrictions would undermine their ability to prevent violence against local populations. The more pluralistic climate in the AU on sovereign responsibility for crimes committed against populations in African states was also reflected in African leaders' changing attitudes to the ICC in the cases of Sudan and Libya. The AU officially rejected ICC accusations of African sovereigns, yet several of the AU's more influential members such as post-revolutionary Egypt and Tunisia, and, in some respects, even South Africa, supported ICC rulings against fellow African leaders.

Considering the AU's peacekeeping inexperience, and the fact that much stronger, richer, and more experienced international organizations have been challenged by the multifaceted concerns of peacekeeping operations, the AU's failure was perhaps not unexpected. It is important to examine whether the transition from the limited-power continental force to the larger, richer, and better-equipped hybrid force generated better results. As the first comprehensive attempt at cooperation between the AU and the UN, the importance of drawing conclusions from the UNAMID experience is unquestionable. Touko Piiparinen, for example, offers several observations on the effectiveness of the hybrid force and future lessons from pace of its deployment:

> One of the most pertinent structural transformations relates to Point 2 of the Action Plan: the example of Darfur proves that the pragmatic shift away from the rigidity of bureaucratic norms and the new division of labor between relevant organizations can contribute effectively to the protection of civilians. Perhaps the area in the current UN PKO system that requires urgent attention and further transformation in order to

> enhance its conflict capacity is Point 5 of the Action Plan (i.e. the ability to implement swift and decisive action, including military intervention). The tardiness of international response to the crisis in Darfur should not be downplayed: since the outbreak of violence in February 2003, more than a year passed before the first international organization, the AU, decided to deploy a military operation to put down the massacres. It took two years until UN troops were deployed in southern Sudan, with only a limited mandate to operate in Darfur. Ironically, the vanguard of the UN forces deployed in Sudan was composed of officers from the Standby High Readiness Brigade. The "high" readiness of the UN to intervene in large-scale human rights violations still requires vast improvements.[6]

Considering the large scale and resources of UNAMID, its performance in Darfur revealed a disappointing gap between the vision to bring peace and security to Darfur, and its actual performance on the ground. One of Eric Reeves' recent reports reveals that almost three years after UNAMID's deployment, little has changed in the force's actual ability to protect Darfurians against violence and atrocities:

> Because a great many actions by the Sudan Armed Forces (SAF) – including attacks on defenseless villages, camp clearances, aerial bombardment of civilians targets, denial of humanitarian access for reasons unrelated to security, torture, and, extrajudicial executions – constitute war crimes under international law, UNAMID is being kept away from many critical scenes of violence and camp displacement. Perhaps the most scandalous example of such obstruction of UNAMID occurred following the massacre in the market area of Tabarat village in North Darfur on September 2, 2010. More than 50 men and boys were killed, most by gunshots at point-blank range. Despite desperately urgent reports carried by survivors to the UNAMID force stationed at nearby Tawilla that evening, UNAMID refused either to intervene or to evacuate the scores of wounded, many of whom subsequently died of their wounds.[7]

AU attempts to resolve the Darfur conflict, however, were not limited to its assignments on the ground. The AU also invested massive efforts in the diplomatic sphere. The events that occurred during the seven rounds of the Abuja talks, and the subsequent signing of the DPA, were widely discussed in this book. One point, however, warrants additional emphasis, as it shows that similar negotiation errors have carried over from Abuja to the current negotiations in Doha.

According to the views of many observers of the final phase of the Abuja talks, some added effort and patience would have made it possible to include all the factions in the final agreement. Instead, the prolonged negotiations led to the fragmentation of the rebel forces, and surrender to the demands of the GoS and its allies led to the signing of the ineffective DPA, which alienated many sectors of Darfurian society. A recent article published in *The Economist* claims that a breakthrough in the negotiations is still possible today:

> Two of Darfur's three big rebel groups this week agreed to sit down at the negotiating table with the Sudanese government. The Justice and Equality Movement (JEM), the best known, and the Liberty and Justice Movement (LJM), a clutch of small rebel outfits, say they will make concessions over how Sudan's wealth and power can be shared. They may even agree to a referendum in which Darfuris could decide their future. The senior UN and African Union (AU) mediator overseeing the talks, Djibril Bassolé, calls the agreement "unprecedented". Immediately afterward, however, he noticed that: "A third rebel group, the Sudan Liberation Army, has failed to show up in Qatar". Also, then as now, it seems that the AU is still supporting more the GoS claims than those of the rebels, such in Thabo Mbeki support in the demand to transfer the negotiations from Doha to Darfur, a claim that was rejected by all the rebel movements, claiming that talks so close to the battle front would be manipulated by the government.[8]

Recent events in Sudan offer some answer to whether Africa has fundamentally changed its position on its responsibility to protect its citizens against the evils of its sovereigns. The recently achieved independence of South Sudan (on 9 July 2011) attests to the people's power to take action against an oppressive and violent sovereign and change their own fate. This historical achievement, which challenged the most sacred African post-colonial principle of the sanctity of colonial borders, probably would not have been accomplished (or at least not with the same speed and efficiency) without the active mediation efforts of IGAD and many AU members, which largely supported the South Sudanese claim against the Northern ruling elite.

The case of Darfur is indicative of what happens in the opposite situation: African leaders were unwilling to consolidate a unified front against the GoS or demand an end to the conflict. As a result, the Darfurians still face a miserable existence today. A more committed stance of the African Union to protect populations who are victims of violence and atrocities, and a less indulgent attitude toward claims of sovereignty coming from oppressive leaders would probably improve the prospects for conflict resolution and transition to the reconstruction phase in the continent's multiple conflict zones.[9]

NOTES

Introduction

1. ICISS, *The Responsibility to Protect, Report of the International Commission on Intervention and State Sovereignty* (Ottawa, December 2001).
2. Mark R. Duffield, *Global governance and the new wars: the merging of development and security* (London, 2001), pp. 1–74.
3. African Union, AU Peace and Security Council (PSC) Communiqué, PSC/MIN/2(XLVI), 10 March 2006.

Chapter 1 Sovereignty versus Intervention in Africa: Historical and Ideological Background

1. Kwame Nkrumah, *Africa Must Unite* (New York, 1972).
2. For detailed studies on the evaluation of the Pan-African discourse on nonintervention, see Colin Legum, *Pan Africanism: A Short Political Guide* (New York, 1962); Peter Olisanwuche Esedebe, *Pan-Africanism: The Idea and Movement* (Washington, DC, 1994). For a discussion of the limits of sovereignty, see Francis M. Deng, "Frontiers of Sovereignty: A Framework of Protection, Assistance, and development for the Internally Displaced", *Leiden Journal of International Law* 8/02 (1995), pp. 249–86.
3. Although it could be claimed that the case of the secessionist efforts of Congo's Katanga region preceded the secession efforts of Biafra from Nigeria, the critical phase of the Congolese conflict notably occurred between 1960 and 1963, prior to the establishment of the OAU. See Adekeye Abedajo, "The Curse of Berlin: Africa's Security Dilemmas", *Internationale Politik und Gesellschaft* 4 (2005): pp. 83–98; W. Scott Thompson and Richard Bissell, "Legitimacy and Authority in the OAU", *African Studies Review* 15/01 (1972), pp. 17–42.

4. Bruce Baker, "Twilight of Impunity for Africa's Presidential Criminals", *Third World Quarterly* 25/8 (2004), pp. 1497–8.
5. Claude E. Welch, "The OAU and the Promotion of Human Rights", *The Journal of Modern African Studies* 29/4 (1991), pp. 535–6.
6. For a detailed description of the development of the Americo-Liberian community and its relations with the indigenous people of Liberia, see Yekutiel Gershoni, *Black Colonialism: The Americo-Liberian Scramble for the Hinterland* (Boulder, CO, 1985).
7. Chike Akabogu, "ECOWAS takes the Initiative", in M. Vogt (ed), *Liberian Crisis and ECOMOG: A Bold Attempt at Regional Peace Keeping* (Lagos, 1992), p. 73.
8. Festus Boahen Aboagye and Alhaji Mohamed Sirjoh Bah, *Tortuous Road to Peace: The Dynamics of Regional, UN and International Humanitarian Interventions in Liberia* (Pretoria, Institute for Security Studies, 2005), "Introduction", pp. 8–9.
9. Ademola Adekele, "The Politics and Diplomacy of Peacekeeping in West Africa: The Ecowas Operation in Liberia", *The Journal of Modern African Studies* 33/04 (1995), pp. 569–93.
10. United National Security Council, "Report of the Secretary-General on Liberia", Security Council documents s/26422, 4.
11. For a detailed description of this case, see Adekele, "The Politics and Diplomacy of Peacekeeping in West Africa", pp. 569–93; Emmanuel Kwesi Aning, "The Challenge of Civil Wars to Multilateral Interventions", *African and Asian Studies* 4/1–2 (2005), pp. 1–20.
12. Aboagye and Bah, *Tortuous Road to Peace*, p. 9.
13. Clement E. Adibe, "The Liberian Conflict and the ECOWAS-UN Partnership", *Third World Quarterly* 18/3 (1997), pp. 471–88.
14. Ian Smillie and Larry Minear, *Charity of Nations* (West Hartford, CT, 2004), pp. 24–5.
15. Ibid., pp. 25–6.
16. Lansana Gberie, *A Dirty War in West Africa* (Bloomington, IN, 2005), pp. 14–15.
17. The term "complex political emergencies" become prevalent in the mid-1990s, when it became clear that the new conflict situations in places such as Somalia and Bosnia required a wider and more tightly coordinated response than had previous intrastate conflicts. See Mark Duffield, *Global Governance and the New Wars: The Merging of Development and Security* (London, 2014), pp. 12, 14, 52, 65, 71, 86, 89, 95–6, 161–3, 244, 250, 252, 254–5.
18. Smillie and Minear, *Charity of Nations*, pp. 26–7.
19. Ibid., pp. 27–8.
20. For a detailed description of the events which emphasizes RUF's role, see Gberie, *Dirty War in West Africa*.
21. David J. Francis, *Uniting Africa: Building Regional Peace and Security Systems* (Surrey, UK, 2006), p. 160.
22. This wording of the agreement eventually triggered UN criticism of the agreement's contents, and subsequently caused US qualms. See Smillie and Minear, *Charity of Nations*, pp. 31–3.

23. Available at http://www.un.org/en/peacekeeping/missions/past/unamsil/background.html (accessed 20 January 2015).
24. Smillie and Minear, *Charity of Nations*, pp. 33–5.
25. Francis, *Uniting Africa*, pp. 161–3.
26. Smillie and Minear claim that international attention to the civil war in Sierra Leone was mainly the result of the sex scandal in the Sierra Leonean aid community. Ibid., pp. 38–40.
27. See, for example, Mahmood Mamdani, *When Victims Become Killers: Colonialism, Nativism, and the Genocide in Rwanda* (Princeton, 2001); Gérard Prunier, *The Rwanda Crisis, 1959–1994: History of a Genocide* (London, 1995).
28. United Nations, "Convention on the Prevention and Punishment of the Crime of Genocide", adopted by Resolution 260 (III) A of the UN General Assembly on 9 December 1948. Article I.
29. Samantha Power, *A Problem from Hell: America and the Age of Genocide* (New York, 2007), p. 343.
30. United Nations Security Council, Resolution 918, S/RES/918, 17 May 1994. Available at http://www.sipri.org/databases/embargoes/un_arms_embargoes/rwanda/918 (accessed 20 January 2015).
31. For the broad context of US attitudes on humanitarian intervention in Africa in the 1990s, see Power, *A Problem from Hell*.
32. UN Security Council, "Special Report of the Secretary General on the United Nations Assistance Mission for Rwanda", Document S/1994/470, 20 April 1994. Available at http://daccess-dds-ny.un.org/doc/UNDOC/GEN/N94/186/70/PDF/N9418670.pdf (accessed 20 January 2015).
33. Romeo Dallaire, "Looking at Darfur, Seeing Rwanda", *New York Times*, 4 October 2004; Jeet Heer, "Romeo Dallaire: Haunted by Genocide". *Boston Globe-Ideas* (4 April 2004).
34. Prunier, *The Rwanda Crisis*, pp. 100–7.
35. Thomas G. Weiss, *Humanitarian Intervention* (Hoboken, NJ, 2012), p. 15.
36. Ibid., p. 18.
37. Allen Gregory Sens, *Somalia and the Changing Nature of Peacekeeping: The Implications for Canada* (Ottawa, 1997).
38. Francis M. Deng and Roberta Cohen, *Masses in Flights: The Global Crisis of Internal Displacement* (Washington, DC, 1998), p. 276.
39. Kofi A. Annan, "Two Concepts of Sovereignty", *The Economist*, 18 September 1999, pp. 49–50.
40. Report of the Secretary-General. Prepared by the UN Web Services Section Department of Public Information in 2005.
41. Thomas G. Weiss, *Humanitarian Intervention* (New York, 2012), pp. 34–5.
42. For a comprehensive discussion of these interventions see Thomas G. Weiss and Don Hubert (eds), *The Responsibility to Protect* (Ottawa, 2001), ch. 4. See also Edward Mortimer, "Under What Circumstances Should the UN Intervene Militarily in a 'Domestic' Crisis?", in O. Otunnu and M. Doyle (eds), *Peacemaking and Peacekeeping for the New Century* (Lanham, MD, 1998), pp. 111–43.

43. Weiss, *Humanitarian Intervention*, pp. 38–9.
44. Chen Kertcher, "Same Agenda, Different Results: The UN Interventions in Cambodia and Somalia after the Cold War", in *International Intervention in Local Conflicts* (London, 2010), pp. 19–33.
45. See, for example, Mark Duffield, "Aid and Complicity", *The Journal of Modern African Studies* 40/01 (2002), pp. 83–104.
46. Weiss, *Humanitarian Intervention*, p. 98.
47. ICISS, *The Responsibility to Protect,* p. viii.
48. UN General Assembly, *A More Secure World* (New York, 2004).
49. For the precedents of these recommendations see Weiss and Hubert, *The Responsibly to Protect*, pp. 29, 30–7, 39–43, 45 (n. 32), 363, 372, 377, 383.
50. Carsten Stahn, "Responsibility to Protect", *The American Journal of International Law* 101/1 (1007), pp. 99–120.
51. Ibid., pp. 118–120.
52. Ibid., p. 106.
53. For a detailed report on the current UN peacekeeping operations around the globe, see "United Nations Current Peacekeeping Operations". Available at www.un.org/en/peacekeeping/operations/current.shtml (accessed 20 January 2015).
54. Omar A. Touray, "The Common African Defence and Security Policy", *African Affairs* 104/417 (2005), pp. 635–56, esp. p. 643.
55. Thomas D. Zweifel, *International Organizations and Democracy: Accountability, Politics, and Power* (Boulder, CO, 2006), p. 148.
56. African Union, Constitutive Act of the African Union, Article 4(h), 11 July 2000.
57. Kelechi A. Kalu, "Resolving African Crises: Leadership role for African States and the African Union in Darfur", *African Journal on Conflict Resolution* 9/1 (2009), p. 17.
58. Baffour Ankomah, "African Union from Non-interference to Non-Indifference", *New African* 460 (2007), pp. 10–13.
59. ICISS, *The Responsibility to Protect*, para. 2.31.
60. Ibid., p. 2.
61. Janice G. Stein, *From Bipolar to Unipolar Order: System Structure and Conflict Resolution* (London, 2010), pp. 6–7.

Chapter 2 Darfur: From Resource-Based Conflicts to Crimes against Humanity

1. Gérard Prunier, *Darfur: The Ambiguous Genocide* (Ithaca, NY, 2007), pp. 88–91.
2. See for example, Prendergast, "Sudan Ravines on the Death, *New York Times*, 15 July 2004, A23.
3. For a detailed description of the events in Darfur during 2003–4, see Alex de Waal, "Counter-Insurgency on the Cheap", *Review of African Political Economy* 31/102 (2004), pp. 25–7; Prunier, *Ambiguous Genocide*, pp. 81–123.

4. For a detailed description of the developments that led to the contemporary situation, see Alex de Waal, "Darfur: The Inside Story," *New African* 461 (28 April 2007); "Counter-Insurgency on the Cheap," p. 25; Julie Flint and Alex de Waal, *Darfur: A Short History of a Long War* (London, 2008), pp. 97–117; Ruth Iyob and Gilbert M. Khadiagala, *Sudan: The Elusive Quest for Peace* (Boulder, CO, 2006); Prunier, *Ambiguous Genocide*, pp. 81–123.
5. Mark Duffield, "The Fallata", in N. O'Neill and J. O'Brien (eds), *Economy and Class in Sudan* (Aldershot, UK, 1988), pp. 122–9.
6. Mahmood Mamdani, "Preliminary Thoughts", *Social Text* 17/3 (1999), pp. 53–62.
7. Alex de Waal, "Who are the Darfurians?", *African Affairs* 104/415 (2005), pp. 181–205.
8. For a detailed study on the development of the history of Darfur, see Rex S. O'Fahey, *The Darfur Sultanate: A History* (New York, 2008).
9. Rex S. O'Fahey, "Islam and Ethnicity in the Sudan", *Journal of Religion in Africa* XXXVI/3 (1996), pp. 258–67.
10. Gabriel Warburg, *Islam, Sectarianism and Politics in Sudan Since the Mahdiyya* (London, 2003), pp. 59–62; Awad al-Sid Karasani, "Beyond Sufism: The case of millennial Islam in Sudan", in L. Brenner (ed), *Muslim identity and social change in Sub-Saharan Africa* (London, 1993), pp. 135–53.
11. M. W. Daly, *Empire on the Nile: The Anglo-Egyptian Sudan, 1989–1934* (Cambridge, UK, 1986), pp. 278–86.
12. Quoted in M. W. Daly, *Darfur's Sorrow: A History of Destruction and Genocide* (Cambridge, UK, 2007), p. 132. For an analysis of the implications of the British colonialism in Darfur see chs 6–7 in this book and Musa A. Abdul-Jalil, Adam Azzain Mohammed, and Ahmed A. Yusuf, "Native Administration and Local Governance in Darfur: past and future", in A. de Waal (ed), *War in Darfur and the Search for Peace* (Cambridge, MA, 2007), pp. 39–76.
13. de Waal, "Who are the Darfurians?", p. 192.
14. The other nationwide census conducted in 2009 is discussed below. For the details of the 1955–6 census, see M. W. Daly, *Darfur's Sorrow*, pp. 178–81.
15. Ibid., p. 180.
16. Ibid.
17. Prunier, *Darfur: The Ambiguous Genocide*, pp. 25–36.
18. John Garang, *John Garang Speaks* (London, 1987), p. 93.
19. Kelechi A. Kalu, "Resolving African Crises: Leadership role for African States and the African Union in Darfur", *African Journal on Conflict Resolution* 9/1 (2009), p. 14.
20. See, for example Karasani, "Beyond Sufism".
21. Ali Ali-Dinar, "Why Khartoum Wants a War in Darfur", *Sudan Tribune*, 30 July 2004.
22. International Crisis Group, *Justice, Peace and the ICC* (London, 2008), p. 2.
23. Roland Marchal, "The Roots of the Darfur Conflict and the Chadian civil war", *Public Culture* 20/3 (2008), pp. 429–36.

24. Ralph Benyamin Neuberger, *Involvement, Invasion, and Withdrawal* (Tel-Aviv, 1982).
25. Flint and de Waal, *Darfur: A Short History of a Long War*, pp. 23–27.
26. Alex de Waal, *Famine That Kills: Darfur, Sudan* (Oxford, UK, 2005); Ray Bush, "Hunger in Sudan: the case of Darfur", *African Affairs* 87/346 (1988), pp. 5–23.
27. Flint and de Waal, *Darfur: A Short History of a Long War*, pp. 7, 38, 41–6, 55, 60–4.
28. For a detailed analysis of al-Turabi's revolutionary ideology, see Abdelwahab El-Effendi, *Turabi's Revolution: Islam and Power in Sudan* (London, 2014).
29. Known in the literature as Abdel Wahid; this name will be used hereinafter.
30. Julie Flint, "Darfur's Armed Movement", A. de Waal (ed), *War in Darfur and the Search for Peace* (Cambridge, MA, 2007), pp. 142–3.
31. Ibid., p. 144.
32. Abdul-Jalil, Mohammed, and Yusuf, "Native Administration and Local Governance in Darfur", pp. 39–76.
33. Flint, "Darfur's Armed Movement", p. 143.
34. Flint and de Waal, "Darfur: A Short History of a Long War", p. 18. For a translated version of the text, see: http://www.sudanjem.com/sudan-alt/english/books/blackbook_part1/blackbook_part1_20040422_bbone.pdf (accessed 15 January 2015).
35. William Wallis, "The Black Book history or Darfur's Darkest Chapter", *Sudan Tribune*, 21 August 2004, p. 16.
36. Suliman Hamid al-Haj, "Darfur: Wad' al-Nuqat fi al-Huruf", *Al-Midan Journal* August (2004), p. 3; quoted in (and trans. by) Mahgoub El-Tigani Mahmoud, "Inside Darfur: Ethnic genocide by a Governance Crisis", 24/2 (2004), pp. 3–17, esp. p. 6.
37. See, for example, John Prendergast, "Sudan Ravines on the Death", *New York Times*, 15 July 2004, A23.
38. Prunier, *The Ambiguous Genocide*, p. xi.
39. Ibid.
40. Referring to the historical attitudes of the elites in Khartoum to Darfur, Alex de Waal coined the term "counter-insurgency on the cheap". See Alex de Waal, "Counter-Insurgency on the Cheap", *Review of African Political Economy* 102 (2004), pp. 716–25.
41. "UNHCR to Resume Protection Activities in South Darfur", *UNHCR News Stories*, 24 November 2004.
42. Brian Steidle and Gretchen Steidle Wallace, *The Devil Came on Horseback: Bearing Witness to the Genocide in Darfur* (Cambridge, MA, 2007), p. 53.
43. Quoted in Richard Cockett, *Sudan: Darfur and the Failure of an Africa State* (New Haven, CT, 2010), pp. 200–1. For additional details on the attack in Tawila, see Flint and de Waal, "Darfur: A Short History of a Long War", pp. 35–6.
44. Cockett, *Sudan*, p. 200.

45. For an analysis of Hilal ideology and activities, see Julie Flint and Alex de Waal, "Ideology in Arms: The Emergence of Darfur's Janjaweed", *Beirut Daily Star,* 30 August 2005.
46. International Crisis Group, "Sudan: Now or Never in Darfur", ICG Africa report No. 80 (2004), p. 8.
47. Samuel Totten and Eric Markusen (eds), *Genocide in Darfur: Investigating the Atrocities in the Sudan* (New York, 2006), chs 9–11.
48. Rob Crilly, "In Darfur, Some Arabs Now Fight Alongside Rebels", *The Christian Science Monitor,* 22 May 2007.
49. See an example of this claim in the organization's website. Available at http://www.sudanjem.com/en/index.php (accessed 15 January 2015).
50. Ruth Iyob and Glbert M. Khadiagala, *Sudan: The Elusive Quest for Peace* (Boulder, CO, 2006), p. 63.
51. Mark Duffield, *Global Governance and the New Wars: The Merging of Development and Security* (London, 2014), pp. 164–5.
52. Letitia Lawson and Donald Rothchild, "Sovereignty Reconsidered", *Current History* 104/682 (2005), pp. 228–35, esp. p. 230.
53. AU Peace and Security Council (PSC) Communiqué, PSC/PR/2(V), 13 April 2004.
54. Alex De Waal, "Sudan: the Turbulent State", in A. de Waal (ed), *War in Darfur and the Search for Peace* (Cambridge, MA, 2007), p. 32.

Chapter 3 Intervention from Theory to Practice: The African Union Mission in Sudan (AMIS)

1. African Union, *Protocol Relating to the Establishment of the Peace and Security Council of the African Union* (2002), p. 3.
2. Adekeye Adebajo, "The peacekeeping travails of the AU and the Regional Economic Communities (RECs)", in John Akokpari, Angela Ndinga-Muvumba, and Timothy Murithi (eds), *The African Union and its Institutions* (Aukland Park, SA, 2008), pp. 132–3.
3. Ibid.
4. African Union, *Protocol Relating to the Establishment of the Peace and Security Council of the African Union*, Article 10 (2002).
5. African Union, *Policy Framework for the Establishment of the African Standby Force and the Military Staff Committee* (2003), p. 2. For a detailed analysis of the initial weaknesses of AMIS operations in Darfur, see L Feinstein, "Darfur and Beyond: What is needed to prevent mass atrocities", Council on Foreign Relations, Report No. 22 (2007), pp. 31–48.
6. African Union, "Report of the chairperson of the commission on the establishment of the continental peace and security architecture and the status of peace processes in Africa", PSC/AHG/3(IX), 25 May 2004. During 2011, the AU's several ASF brigades and rapid-response forces can be deployed quickly to

stop genocide. See Stephen F. Burgess, "Comments on the Mass Atrocity Response Operations (MARO) Handbook", *Genocide Studies and Prevention* 6/1 (2011), pp. 66–9.

7. African Union, *Protocol Relating to the Establishment of the Peace and Security Council of the African Union*, Article 10 (2002).
8. African Union, *Protocol Relating to the Establishment of the Peace and Security Council of the African Union*, Article 10.
9. Hugo Slim, "Dithering over Darfur? A preliminary review of the international response", *International Affairs* 80/5 (2004), pp. 811–28.
10. Musifiky Mwanasali, "From non-interference to non-indifference: The emerging doctrine of conflict prevention in Africa", in J. Akokpari, A. Ndinga-Muvumba, and Y. Murithi (eds), *The African Union and its Institutions* (Aukland Park, SA, 2008), pp. 47–9.
11. African Union. "Report of the Chairperson of the Commission on the Situation in the Sudan (Crisis in Darfur)", PSC/PR/2(V), 13 April 2004.
12. Ibid. See also *UN News Center*, "Sudan: Annan hails signing of humanitarian ceasefire accord". Available at http://www.un.org/apps/news/story.asp?NewsID=10364&Cr=sudan&Cr1=#.VL4ZK0eUeCk (accessed 15 January 2015).
13. AU Press Release - 61/2004 (19 June 2004).
14. Moyiga Nduru, "Foreign troops run gauntlet", *Sudan Tribune*, 16 August 2004.
15. Ibid.
16. Emily Wax, "In Darfur, Rwandan soldiers relive their past again", *Washington Post*, 7 August 2005.
17. African Union, "Communique of the Peace and Security Council (Darfur)", PSR/PR/Comm. (XVII), 20 October 2004.
18. Ibid.
19. William G. O'Neill and Violette Cassis, *Protecting Two Million Internally Displaced: The Successes and Shortcomings of the African Union in Darfur* (Washington, DC, 2005), pp. 17–19. For the arrival of the first troops in Sudan, see also a series of articles in the *New York Times*: Warren Hoge, "African Union to send troops in bid to curb Sudan violence" (24 September 2004); Somini Sengupta, "Sudan agrees to allow 3,500 African Union Troops into Darfur" (2 October 2004), and "From rare glimpse inside militia camp, clear ties to Sudan" (21 October 2004).
20. *The Economist*, "An agreement, sort of", 13 November 2004.
21. See Guiding Principles on Internal Displacement, UN Doc. E/CN.4/1998/53/Add.2, Available at http://www1.umn.edu/humanrts/instree/GuidingPrinciplesonInternalDisplacement.htm (accessed 22 January 2015).
22. Ibid. The majority of the displaced persons were mainly from the Zaghawa, Fur and Masalit tribes, and were located around Kutum in North Darfur, and Wadi Saleh in West Darfur.
23. For a detailed discussion of AMIS successes and failures in dealing with the IDP problem in Darfur, see O'Neill and Cassis, *Protecting Two Million Internally Displaced*, pp. 17–19.

24. International Crisis Group, "The AU's mission in Darfur: Bridging the gaps," 6 July 2005, p. 6.
25. Sally Chin and Jonathan Morgenstein, "No power to protect: The African Union Mission in Sudan", *Refugees International* November (2005), p. 8.
26. O'Neill and Cassis, *Protecting Two Million Internally Displaced*, p. 35.
27. International Crisis Group, "The AU's mission in Darfur: Bridging the gaps", p. 5.
28. For a more comprehensive review of AMIS's tasks, see O'Neill and Cassis, *Protecting Two Million Internally Displaced*, pp. 35–49.
29. UN Security Council, "Monthly Report of the Secretary-General on Darfur", S/2005/467, 18 July 2005, p. 11.
30. African Union, Press Release No. 39/2005, 15 July 2005.
31. Mahmood Mamdani, *Saviors and Survivors: Darfur, Politics, and the War on Terror* (New York, 2010), p. 38.
32. Alex de Waal, "Darfur elusive peace", in A. de Waal (ed), *War in Darfur and the Search for Peace* (Cambridge MA, 2007), p. 337.
33. For testimonies of rape collected in the refugee camps in Sudan, see Samuel Totten and Eric Markusen (eds), *Genocide in Darfur: Investigating the Atrocities in the Sudan* (London, 2013). See also Médicins sans Frontières, "The crushing burden of rape", briefing paper, 2005.
34. IRIN, "Sudan: Interview with Amb Baba Kingibe", 15 May 2005. Available at http://www.irinnews.org/report/55494/sudan-interview-with-amb-baba-gana-kingibe-head-of-amis (accessed 20 January 2015).
35. Chin and Morgenstein, "No power to protect", p. 8.
36. Available at http://www.amis-sudan.org/history.html (emphasis added) (accessed 20 January 2015).
37. Eric Reeves, "Things are looking greatly better in Darfur". *Sudan Tribune,* 16 February 2005.
38. Chin and Morgenstein, "No power to protect", p. 1.
39. International Crisis Group, "Garang's death", 9 August 2005; "South Sudan and Darfur", 11 August 2005.
40. Chin and Morgenstein, "No power to protect", p. 2. Although Darfur hosted the largest humanitarian effort in that period (with approximately 14,000 aid workers and 85 NGOs operating in the area), the deteriorating security conditions limited the access of Darfur's population to humanitarian aid. This had a critical impact on the situation. See for example, "Darfur: Peacekeeper deaths raise concerns", *USA Today*, 1 October 2007.
41. Baffour Ankomah, "African Union: From Non-interference to non-indifference", *New African* 460 (2007), pp. 10–13.
42. Alhaji M.S. Bah and Ian Johnston, "Peacekeeping in Sudan: The dynamics of protection, partnerships and inclusive politics", *New York, Center on International Cooperation* (2007), pp. 7–8.
43. EU Council Secretariat, *Factsheet*. Available at http://www.consilium.europa.eu/uedocs/cmsUpload/080109-Factsheet8-AMISII.pdf (accessed 20 January 2015).

44. GAO Report to Congressional Requests, "Darfur Crisis: Progress in aid and peace monitoring threatened by ongoing violence and operational challenges", (2006), p. 45.
45. International Crisis Group, "The EU partnership in Darfur: Not yet a winning combination", *Africa Report* 99 (2005).
46. African Union, "Brief on the Security Situation in Central African Republic (CAR) and the Visit of an AU Mission to the Region", PSC/PR/2 (XLVI), 10 March 2006.
47. Susan E. Rice, "Why Darfur can't be left to Africa", *Washington Post*, 7 August 2005.
48. Ibid. See also "Wesley Clark: NATO forces needed in Darfur", *NPR Morning Edition*, 22 August 2005. Available at http://www.npr.org/templates/story/story.php?storyId=4809638 (accessed 20 January 2015).
49. International Crisis Group, "The AU's mission in Darfur", p. 7.
50. Brian Steidle and Gretchen Steidle Wallace, *The Devil Came on Horseback: Bearing Witness to the Genocide in Darfur* (New York, 2007), p. 63.
51. International Crisis Group, "The AU's mission in Darfur", p. 7.
52. Ibid.
53. Craig Timberg, "Rebels may abandon Darfur pact", *Washington Post*, 14 September 2006, A14.
54. Chin and Morgenstein, "No power to protect", pp. 13–14.
55. Seth Appiah-Mensah, "AU's critical assignment in Darfur: Challenges and constraints", *African Security Review* 14/2 (2005), pp. 7–8.
56. Catherine Guicherd, *The AU in Sudan: Lessons for the African Standby Force*, IPA meeting report, 2006, p. 21.

Chapter 4 From Abéché to Abuja: The African Union Mediation Efforts

1. http://www.africa-union.org/root/au/AboutAu/Constitutive_Act_en.htm#Article4 (link no longer working).
2. For an analysis of the Comprehensive Peace Agreement (CPA) on the negotiations on the Darfur conflict, see Azzain Mohamed, "The comprehensive peace agreement and Darfur", in A. de Waal (ed), *War in Darfur* (Cambridge, MA, 2007), pp. 199–213.
3. "Sirte Summit", *Al-Ray Al-A'm*, 6 October 2004.
4. "Opening of the quintuple summit in Tripoli", *Al-Ray Al-A'm*, 17 October 2004.
5. Dawit Toga, "The African Union mediation and the Abuja talks", in A. de Waal (ed), *War in Darfur and the Search for Peace* (Cambridge, MA, 2007), p. 221.
6. Alexander Ramsbotham, "Peacekeeping mission updates: January–June 2009", *International Peacekeeping* 17/1 (2010), pp. 124–37.
7. Toga, "The African Union mediation", p. 222.

8. African Union Peace and Security Council (Darfur) Communiqué, SC/Min/Comm. (XXXIV)–(iii), 3 July 2005.
9. "Sudan: UN envoy confesses its shortcomings", *Indian Ocean Newsletter*, 25 December 2004.
10. African Union Peace and Security Council (Darfur) Communiqué, PSR/PR/Comm. (XVII), 20 October 2004.
11. For an analysis of the events in the third round of the Abuja talks, see Toga, "The African Union Mediation", pp. 223–9.
12. Ibid., pp. 230–2.
13. Alex de Waal, "Briefing: Darfur, Sudan: Prospects for peace", *African Affairs* 104/414 (2005), pp. 127–35, esp. p. 130.
14. Julie Flint and Alex de Waal, *Darfur: A Short History of a Long War* (London, 2005), p. 95.
15. Dave Clark, "Sudan peace talks deadlocked", *Agence France-Presse*, 24 August 2004.
16. See, for example "Sudan peace talks delayed as rebels refuse demobilisation", *Agence France-Presse*, 15 August 2004; "Darfur peace talks restart", *Xinhua News Agency*, 26 October 2004.
17. Julie Flint, "Darfur's armed movements", in A. de Waal, *War in Darfur*, pp. 170–2.
18. Katherine Houreld, "Sudan: Rebel with a cause?", *Mail and Guardian*, 15 October 2014.
19. Flint, "Darfur's armed movements", p. 164.
20. Ibid., p. 141.
21. Ibid., p. 158.
22. Toga, "The African Union mediation", pp. 235–40.
23. Laurie Nathan, "The making and unmaking of the Darfur peace agreement", in A. de Waal, *War in Darfur*, pp. 245–66.
24. Ibid., p. 249.
25. Abaker Mohamed Abuelbashar, "On the failure of the Darfur peace talks in Abuja", *Sudan Tribune*, 25 August 2006.
26. Thilo Thielke and Volkhard Windfuhr, "The black Janjaweed", *Spiegel Online International*, 6 August 2006.
27. "AU reacts to ICG report on Darfur peace deal", *Sudan Tribune*, 26 June 2006.
28. AU Peace and Security Council (Darfur) Communiqué PSC/PR/Comm. (XLIII), 22 November 2005.
29. Author's Interview with Abdourahman A. Ibrahim, 4 February 2011.
30. Alex de Waal, "Darfur deadline: The final days of the Abuja peace process", in *War in Darfur*, p. 267.
31. Ibid.
32. Africa Action, "A chronology of international failures", 20 June 2006, p. 6.
33. Ibid. p. 12.
34. Tom Clonan, "An African solution to an African problem?", *Irish Times*, 9 October 2006.

35. Statement by Dr Salim Ahmed Salim, African Union Special Envoy and Chief Mediator for the Inter-Sudanese Peace Talks on the Conflict in Darfur, Abuja, 4 February 2006. Available at http://www.sudantribune.com/spip.php?page=imprimable&id_article = 13928 (accessed 20 January 2015).
36. African Union Peace and Security Council (Darfur) Communiqué. PSC/MIN/Comm/1 (LI), 15 May 2006.
37. Gethin Chamberlin, "Peacekeepers in Darfur", *Sunday Telegraph*, 5 November 2005.
38. "African Union warns militias in Darfur", *PANA*, 19 December 2006. It is important to note, however, that subsequent AMIS investigations discovered that several of the attacks originally attributed to the rebels' movements were actually committed by the Janjaweed.
39. Gerard Prunier, "Sudan: Genocide in Darfur", *Le Monde Diplomatique* (2007), p 1. Available at http://mondediplo.com/2007/03/08darfur (accessed 20 January 2015).
40. Alex de Waal, "Darfur elusive peace", in *War in Darfur,* p. 369. See also his chapter, "Darfur deadline", pp. 267–83.
41. For a detailed analysis of the Abuja talks, see Steven Wöndu and Ann Mosely Lesch, *Battle for Peace in Sudan: An Analysis of the Abuja Conferences, 1992–1993* (Lanham, MD, 2000).
42. For a detailed description of IGAD's diplomatic initiatives in this case, see Ruth Iyob and Gilbert M. Khadiagala, *Sudan: The Elusive Quest for Peace* (Boulder, CO, 2006), ch. 5; Abdelwahab El-Effendi, "The impasse in the IGAD peace process for Sudan: The limits of regional peacemaking?", *African Affairs* 100/401 (2001), pp. 581–99.
43. That year, IGADD changed its name by dropping "Drought" and became known as IGAD.
44. AU Peace and Security Council (Sudan) Communiqué, PSC/PR/Comm (LXXXIX), 24 August 2007.
45. For a comparative study on the Southern and Western civil wars, see Robert O. Collins, *Civil Wars and Revolution in the Sudan: Essays on the Sudan, Southern Sudan and Darfur, 1962–2004* (Los Angeles, 2005).

Chapter 5 The Government of Sudan Responds to African Union Intervention

1. "The African Union defines the mission of its peacekeeping", *Al-ray al-a'm*, 16 August 2004; "Negotiations between the Government and the African Union", *Al-ray al-a'm*, 18 September 2004; "African Union's Peace and Security Council extended the mission of AMIS", *Al-Shari al-Siasi*, 16 February 2006.
2. "The Third AU Summit ended with a call", *Asharq Alawsat*, 9 July 2004.
3. "AU humanitarian delegation tour in Darfur", *Al-ray al-a'm*, 16 August, 2004.

4. "Advance party of the African Keeping forces arrived at Al-Fasher", *Al-ray al-a'm*, 15 August 2004.
5. "The African Union postpones the decision". Available at http://www.sudaneseonline.com/anews/jul9–34783.html (accessed 20 January 2015).
6. Ibid., pp. 28–9.
7. "Accusations in Sudan", *Sudaneseonline*, 19 August 2004.
8. "The GoS and the AU are negotiating", *Asharq Alawsat*, 29 September 2004.
9. "The government announced its conditional approval", *Al-ray al-a'm*, 26 August 2004.
10. "Khartoum respond partly to Blair's demands", *Asharq Alawsat*, 8 October 2004.
11. See, for example "The GoS and the AU are negotiating", *Asharq Alawsat*, 29 September 2004.
12. "AU chairperson announced", *Al-Ray Al-A'm*, 16 October 2004.
13. Cited in Ruth Iyob and Gilbert M. Khadiagala, *Sudan: The Elusive Quest for Peace* (Boulder, CO, 2006), p. 103. Neo-colonial rhetoric was used again by al-Bashir in 2009, while explaining the reasons for the expulsion of humanitarian organizations after the International Criminal Court (ICC) issued an arrest warrant against him, as will be described in greater detail in Chapter 7 in this book.
14. "Enhancement of the international pressures", *Asharq Alawsat*, 25 July 2004.
15. "Khartoum is warning US", *Asharq Alawsat*, 10 July 2004.
16. "Sudan accuses the UN", *Asharq Alawsat*, 2 April 2005.
17. See, for example "Delegation of the armed groups", *Al-Ray Al-A'm*, 3 March 2005.
18. Thomas G. Weiss, *Humanitarian Intervention* (Cambridge, UK, 2013), p. 26.
19. "Temperamental debate", *Asharq Alawsat*, 15 October 2004.
20. "The Sudanese Minister of Information", *Asharq Alawsat*, 10 May 2005.
21. Quoted in Rex S. O'Fahey, "Some recent publications of and about the Sudan", *Sudanic Africa* 16 (2005). pp.137–53.
22. Iyob and Khadiagala, *Sudan: The Elusive Quest for Peace*, p. 184.
23. "The AU Expressed Resentment", *Al-Ray Al-A'm*, 17 September 2004.
24. Itai Madamombe, "Darfur crisis challenges Africa, world", *Africa Renewal* 18/4 (2005), p. 3.
25. The leaders came from Libya, Sudan, Egypt, Chad, Nigeria, Eritrea, and Gabon. See "Darfur summit convenes in Libya", *Libyan Jamahiriya Broadcasting Corporation*, 17 May 2005.
26. "The African Union to the Security Council", *Asharq Alawsat*, 7 March 2005.
27. Susan E. Rice, "Why Darfur can't be left to Africa", *The Washington Post*, 7 August 2005.
28. Brian Steidle and Gretchen Steidle Wallace, *The Devil Came on Horseback: Bearing Witness to the Genocide in Darfur* (New York, 2007), p. 52.
29. See, for example Andrew England, "Darfur's Green Berets", *Sudan Tribune*, 25 September 2004.
30. Mahgoub El-Tigani Mahmoud, "Inside Darfur: Ethnic genocide by a governance crisis", *Comparative Studies of South Asia, Africa and the Middle East* 24/2 (2004), pp. 3–17.

31. See, for example "Ethiopia, Egypt, Sudan agree", *BBC Monitoring Africa*, 19 April 2005, p. 1.
32. It is interesting to note that Gamal Nkrumah is the son of Kwama Nkrumah, the first Ghanaian president, who envisioned the idea of the "United States of Africa" (see Chapter 1 in this book). For several examples of Gamal's coverage of Darfur, see "An unequal Sudan", *Al-Ahram Weekly Online*, 1 June 2006; "Get a move on", *Al-Ahram Weekly Online*, 27 September 2007.
33. AU Peace and Security Council (Darfur) Communiqué, PSR/PR/Comm. (XVII), 20 October 2004.
34. Nadim Hasbani, "About the Arab stance", *Al-Hayat*, 21 March 2007.
35. "Arab League's Secretary General", *Asharq Alawsat*, 18 April 2005.
36. "Why Darfur can't be left to Africa", *The Washington Post*, 7 August 2005.
37. "Jan Pronk: The numbers of the AU troops", *Asharq Alawsat*, 30 September 2005.
38. "The African Union blames Sudan with involvement in latest attacks in Darfur", *Asharq Alawsat*, 2 October 2005.
39. "Khartoum demands that the AU expel", *Asharq Alawsat*, 11 October 2005.
40. Craig Timberg, "Rebels may abandon Darfur pact", *Washington Post*, 14 September 2006, a14.
41. "Al-Bashir and Konaré are supporting", *SudaneseOnline.com*, 15 February 2006.
42. "Baba Kingibe, Head of AMIS", *SudaneseOnline.com*, 6 February 2006.
43. "*Janjaweed*'s senior commander", *SudaneseOnline.com*, 7 February 2006.
44. AU Peace and Security Council Communiqué, PSC/MIN/2(XLVI), 10 March 2006.
45. "Sudanese minister: A role to the UN in Darfur – only after achieving peace agreement", *SudaneseOnline.com*, 6 March 2006.
46. Ibid.
47. Ibid.
48. "The Arab League criticized", *SudaneseOnline.com*, 18 February 2006.
49. Alex de Waal, "Sudan: The turbulent state", in *War in Darfur and the Search for Peace. Studies in Global Equity* (Cambridge, MA, 2007), pp. 11–16.
50. "DUP's Chairperson, Muhammad Othman al-Mirghani", *SudaneseOnline.com*, 3 March 2006.
51. For a review of his rising popularity, see Kwame Nkrumah, "Sadig Al-Mahdi", *Al-Ahram Weekly*, 5–21 July 2004.
52. "Al-Mahdi criticized the GoS's mistakes", *Asharq Alawsat*, 6 January 2005.
53. One example was the following news item: "Opposition Popular Congress Party (PCP) led by the veteran Islamist Hassan Al-Turabi has threatened to work towards overthrowing the ruling National Congress Party (NCP) if the latter continues to dismiss demands to for reforms and a transitional government." See "Sudan's Islamic opposition party threatens", *Sudan Tribune*, 2 December 2010. A recent statement by al-Turabi exemplifies his relationship with and Darfur: "What happened in Tunisia is a reminder. This is likely to happen in Sudan [...] If it doesn't, then there will be a lot of bloodshed. The whole

country is armed. In the towns, it will be a popular uprising, but in Darfur, and in Kordofan as well, they have weapons." Cited in "Al-Turabi Arrested in Khartoum", *Aljazeera*, 21 January 2011.

54. Cited in "Al-Turabi attacks the foreign presence in Sudan", *Sudaneseonline.com*, 1 January 2006.
55. "Al-Turabi: The international forces are the drugs", *Alwatan Sudan*, 22 April 2007.
56. Amber Henshaw, "Assault heralds change", *BBC News*, 12 May 2008.
57. Human Rights Watch, "Sudan's chairmanship would discredit", 18 January 2006.
58. Cited in http://www.sudaneseonline.com/anews2006/jan27–37165.shtml (accessed 20 January 2012).
59. See WilliamWallis, "President of Sudan's bid", *Financial Times*, 30 January 2007; "African Union Picks Ghanaian", *Associated Press*, 30 January 2007. For the accusation that Washington was involved in the first rejection, see "Washington puts pressure on African states", *Alwatan Sudan*, 1 February 2006.

Chapter 6 The Transition to UNAMID – A Hybrid Force Experiment

1. "Powell declares genocide in Sudan", *BBC News*, 9 September 2004.
2. Cited in Eric Reeves, "Darfur and international justice", *Dissent* 56/3 (2009), pp. 13–18, esp. 15. The debate concerning the terminology of the events in Darfur, genocide or otherwise, is the topic of an extensive discussion in Chapter 7 in this book).
3. Report of the International Commission of Inquiry on Darfur to the United Nations Secretary-General, 25 January 2005.
4. For a detailed description of the worsening situation in Darfur during 2007, see Eric Reeves, "Genocide without end?", *Dissent* 54/3 (2007), pp. 8–13.
5. James Kurth, "Humanitarian intervention after Iraq: Legal ideals vs. military realities", *Orbis* 50/1 (2006), pp. 87–101.
6. Nick Grono, "Briefing-Darfur", *African Affairs* 105/421 (2006), pp. 621–31, esp. p. 628. See also African Action, "The ties that bind Bush and Bashir", April 2008. Available at: http://reliefweb.int/report/sudan/sudan-ties-bind-bush-and-bashir (accessed 20 January 2015).
7. Susan R. Rice, "Why Darfur can't be left to Africa", *The Washington Post*, 7 August 2005.
8. Matthew Lipmann, "Darfur: The Politics of genocide denial syndrome", *Journal of Genocide Research* 9/2 (2007), pp. 193–213.
9. Alex J. Bellamy, "Responsibility to protect or Trojan horse? The crisis in Darfur and humanitarian intervention after Darfur", *Ethic and International Affaires* 19/2 (2005), pp. 31–53. For a detailed analysis of the rising power of China in Africa using "political warfare" as a means to undermine US influence there, see Donovan C. Chau, "Political warfare in Sub-Saharan Africa: U.S. capabilities

and Chinese Operations in Ethiopia, Kenya, Nigeria, and South Africa", Monograph Information for the Defense Community, 2007.

10. Ted Dagne, *Sudan: The Crisis in Darfur and Status of the North-South Peace Agreement* (Collingdale, PA, 2010), p. 24.
11. Bellamy, "Responsibility to protect or Trojan Horse?".
12. African Union Peace and Security Council (Darfur) Communiqué, PSR/PR/Comm. (XVII), 20 October 2004.
13. Cited in Dagne, *Sudan: The Crisis in Darfur*, p. 24.
14. Moshe Terdman, *Somalia at War: Between Radical Islam and Tribal Politics* (Tel-Aviv, 2008), pp. 35–44.
15. Available at http://www.un.org/en/documents/charter/chapter7.shtml (accessed 20 January 2015).
16. Terdman, *Somalia at War*, pp. 35–44.
17. Cited in "Somalia: UNOSOM I", available at http://www.un.org/Depts/DPKO/Missions/unosomi.htm (accessed 20 January 2015).
18. For a review of these analysts, see Chen Kertcher, "Same Agenda, Different Results: The UN Interventions in Cambodia and Somalia after the Cold War", U. Raby (ed), *International Intervention in Local Conflicts: Crisis Management and Conflict Resolution since the Cold War* (London, 2010), pp. 28–9.
19. Images regarding the events of this battle were also influenced by the popular movie "Black Hawk Down", directed by Ridley Scott in 2001.
20. "Somalia – UNOSOM II". Available at http://www.un.org/Depts/DPKO/Missions/unosom2p.htm (accessed 20 January 2015).
21. Nsongurua J. Udombana, "Still playing dice with lives", *Third World Quarterly* 28/1 (2007), pp. 97–116.
22. For a recent and comprehensive discussion of these issues, see Sara A. Arola, *Humanitarian Aid: Problems and Solutions* (MA thesis, Webster University, 2008).
23. Henri Boshoff, "Burundi: The African Union's first mission", *Institute for Security Studies* 9 June 2011. Available at http://hdl.handle.net/123456789/31434 (accessed 20 January 2015).
24. African Union, "Brief on the security situation in Central African Republic (CAR) and the visit of an AU Mission to the Region", PSC/PR/2 (XLVI), 10 March 2006.
25. Security Council Resolution 1679, 16 May 2006, S/Res/1679.
26. For a detailed discussion of the failure of Resolution 1706, see Udombana, "Still playing dice with lives".
27. Kassa A. Meron (Political Officer, Joint Mediation Support Team {JMST}, Addis Ababa), in discussion with the author, 3 February 2011.
28. Dr Dawit Toga (Political Analyst, Conflict Management Division, African Union), in discussion with the author, 3 February 2011.
29. Katherine N. Andrews and Victoria N. Holt, *United Nations-African Union Coordination on Peace and Security in Africa* (Washington, DC, 2007), pp. 7–8.
30. "Sudan: New hope for Darfur", *IRIN,* 20 April 2007.

31. Eric Reeves, "What alternative to UNAMID will provide security for Darfur?", *Sudan Tribune*, 1 January 2008.
32. Eric Reeves, "UN Security Council Resolution 1706", 31 August 2006." Available at http://sudanreeves.org/2007/05/14/un-security-council-resolution-1706-august-31–2006/ (accessed 20 January 2005).
33. "Sudan is threatening to Quit", *SudaneseOnline.com*, 3 March 2006.
34. Africa Action, "A chronology of international failures on Darfur", 20 June 2006, p. 16.
35. According to *Al-Hayat*, the Sudanese President expressed his consent to the plan during a meeting with US Special President Envoy, in return for a declaration by the Security Council that the Abuja Agreement would be the basis for any future negotiations between the government and the rebels. See "Al-Bashir Will announce to the UN", *Al-Hayat,* 22 December 2006.
36. Alex de Waal, "From bad to worse in Sudan", *Los Angeles Times*, 13 October 2007.
37. Richard Dowden, "China's healing power", *Time,* 13 August 2007.
38. In spite of the important role played by Save Darfur Coalition and other NGOs in raising awareness of Darfur, this book will not go into detail on this subject. For an extensive review of their activities and influence, see Rebecca Hamilton and Chad Hazlett, "Not on our watch: The emergence of the American Movement for Darfur", in A. de Waal (ed), *War in Darfur and the Search for Peace* (Cambridge, 2007), pp. 337–66.
39. Onwuka Nzeshi, "Nigeria: Group wants Nigeria to boycott Olympics", *This Day* (Nigeria), 13 April 2008.
40. J Stephen Morrison, "Will Darfur steal the Olympic spotlight?", *Washington Quarterly* 31/3 (2008), pp. 181–91, esp. 186–7.
41. Ibid.
42. Andrews and Holt, *United Nations-African Union*, p. 8 (emphasis added).
43. Kelly Campbell, "Negotiating peace in Darfur", United States Institute of Peace 2008. Available at http://www.usip.org/publications/negotiating-peace-in-darfur (accessed 20 January 2015).
44. African Union, "Report of the Chairperson of the Commission and the Secretary-General of the United Nations on the hybrid operation in Darfur", PSC/PR/2 (LXXIX), 22 June 2007.
45. Ibid., para. 16.
46. Ibid., para. 37.
47. Ibid., paras 38–9.
48. African Union, "The Chairperson of the African Union Commission and the UN Secretary-General appoint Rodolphe Adada of the Republic of Congo as Joint AU-UN Special Representative for Darfur". News release, 8 May 2007.
49. African Union, "Press Statement by Rodolphe Adada, the UN–AU Joint Special Representative for Darfur (UNAMID) on the First Day of the Mission in its El Fasher Headquarters." News release, 31 October 2007.
50. Press Release, African Union, Addis Ababa, 23 May 2007.

51. "The humanitarian crisis in the Darfur-Chad-Central African Republic triangle has deteriorated to unprecedented levels in recent months, with increasing spillover from the conflict in Darfur to Chad and CAR." See UN Office for the Coordination of Humanitarian Affairs, "Humanitarian space shrinking rapidly in Darfur-Chad-CAR: Ban Ki-Moon calls for peace-keepers to Chad and CAR as crisis spreads", *Humanitarian Newsmaker* 1/1 (2007).
52. African Union, "Press Statement of the Peace and Security Council on the Joint Mission to the Sudan of the AU and the UN Special Envoys for Darfur", PSC/PR/Comm. (LXX), 12 February 2007.
53. Ibid.
54. Silvia Spring, "Interview with Martin Luther Agwai", *Newsweek*, 15 October 2007, p. 66 (emphasis added).
55. Col. Michael K. Amuzu (Head of Darfur Desk, Peace and Security Department, African Union Commission (in discussion with the author, 1 February 2011).
56. Michael Fleshman, "Darfur: An experiment in African peacekeeping: Is African Union-UN Hybrid a model for the future? *Africa Renewal*, December 2010, p. 19.
57. "Australia's leader accuses Sudan of obstructing peacekeepers in Darfur", *Sudan Tribune*, 29 March 2008. Available at http://www.sudantribune.com/spip.php?iframe&page=imprimable&id_article = 26558 (accessed 20 January 2015).
58. Although this claim could be considered a return to the old rhetoric of "African solutions to African problems", it was not rejected by the AU chairman. See "Al-Basir: We are committed to cooperate with the AU and the UN for the sake of the success of the Hybrid Forces", *Alwatan Sudan*, 2 October 2007.
59. "Sudanese Leader, Tanzanian Defense Minister discuss Darfur", *BBC Monitoring Middle East-Political*, 1 May 2008.
60. "Sudan: humanitarian crisis in Darfur worsening", *Africa News,* 24 April 2008.
61. "Sudan: Obama backs AU–UN mission", *Africa News*, 2 March 2009.
62. Cited in Fleshman, "Darfur: An experiment", p. 20.
63. Report of the Secretary-General on the deployment of the African Union-United Nations Hybrid Operation in Darfur", Available at http://www.un.org/en/ga/search/view_doc.asp?symbol=S/2009/297.
64. Richard Cockett, *Sudan: Darfur and the Failure of an African State* (New Haven, CT, 2010), p. 233.
65. Ibid., pp. 234–5.
66. African Union Peace and Security Council (Darfur) Communiqué, SC/PR/Comm. (CCLXXXVI), 19 July 2011.
67. "An uphill struggle for peace in Darfur", *Los Angeles Times*, 27 April 2008.
68. Amber Henshaw, "Slow start to fledgling Darfur mission", *BBC Monitoring Africa*, 3 March 2008.
69. "Sudan-Ugandan shot dead in Darfur", *African Action*, 29 May 2008.
70. Simon Haselock, "Pessimism hangs over Darfur (Sudan)", *New African* 476 (August–September 2008), p. 2.

71. "Conflict, peace and security", *Africa News*, 10 March 2009.
72. UNAMID Facts and Figures, *UNAMID Information Kit*, 30 January 2011, p. 14.
73. Ibid. In one incident, two female staff members of the Irish NGO GOAL were abducted from their residence in Northern Darfur on 9 July 2009 and released on 18 October 2009.
74. Michael Fleshman, "Darfur: Another tough job", *Africa Renewal*, 8 September 2010.
75. Andrews and Holt, *United Nations-African Union Coordination*, p. 8.
76. UNAMID Facts and Figures, p. 3.
77. See one of the detailed reports in this context: "Darfur crisis: Progress in aid and peace monitoring threatened by ongoing violence and operational challenges", GOA Report to Congressional Requests, p. 45.
78. "Sudan: Humanitarian crisis in Darfur worsening", *African News*, 24 April 2008.
79. UNAMID Facts and Figures, *UNAMID Information Kit*, 30 January 2011, p. 3.
80. Mahmoud A. Suleiman, "Oil for blood: Chinese are unwelcome in Darfur", Available at http://www.sudantribune.com/spip.php?page=imprimable&id_article = 25047 (accessed 8 September 2015).
81. UNAMID, "UNAMID DJSR encourages IDPs Sheiks in Kalma IDPs camp to find joint solution to security problems", 2 December 2008.
82. "African Union-UN Blue Helmets", *UN News Center*, 22 February 2009.
83. African Union, "Briefing note: Mitigating vulnerabilities of women and children in armed conflicts", PSR/PR/3 (CCXXIII), 30 March 2010 (emphasis added).
84. "Five years on: No justice", *Human Rights Watch*, 6 April 2008.
85. Ibid.
86. "UNAMID peacekeepers complete training", *Xinhua News Agency*, 27 March 2009.
87. "Sudan; Peacekeepers probe gender-based crimes", *Africa News*, 18 August 2009.
88. "Activities promoting women's rights in Nyala", *UNAMID Daily Media Brief*, 9 December 2010.
89. "Women ambassadors discuss gender issues in North Darfur", *UNAMID Press Release* (El Fasher), 14 April 2010.
90. AU Peace and Security Council (PSC) Communiqué, PSR/PR/Comm. PSC/PR/3 (CCXXIII), 30 March 2010.
91. See UNAMID's recent decision to dispatch a human rights team to the South Darfurian village of Amar Jadeed to investigate recent allegations of widespread rape: "Sudan: UN civilian protection officials", *UN News Center*, 16 March 2011.
92. Security Council Resolution 1809, S/RES/1809 (2008).
93. UN General Assembly. "Report of the African Union–United Nations Panel on Modalities for Support to African Union Peacekeeping Operations", Document A/63/666-S/2008/813, 31 December 2008.
94. Ibid., para. 25.

Chapter 7 Darfur and Sudan from the ICC Ruling to Southern Independence – 2009–11

1. Manisuli Ssenyonjo, "The International Criminal Court arrest warrant", *International and Comparative Law Quarterly* 59/01 (2010), pp. 205–25.
2. Victor Peskin, "Caution and confrontation in the International Criminal Court's pursuit of accountability in Uganda and Sudan", *Human Rights Quarterly* 31/3 (2009), pp. 655–91, esp. 655–7.
3. UN Security Council, Resolution 1593, 31 March 2005.
4. Cited in Nadim Hasbani, "About the Arab stance vis-à-vis Darfur", *Al-Hayat*, 21 March 2007.
5. International Criminal Court, "Warrant of arrest for Ahmad Harun"; "Warrant of arrest for Ali Muhammad Ali Abd-Al-Rahman ('Ali Kushayb')." Available at http://www.icc-cpi.int/en_menus/icc/situations%20and%20cases/situations/situation%20icc%200205/related%20cases/icc%200205%200107/Pages/darfur_%20sudan.aspx (accessed 20 January 2014).
6. For a comprehensive discussion in this issue, see Peskin, "Caution and confrontation", pp. 655–91.
7. Ibid., p. 673.
8. International Criminal Court, "ICC issues a warrant of arrest for Omar Al Bashir, President of Sudan", Press Release, ICC-CPI-20090304-PR39, 4 March 2009.
9. Ibid.
10. "Sudan: AU Calls on UN Security Council to Delay ICC Decision", *BBC Monitoring Middle East-Political*, 22 July 2008.
11. AU Peace and Security Council (PSC) Communiqué, PSR/PR/Comm. (CLXXV), 5 March 2009.
12. Irit Back, "The ICC arrest warrant against Omar al-Bashir", *Tel Aviv Notes*, 1 June 2009.
13. AU Peace and Security Council (PSC) Communiqué, PSR/PR/Comm. (CLXXV), 5 March 2009.
14. "Ugandan President does not condemn ICC", *Sudan Tribune*, 2 August 2008.
15. "South Africa U-turns on ICC defiance", *African Business,* October 2009, p. 2.
16. See, for example, special edition of *New African*, July 2009.
17. AU Peace and Security Council (PSC) Communiqué, SC/PR//COMM (CXCCVIII) 21 July 2009.
18. Richard Cockett, *Sudan: Darfur and the Failure of an African State* (New Haven, CT, 2010), pp. 277–8.
19. "A Sudanese presidential assistant", *Alwatan Sudan*, 1 March 2009. Available at http://www.alwatansudan.com/index.php?type=3&id = 14623 (accessed 22 January 2015).
20. "Expulsion of NGOs", *BBC Monitoring Middle East-Political*, 5 March 2009.

21. Ahmed Al-Sharif, "The Court in Hague", *Alwatan Sudan*, 10 March 2009.
22. "An Arab and Muslim delegation", *Alwatan Sudan*, 7 March 2009.
23. Abd al-Rahman Daud, Editorial, *Alwatan Sudan*, 17 March 2009.
24. Ibid.
25. International Crisis Group, "Sudan: Justice, peace and the ICC", 17 July 2009, pp. 18–19.
26. Eric Reeves, "Darfur and international justice", *Dissent* 56/3 (2009), pp. 13–18, esp. p. 14.
27. Edward Mortimer, "Under what circumstances should the UN intervene militarily in a 'domestic' crisis?", in O. Oyunnu and M. Doyle (eds), *Peacemaking and Peace Keeping in the New Century* (Lanham, MD, 1998).
28. For the consultations in Doha prior to the ICC arrest warrant and the concerns over the ICC decision, see "Statement issued by the Afro Arab Ministerial Committee, Doha", *African Union*, 14 January 2009.
29. Nadia Sarwar, "Darfur crisis: Why has the UN failed?", *Strategic Studies* 4/XXIX (2009), p. 8.
30. "The GoS exposed the names", *Alwatan Sudan*, 8 March 2009.
31. "An Editorial", *Alwatan Sudan*, 13 March 2009.
32. AU Peace and Security Council (PSC) Communiqué, SC/AHG/COMM.1 (CCVII), 29 October 2009 (emphasis added). See also "African Union report calls", *Alwatan Sudan*, 24 October 2009.
33. AU Peace and Security Council (PSC) Communiqué, SC/AHG/COMM.1 (CCVII), 29 October 2009.
34. "Preliminary Statement", *The Carter Center Election Observation Mission in Sudan Presidential, Gubernatorial, and Legislative Elections*, April 2010. Available at http://www.cartercenter.org/news/pr/sudan-041710.html (accessed 22 January 2015).
35. Ibid.
36. Ibid.
37. AU Peace and Security Council (PSC) Communiqué, PSC/PR/Comm.1 (CCXIII), 22 December 2009.
38. Although it can be argued that Eritrea's secession from Ethiopia was a precedent for the Southern Sudan referendum, it was not quite the same case, as Ethiopia was not colonized during the colonial partition of Africa in the late nineteenth century, and annexed Eritrea only in 1952.
39. Scopus S. Poggo, *The First Sudanese Civil War: Africans, Arabs, and Israelis in the Southern Sudan, 1955–1972* (Basingstoke, UK, 2011), p. 86.
40. "Sudan; AU Commission Chairman urges country", *African News*, 27 September 2010.
41. AU Peace and Security Council (PSC) Communiqué, PSC/AHG/3(CCL), 30 November 2010 (italics added).
42. Zeinab Saleh, "Mission interrupted: Khartoum asks UN mission to leave Sudan", *Sudan Votes*, 5 June 2011.

Chapter 8 The Arab Spring, Darfur, and Beyond

1. Irit Back, "The Arab Spring and Sub-Saharan Africa", *Tel Aviv Notes* 10 (2011), pp. 1–4.
2. Larry Diamond, "Why are there no Arab democracies?", *Journal of Democracy* 21/1 (2010), pp. 93–112.
3. Ibid., pp. 101–2.
4. Irit Back, "Beyond Zimbabwe: The African discourse on dictatorship and democracy", *Tel Aviv Notes*, 6 August 2008.
5. AU Peace and Security Council (PSC) Press Release, PSC/PR/BR (CCLI), 4 December 2010.
6. Ibid.
7. "Côte d'Ivoire: Briefing", *IRIN*, 15 February 2011.
8. Lisa Anderson, "Demystifying the Arab Spring: Parsing the differences between Tunisia, Egypt, and Libya", *Foreign Affairs* 90/2 (2011), p. 6.
9. Security Council Resolution 1973, 17 March 2011; S/RES/1973 (2011).
10. Ibid.
11. "Libya Resolution", *Guardian*, 17 March 2011.
12. African Union, "Press Statement on the Situation in (Libya)", PSC/PR/BR.1 (CCLXVIII), 23 March 2011.
13. African Union, "Press Statement on the Situation in (Libya)", SC/MIN/ COMM.2 (CCLXXV), 23 April 2011.
14. Ibid.
15. "African Union 'ignored'", *BBC Hardtalk*, 25 March 2011.
16. "Libya; South Africa accuses NATO", *Africa News*, 15 June 2011 (emphasis added).
17. International Criminal Court, "Warrant of Arrest for Muammar Mohammed Abu Minyar Gaddafi (Muammar Gaddafi)", 27 June 2011.
18. Ibid., 48.
19. "The International Criminal Court bears its teeth", *Economist,* 14 May 2011, pp. 47–8.
20. Ken Menkhaus, "Governance without government in Somalia: Spoilers, state building, and the politics of coping", *International Security* 31/3 (2006–7), pp. 74–106, esp. p. 83.
21. Ibid., p. 80.
22. During two years, the TFG could not remain in Somalia for security reasons. See "IGAD to Deploy Peacekeepers", *IRIN*, 16 March 2005.
23. Anneli Botha, "Who's who in the Somali quagmire?", *The African Org.* 2010, 9, pp. 15–17. For background on the rise of the ICU and the Ethiopian and American responses, see also A. de Waal (ed), *Islamism and its Enemies in the Horn of Africa* (Bloomington, IN, 2004), pp.182–257.
24. Cecilia Hull and Emma Svensson, *African Union Mission in Somalia* (Stockholm, 2008), p. 22.
25. UN Security Council, "Resolution 1744", S/RES/1744 (2007).

26. AU Peace and Security Council (Somalia) Communiqué, PSC/PR/Comm. (LXIX), 19 January 2007.
27. P. D. Williams, "The African Union mission in Somalia: Decision time", *Stockholm International Peace Research Institute,* 10 December 2010.
28. Hull and Svensson, *African Union Mission in Somalia*, p. 8.
29. Ibid., pp. 27–8.
30. Jakkie Cilliers, Henri Boshoff, and Festus B. Aboagye, "Troop surge in Somalia won't solve anything", *The African.org* (October–November 2010). Available at http://www.biyokulule.com/view_content.php?articleid=3038 (accessed 20 January 2015).
31. See, for example, "UN 'disturbed' over Somali hunger crisis", *Aljazeera*, 5 July 2011.
32. Hull and Svensson, *African Union Mission in Somalia*, pp. 28–9.
33. Cilliers, Boshoff, and Aboagye, "Troop surge in Somalia".
34. Cited in Hull and Svensson, *African Union Mission in Somalia*, p. 32.

Conclusion

1. Letitia Lawson and Donald Rothschild, "Sovereignty reconsidered", *Current History* 104/682 (2005), pp. 228–35, esp. p. 229.
2. Ibid.
3. Ibid., pp. 232–3.
4. The report written as a result of this seminar was published as Catherine Guicherd, *The AU in Sudan: Lessons for the African Standby Force*, IPA meeting report 2006. Available at http://www.ipinst.org/media/pdf/publications/au_in_sudan_eng2.pdf (accessed 22 January 2015). One example shows clearly how AMIS was also plagued by a lack of basic management skills: "The absence of benchmarks, with the consequence that commanders and mission leaders have been unable to know whether they had reached their goals" (pp. 4–5). Although this issue might be perceived as negligible under other circumstances, it was extremely crucial to understand AMIS' performance on ground.
5. African Union, "Report on the Status of the Establishment of the Continental Peace and Security Architecture" (PSC/PR/3) LVII), 21 June 2006.
6. John Piiparinen, "The lessons of the Darfur for the future of humanitarian intervention", *Global Governance* 13/3 (July–September 2007), pp. 365–9.
7. Eric Reeves, "What we learn of UNAMID", *Sudanreeves. Org*, 18 September 2010.
8. "A deal over Darfur?" *Economist*, 3 February 2011.
9. To quote a recent UNAMID publication: "It is only through comprehensive and sustainable peace that UNAMID can fully and effectively implement its mandate in Darfur and maximize its capacity to bring succor and hope to the sufferings of civilians." UNAMID, "Prospects for peace in Darfur- A significant step forward", *UNAMID Publication for the People of Darfur – Voices of Darfur* (July–August 2011), p. 15.

BIBLIOGRAPHY

Abdul-Jalil, Mussa A., Adam Azzain Mohammed, and Ahmed A. Yusuf, "Native administration and local governance in Darfur: Past and future", in A. de Waal, *War in Darfur and the Search for Peace* (Cambridge MA, 2007), pp. 39–76.

Abedajo, Adekeye, "The curse of Berlin: Africa's security dilemmas", *Internationale Politik und Gesellschaft* 4 (2005), pp. 83–98.

——— "The peacekeeping travails of the AU and the Regional Economic Communities (RECs)", in J. Akokpari, A. Ndinga-Muvumba, and T. Murithi (eds), *The African Union and its Institutions* (Aukland Park, SA, 2008), pp. 132–3.

Aboagye, Festus Boahen and Alhaji Mohamed Sirjoh Bah, *Tortuous Road to Peace: The Dynamics of Regional, UN and International Humanitarian Interventions in Liberia* (Pretoria, Institute for Security Studies, 2005).

Abuelbashar, Abaker Mohamed, "On the failure of the Darfur peace talks in Abuja", *Sudan Tribune*, 25 August 2006.

Adekele, Ademola, "The politics and diplomacy of peacekeeping in West Africa: The Ecowas Operation in Liberia", *The Journal of Modern African Studies* 33/04 (1995), pp. 569–93.

Adibe, Clement E., "The Liberian conflict and the ECOWAS–UN partnership", *Third World Quarterly* 18/3 (1997), pp. 471–88.

Africa Action, "A chronology of international failures on Darfur", 20 June 2006.

——— "The ties that bind Bush and Bashir", April 2008. Available at http://reliefweb.int/report/sudan/sudan-ties-bind-bush-and-bashir (accessed 20 January 2015).

African Union Peace and Security Council (Darfur) Communiqué, PSC/PR/2(V), 13 April 2004.

——— PSR/PR/Comm. (XVII), 20 October 2004.

——— SC/Min/Comm. (XXXIV)–(iii), 3 July 2005.

——— PSC/PR/Comm. (XLIII), 22 November 2005.

——— PSC/MIN/2(XLVI), 10 March 2006.

——— PSC/MIN/Comm/1 (LI), 15 May 2006.

——— PSC/PR/Comm. (LXIX), 19 January 2007.

——— PSC/PR/Comm. (LXXXIX), 24 August 2007.

——— PSR/PR/Comm. (CLXXV), 5 March 2009.

——— PSR/PR/Comm. PSC/PR/3 (CCXXIII), 30 March 2010.

——— SC/PR//COMM (CXCCVIII), 21 July 2009.

——— SC/AHG/COMM.1 (CCVII), 29 October 2009 (emphasis added). See also "African Union Report Calls", *Alwatan Sudan*, 24 October 2009.

——— PSC/PR/Comm.1 (CCXIII), 22 December 2009.

——— PSC/AHG/3 (CCL), 30 November 2010 (italics added).

——— PSC/PR/BR (CCLI), 4 December 2010.

——— SC/PR/Comm. (CCLXXXVI), 19 July 2011.

African Union, "Brief on the security situation in Central African Republic (CAR) and the visit of an AU mission to the region", PSC/PR/2 (XLVI), 10 March 2006.

——— "Briefing note: Mitigating vulnerabilities of women and children in armed conflicts", PSR/PR/3 (CCXXIII), 30 March 2010 (emphasis added).

——— Constitutive Act of the African Union, Article 4(h), 11 July 2000.

——— *Policy Framework for the Establishment of the African Standby Force and the Military Staff Committee* (2003).

——— Press Release No. 39/2005, 15 July 2005.

——— *Protocol Relating to the Establishment of the Peace and Security Council of the African Union*, Article 10 (2002).

——— "Press statement by Rodolphe Adada, the UN–AU Joint Special Representative for Darfur (UNAMID) on the first day of the mission in its El Fasher headquarters", News release, 31 October 2007.

——— "Press statement of the Peace and Security Council on the joint mission to the Sudan of the AU and the UN special envoys for Darfur", PSC/PR/Comm. (LXX), 12 February 2007.

——— "Press statement on the situation in (Libya)", PSC/PR/BR.1 (CCLXVIII), 23 March 2011.

——— "Press statement on the situation in (Libya)", SC/MIN/COMM.2 (CCLXXV), 23 April 2011.

——— Press Release 61/2004, 19 June 2004.

——— Protocol Relating to the Establishment of the Peace and Security Council of the African Union, Article 10.

——— "Report of the Chairperson of the Commission on the Situation in the Sudan (Crisis in Darfur)", PSC/PR/2(V), 13 April 2004.

——— "Report of the Chairperson of the Commission on the Establishment of the Continental Peace and Security Architecture and the status of peace processes in Africa", PSC/AHG/3(IX), 25 May 2004.

——— "Report on the status of the establishment of the Continental Peace and Security Architecture", PSC/PR/3(LVII), 21 June 2006.

——— "Report of the Chairperson of the Commission and the Secretary-General of the United Nations on the hybrid operation in Darfur", PSC/PR/2 (LXXIX), 22 June 2007.

——— "Statement issued by the Afro Arab ministerial committee, Doha", 14 January 2009.

——— "The Chairperson of the African Union Commission and the UN Secretary-General appoint Rodolphe Adada of the Republic of Congo as Joint AU–UN Special Representative for Darfur." News release, 8 May 2007.

Akabogu, Chike, "ECOWAS takes the initiative", in M. Vogt (ed), *Liberian Crisis and ECOMOG: A Bold Attempt at Regional Peace Keeping* (Lagos, 1992), p. 73.

Ali-Dinar, Ali, "Why Khartoum wants a war in Darfur", *Sudan Tribune*, 30 July 2004.

Al-Sharif, Ahmed, "The Court in Hague", *Alwatan Sudan*, 10 March 2009.

Anderson, Lisa, "Demystifying the Arab Spring: Parsing the differences between Tunisia, Egypt, and Libya", *Foreign Affairs* 90/2 (2011), p. 6.

Andrews, Katherine N. and Victoria N. Holt, *United Nations-African Union Coordination on Peace and Security in Africa* (Washington, DC, 2007).

Aning, Emmanuel Kwesi. "The challenge of civil wars to multilateral interventions – UN, ECOWAS, and complex political emergencies in West Africa: A critical analysis", *African and Asian Studies* 4/1–2 (2005), pp. 1–20.

Ankomah, Baffour, "African Union from non-interference to non-indifference", *New African* 460 (2007), pp. 10–13.

Annan, Kofi A., "Two concepts of sovereignty", *The Economist,* 18 September 1999, pp. 49–50.

Appiah-Mensah, Seth. "AU's critical assignment in Darfur: Challenges and constraints", *African Security Review* 14/2 (2005), pp. 7–8.

Arola, Sara A., *Humanitarian Aid: Problems and Solutions* (MA thesis, Webster University, 2008).

Associated Press, "African Union picks Ghanaian", 30 January 2007.

Back, Irit, "The ICC Arrest Warrant against Omar al-Bashir", *Tel Aviv Notes*, 1 June 2009.

——— "Beyond Zimbabwe: The African Discourse on Dictatorship and Democracy, *Tel Aviv Notes*, 6 August 2008.

——— "The Arab Spring and Sub-Saharan Africa", *Tel Aviv Notes* 10 (2011), pp. 1–4.

Bah, Alhaji M.S. and Ian Johnston. "Peacekeeping in Sudan: The dynamics of protection, partnerships and inclusive politics", *New York, Center on International Cooperation* (2007), pp. 7–8.

Baker, Bruce, "Twilight of impunity for Africa's presidential criminals", *Third World Quarterly* 25/8 (2004), pp. 1497–8.

Bellamy, Alex J. "Responsibility to protect or Trojan horse? The crisis in Darfur and humanitarian intervention after Darfur", *Ethic and International Affaires*, 19 (2), 2005. pp. 31–53.

Boshoff, Henri, "Burundi: The African Union's first mission", *Institute for Security Studies*, 9 June 2011. Available at http://hdl.handle.net/123456789/31434 (accessed 20 January 2015).

Botha, Anneli. "Who's who in the Somali quagmire?", *The African.org* 9 (2010), pp. 15–17.

Burgess, Stephen F., "Comments on the Mass Atrocity Response Operations (MARO) Handbook", *Genocide Studies and Prevention* 6/1 (2011), pp. 66–9.

Bush, Ray, "Hunger in Sudan: The case of Darfur", *African Affairs* 87/346 (1988), pp. 5–23.

Campbell, Kelly, "Negotiating peace in Darfur", *United States Institute of Peace* (2008). Available at http://www.usip.org/publications/negotiating-peace-in-darfur (accessed 20 January 2015).

Carter Center, "Preliminary statement", April 2010. Available at http://www.cartercenter.org/news/pr/sudan-041710.html (accessed 22 January 2015).

Chamberlain, Gethin, "Peacekeepers in Darfur", *Sunday Telegraph*, 5 November 2005.

Chau, Donovan C., "Political warfare in Sub-Saharan Africa: U.S. Capabilities and Chinese operations in Ethiopia, Kenya, Nigeria, and South Africa", Monograph Information for the Defense Community, 2007.

Chin, Sally, and Jonathan Morgenstein, "No power to protect: The African Union mission in Sudan", *Refugees International* November (2005), p. 8.

Cilliers, Jakkie, Henri Boshoff, and Festuus B. Aboagye, "Troop surge in Somalia won't solve anything", *The African.org* (Oct.–Nov. 2010).

Clark, Dave, "Sudan peace talks deadlocked", *Agence France-Presse*, 24 August 2004.

Clonan, Tom, "An African solution to an African problem?" *Irish Times*, 9 October 2006.

Cockett, Richard, *Sudan: Darfur and the Failure of an African State* (New Haven, CT, 2010), p. 233.

Collins, Robert O., *Civil Wars and Revolution in the Sudan: Essays on the Sudan, Southern Sudan and Darfur, 1962–2004* (Los Angeles, 2005).

Crilly, Rob, "In Darfur, some Arabs now fight alongside rebels", *The Christian Science Monitor*, 22 May 2007.

Dagne, Ted, *Sudan: The crisis in Darfur and status of the North-South peace agreement* (Collingdale, PA, 2010).

Dallaire, Roméo, "Looking at Darfur, seeing Rwanda", *New York Times*, 4 October 2004.

Daly, M.W., *Empire on the Nile: The Anglo-Egyptian Sudan, 1989–1934* (Cambridge, UK, 1986).

——— *Darfur's Sorrow: A History of Destruction and Genocide* (Cambridge, UK, 2007).

Daud, Abd al-Rahman, Editorial, *Alwatan Sudan*, 17 March 2009.

de Waal, Alex (ed), *Islamism and its Enemies in the Horn of Africa* (Bloomington, IN, 2004).

——— *War in Darfur and the Search for Peace* (Cambridge MA, 2007).

de Waal, Alex, "Counter-insurgency on the cheap", *Review of African Political Economy* 31/102 (2004), pp. 25–7.

——— "Briefing: Darfur, Sudan: Prospects for peace", *African Affairs* 104/414 (2005), pp. 127–35.

——— "Who are the Darfurians?", *African Affairs* 104/415 (2005), pp. 181–205.

——— *Famine That Kills: Darfur, Sudan* (Oxford, UK, 2005).

——— "Sudan: The turbulent state", in *War in Darfur and the Search for Peace. Studies in Global Equity* (Cambridge, MA, 2007), pp. 11–16.

——— "Darfur's elusive peace", in A. Waal (ed), *War in Darfur and the Search for Peace* (Cambridge MA, 2007), pp. 367–88.

——— "Darfur: The inside story", *New African* 461 (April 2007), p. 28.

——— "From bad to worse in Sudan", *Los Angeles Times*, 13 October 2007.

——— "Darfur deadline: The final days of the Abuja peace process", in *War in Darfur and the Search for Peace. Studies in Global Equity* (Cambridge, MA, 2007), pp. 267–83.

Deng, Francis M., "Frontiers of sovereignty: A Framework of protection, assistance, and development for the internally displaced", *Leiden Journal of International Law* 8/02 (1995), pp. 249–86.

Deng, Francis M. and Roberta Cohen, *Masses in Flights: The global crisis of internal displacement* (Washington, DC, 1998).

Diamond, Larry, "Why are there no Arab democracies?", *Journal of Democracy* 21/1 (2010), pp. 93–112.
Dowden, Richard. "China's healing power", *Time,* 13 August 2007.
Duffield, Mark, "Aid and complicity", *The Journal of Modern African Studies* 40/01 (2002), pp. 83–104.
——— *Global governance and the new wars: the merging of development and security* (London, 2001).
——— "The Fallata", in N. O'Neill and J. O'Brien (eds), *Economy and Class in Sudan* (Aldershot, UK, 1988).
Economist, "An Agreement, Sort of", 13 November 2004.
El-Effendi, Abdelwahab, "The impasse in the IGAD peace process for Sudan: The limits of regional peacemaking?", *African Affairs* 100/401 (2001), pp. 581–99.
——— *Turabi's Revolution: Islam and Power in Sudan* (London, 2014).
El-Tigani Mahmoud, Maghoub, "Inside Darfur: Ethnic genocide by a governance crisis", *Comparative Studies of South Asia, Africa and the Middle East* 24/2 (2004), pp. 3–17.
England, Andrew, "Darfur's Green Berets", *Sudan Tribune*, 25 September 2004.
EU Council Secretariat, *Factsheet*. Available at http://www.consilium.europa.eu/uedocs/cmsUpload/080109-Factsheet8-AMISII.pdf (accessed 20 January 2015).
Feinstein, Lee, "Darfur and beyond: What Is needed to prevent mass atrocities", Council on Foreign Relations, Report 22 (2007), pp. 31–48.
Fleshman, Michael, "Darfur: An experiment in African peacekeeping: Is African Union–UN Hybrid a model for the future? *Africa Renewal*, December 2010.
——— "Darfur: Another Tough Job", *Africa Renewal*, September 2010.
Flint, Julie, "Darfur's Armed Movements", in A. de Waal, *War in Darfur and the Search for Peace* (Cambridge, MA: 2007), pp. 170–2.
Flint, Julie and Alex de Waal, *Darfur: A Short History of a Long War* (London, 2005).
——— "Ideology in Arms: The Emergence of Darfur's Janjaweed", *Beirut Daily Star,* 30 August 2005.
Francis, David J., *Uniting Africa: Building Regional Peace and Security Systems* (Surrey, UK, 2006).
GAO Report to Congressional Requests, "Darfur crisis: Progress in aid and peace monitoring threatened by ongoing violence and operational challenges" (2006), p. 45.
Garang, John, *John Garang Speaks* (London, 1987).
Gberie, Landana, *A Dirty War in West Africa* (Bloomington, IN, 2005).
Gershoni, Yekutiel, *Black Colonialism: The Americo-Liberian Scramble for the Hinterland* (Boulder, CO, 1985).
Grono, Nick, "Briefing-Darfur", *African Affairs* 105/421 (2006), pp. 621–31.
Guicherd, Catherine, *The AU in Sudan: Lessons for the African Standby Force,* IPA meeting report 2006. Available at http://www.ipinst.org/media/pdf/publications/au_in_sudan_eng2.pdf (accessed 22 January 2015).
Guiding Principles on Internal Displacement, UN Doc. E/CN.4/1998/53/Add.2. Available at http://www1.umn.edu/humanrts/instree/GuidingPrinciplesonInternalDisplacement.htm (accessed 22 January 2015).
Hamid al-Haj, Suliman, "Darfur: Wad' al-Nuqat fi al-Huruf", *Al-Midan Journal* August (2004), p. 3; quoted in (and trans. by) Mahgoub El-Tigani Mahmoud, "Inside Darfur: Ethnic genocide by a governance crisis", 24/2 (2004), pp. 3–17.

Hamilton, Rebecca and Chad Hazlett, "Not on our watch: The emergence of the American Movement for Darfur", in A. de Waal (ed), *War in Darfur and the Search for Peace* (Cambridge, 2007), pp. 337–66.

Hasbani, Nadim, "About the Arab stance vis-à-vis Darfur", *Al-Hayat*, 21 March 2007.

Haselock, Simon, "Pessimism hangs over Darfur (Sudan)", *New African* 476 (August–September 2008), p. 2.

Heer, Jeet, "Romeo Dallaire: Haunted by genocide", *Boston Globe-Ideas* (4 April 2004).

Henshaw, Amber, "Slow start to fledgling Darfur mission", *BBC Monitoring Africa*, 3 March 2008.

——— "Assault heralds change", *BBC News*, 12 May 2008.

Hoge, Warren, "African Union to send troops in bid to curb Sudan violence", New York Times, 24 September 2004.

Houreld, Katherine., "Sudan: Rebel with a cause?", *Mail and Guardian*, 15 October 2014.

Hull, Cecilia and Emma Svensson, *African Union Mission in Somalia* (Stockholm, 2008).

Human Rights Watch, "Sudan's Chairmanship would Discredit", 18 January 2006.

ICISS, *The Responsibility to Protect, Report of the International Commission on Intervention and State Sovereignty* (Ottawa, December 2001).

International Criminal Court, "ICC issues a warrant of arrest for Omar Al Bashir, President of Sudan", Press Release, ICC-CPI-20090304-PR39, 4 March 2009.

——— "Warrant of arrest for Muammar Mohammed Abu Minyar Gaddafi (Muammar Gaddafi)", 27 June 2011.

——— "Warrant of arrest for Ahmad Harun"; "Warrant of arrest for Ali Muhammad Ali Abd-Al-Rahman ('Ali Kushayb')." Available at http://www.icc-cpi.int/en_menus/icc/situations%20and%20cases/situations/situation%20icc%200205/related%20cases/icc%200205%200107/Pages/darfur_%20sudan.aspx (accessed 20 January 2014).

International Crisis Group, "Sudan: Now or never in Darfur", ICG Africa Report No. 80 (2004), p. 8.

——— "The AU's Mission in Darfur: Bridging the Gaps", 6 July 2005, p. 6.

——— "Garang's Death", 9 August 2005.

——— "South Sudan and Darfur", 11 August 2005.

——— "The EU partnership in Darfur: Not yet a winning combination", *Africa Report*, 99 (October 2005).

——— *Justice, Peace and the ICC* (London, 2008), p. 2.

——— "Sudan: Justice, peace and the ICC", 17 July 2009, pp. 18–19.

IRIN, "Sudan: Interview with Amb Baba Kingibe", 15 May 2005. Available at http://www.irinnews.org/report/55494/sudan-interview-with-amb-baba-gana-kingibe-head-of-amis (accessed 20 January 2015).

Iyob, Ruth and Gilbert M. Khadiagala, *Sudan: The Elusive Quest for Peace* (Boulder, CO, 2006).

Kalu, Kelechi A. "Resolving African crises: Leadership role for African states and the African Union in Darfur", *African Journal on Conflict Resolution* 9/1 (2009), 9–39.

Karasani, A.a.a., "Beyond Sufism: The case of millennial Islam in Sudan", in L. Brenner (ed), *Muslim Identity and Social Change in Sub-Saharan Africa* (London, 1993), pp. 135–53.

Kertcher, Chen, "Same agenda, different results: The UN interventions in Cambodia and Somalia after the Cold War", in U. Rabi (ed), *International Intervention in Local Conflicts: Crisis Management and Conflict Resolution since the Cold War* (London, 2010), pp. 19–33.

Kurth, James, "Humanitarian intervention after Iraq: Legal ideals vs. military realities", *Orbis* 50/1 (2006), pp. 87–101.

Lawson, Letita and Donald Rothchild, "Sovereignty reconsidered", *Current History* 104/682 (2005), pp. 228–35.

Legum, Colin, *Pan Africanism: A Short Political Guide* (New York, 1962).

Lipmann, Matthew, "Darfur: The politics of genocide denial syndrome", *Journal of Genocide Research* 9/2 (2007), pp. 193–213.

Madamombe, Itai, "Darfur crisis challenges Africa, World", *Africa Renewal* 18/4 (2005), p. 3.

Mamdani, Mahmood, "Preliminary thoughts", *Social Text* 17/3 (1999), pp. 53–62.

——— *When Victims Become Killers: Colonialism, Nativism, and the Genocide in Rwanda* (Princeton, 2001).

——— *Saviors and Survivors: Darfur, Politics, and the War on Terror* (New York, 2010).

Marchal, Roland, "The roots of the Darfur conflict and the Chadian civil war", *Public Culture* 20/3 (2008), pp. 429–36.

Médicins sans Frontières, "The crushing burden of rape", Briefing paper, 2005.

Menkhaus, Ken, "Governance without government in Somalia: Spoilers, state building, and the politics of coping", *International Security* 31/3 (2006–7), pp. 74–106.

Mohamed, Azzain, "The Comprehensive Peace Agreement and Darfur", in A. de Waal (ed), *War in Darfur and the Search for Peace* (Cambridge, MA, 2007), pp. 199–213.

Morrison, J. Stephen, "Will Darfur steal the Olympic spotlight?", *Washington Quarterly* 31/3 (2008), pp. 181–91.

Mortimer, Edward, "Under what circumstances should the UN Intervene militarily in a 'domestic' crisis?", in O. Otunnu and M. Doyle (eds), *Peacemaking and Peacekeeping for the New Century* (Lanham, MD, 1998), pp. 111–43.

Mwanasali, Musifiky, "From non-interference to non-indifference: The emerging doctrine of conflict prevention in Africa", in J. Akokpari, A. Ndinga-Muvumba, and Y. Murithi (eds), *The African Union and its Institutions* (Aukland Park, SA, 2008), pp. 47–9.

Nathan, Laurie, "The making and unmaking of the Darfur peace agreement", in A. de Waal (ed), *War in Darfur and the Search for Peace* (Cambridge, MA: 2007), pp. 245–66.

Nduru, Moyiga, "Foreign troops run gauntlet", *Sudan Tribune*, 16 August 2004.

Neuberger, Ralph Benyamin, *Involvement, Invasion, and Withdrawal* (Tel-Aviv, 1982).

Nkrumah, Kwame, *Africa Must Unite* (New York, 1972).

——— "Sadig Al-Mahdi", *Al-Ahram Weekly*, 5–21 July 2004.

NPR Morning Edition, "Wesley Clark: NATO Forces Needed in Darfur", 22 August 2005.

Nzeshi, Onwuka, "Nigeria: Group wants Nigeria to boycott Olympics", *This Day* (Nigeria), 13 April 2008.

O'Fahey, Rex S., "Islam and ethnicity in the Sudan", *Journal of Religion in Africa* XXXVI/3 (1996), pp. 258–67.

——— *Some Recent Publications of and about* the Sudan, *Sudanic Africa* 16 (2005), p. 137–53.

——— *The Darfur Sultanate: A History* (New York, 2008).

O'Neill, William G. and Violette Cassis, *Protecting Two Million Internally Displaced: The Successes and Shortcomings of the African Union in Darfur* (Washington, DC, 2005).

Olisanwuche Esedebe, Peter, *Pan-Africanism: The Idea and Movement* (Washington, DC, 1994).

Peskin, Victor, "Caution and confrontation in the International Criminal Court's pursuit of accountability in Uganda and Sudan", *Human Rights Quarterly* 31/3 (2009), pp. 655–91.

Piiparinen, John, "The lessons of the Darfur for the Future of humanitarian intervention", *Global Governance* 13/3 (July–September 2007), pp. 365–69.

Poggo, Scopus S., *The First Sudanese Civil War: Africans, Arabs, and Israelis in the Southern Sudan, 1955–1972* (Basingstoke, UK, 2011).

Power, Samantha, *A Problem from Hell: America and the Age of Genocide* (New York, 2007).

Prendergast, John, "Sudan ravines on the death", *New York Times*, 15 July 2004 A23.

Press Release, African Union, Addis Ababa, 23 May 2007.

Prunier, Gérard, *The Rwanda Crisis, 1959–1994: History of a Genocide* (London, 1995).

——— "Sudan: Genocide in Darfur", *Le Monde Diplomatique* (2007), p. 1. Available at http://mondediplo.com/2007/03/08darfur (accessed 20 January 2015).

Ramsbotham, Alexander, "Peacekeeping mission updates: January–June 2009", *International Peacekeeping* 17/1 (2010), pp. 124–37.

Reeves, Eric, "Things are looking greatly better in Darfur." *Sudan Tribune,* 16 February 2005.

——— "UN Security Council Resolution 1706, August 31, 2006." Available at: http://sudanreeves.org/2007/05/14/un-security-council-resolution-1706-august-31-2006/ (accessed 20 January 2005).

——— "Genocide without end?" *Dissent* 54/3 (2007), pp. 8–13.

——— "What alternative to UNAMID will provide security for Darfur?", *Sudan Tribune*, 1 January 2008.

——— "Darfur and international justice", *Dissent* 56/3 (2009), pp. 13–18.

——— "What we learn of UNAMID", *Sudanreeves.org*, 18 September 2010.

Report of the International Commission of Inquiry on Darfur to the United Nations Secretary-General, 25 January 2005.

Rice, Susan E., "Why Darfur can't be left to Africa", *Washington Post*, 7 August 2005.

Saleh, Zeinab, "Mission interrupted: Khartoum asks UN mission to leave Sudan", *Sudan Votes*, 5 June 2011.

Sarwar, Nadia. "Darfur crisis: Why has the UN failed?", *Strategic Studies* 4/XXIX (2009), p. 8.

Sengupta, Somini, "Sudan agrees to allow 3,500 African Union troops into Darfur", *New York Times* (2 October 2004).

——— "From rare glimpse inside militia camp, clear ties to Sudan. *New York Times*, (21 October 2004).

Sens, Allen Gregory, *Somalia and the Changing Nature of Peacekeeping: The Implications for Canada* (Ottawa, 1997).

Slim, Hugo, "Dithering over Darfur? A preliminary review of the international response", *International Affairs* 80/5 (2004), pp. 811–28.

Smillie, Ian, and Larry Minear, *Charity of Nations* (West Hartford, CT, 2004).

Spring, Silivia, "Interview with Martin Luther Agwai", *Newsweek*, 15 October 2007, p. 66.

Ssenyonjo, Manisuli, "The International Criminal Court Arrest Warrant", *International and Comparative Law Quarterly* 59/01 (2010), pp. 205–25.

Stahn, Carsten, "Responsibility to protect", *The American Journal of International Law* 101/1 (1007), pp. 99–120.

Steidle, Brian and Gretchen Steidle Wallace, *The Devil Came on Horseback: Bearing Witness to the Genocide in Darfur* (Cambridge, MA, 2007).

Stein, Janice G., "From bipolar to unipolar order: System structure and conflict resolution", in U. Rabi (ed), *International Intervention in Local Conflicts: Crisis Management and Conflict Resolution since the Cold War* (London, 2010), pp. 3–8.

Suleiman, Mahmoud A. "Oil for blood: Chinese are unwelcome in Darfur", Available at http://www.sudantribune.com/spip.php?page=imprimable&id_article=25047 (accessed 20 January 2015).

Terdman, Moshe, *Somalia at War: Between Radical Islam and Tribal Politics* (Tel-Aviv, 2008).

Thielke, Thilo and Volkhard Windfuhr, "The black janjaweed", *Spiegel Online International*, 6 August 2006.

Thompson, W. Scott and Richard Bissell, "Legitimacy and authority in the OAU", *African Studies Review* 15/01 (1972), pp. 17–42.

Timberg, Craig, "Rebels may abandon Darfur Pact", *Washington Post*, 14 September 2006, p. A14.

Toga, Dawit, "The African Union mediation and the Abuja talks", in A. de Waal (ed), *War in Darfur and the Search for Peace* (Cambridge MA, 2007).

Totten, Samuel and Eric Markusen (eds), *Genocide in Darfur: Investigating the Atrocities in the Sudan* (New York, 2006).

Touray, Omar A., "The common African defence and security policy", *African Affairs* 104/417 (2005), pp. 635–56.

Udombana, Nsongurua J., "Still playing dice with lives", *Third World Quarterly* 28/1 (2007), pp. 97–116.

United Nations, "Convention on the Prevention and Punishment of the Crime of Genocide", Adopted by Resolution 260 (III) A of the UN General Assembly on 9 December 1948. Article I.

United Nations Department of Public Information, "Somalia: UNOSOM I." Available at http://www.un.org/Depts/DPKO/Missions/unosomi.htm (accessed 20 January 2015).

United Nations General Assembly, *A More Secure World* (New York, 2004).

——— "Report of the African Union-United Nations panel on modalities for support to African Union peacekeeping operations", Document A/63/666-S/2008/813, 31 December 2008.

United Nations News Center, "Sudan: Annan Hails Signing of Humanitarian Ceasefire Accord." Available at http://www.un.org/apps/news/story.asp?NewsID=10364&Cr=sudan&Cr1=#.VL4ZK0eUeCk (accessed 15 January 2015).

United Nations Office for the Coordination of Humanitarian Affairs, "Humanitarian Space Shrinking Rapidly in Darfur-Chad-CAR: Ban Ki-Moon Calls for Peace-keepers to Chad and CAR as Crisis Spreads", *Humanitarian Newsmaker* l/1 (2007).

United Nations Security Council, "Monthly Report of the Secretary-General on Darfur", S/2005/467, 18 July 2005, p. 11.

——— "Report of the Secretary-General on Liberia", Security Council documents s/26422, 4.

——— Resolution 918, S/RES/918, 17 May 1994. Available at http://www.sipri.org/databases/embargoes/un_arms_embargoes/rwanda/918 (accessed 20 January 2015).

——— Resolution 1593, 31 March 2005.

——— Resolution 1679, 16 May 2006, S/Res/1679.

——— Resolution 1744, S/RES/1744 (2007).

——— Resolution 1809, S/RES/1809 (2008).

——— Resolution 1973, 17 March 2011, S/RES/1973 (2011).

——— "Special Report of the Secretary General on the United Nations Assistance Mission for Rwanda", Document S/1994/470, 20 April 1994. Available at http://daccess-dds-ny.un.org/doc/UNDOC/GEN/N94/186/70/PDF/N9418670.pdf (accessed 20 January 2015).

UNAMID Facts and Figures, *UNAMID Information Kit*, 30 January 2011, p. 14.

UNAMID, "Prospects for peace in Darfur", *UNAMID Publication for the People of Darfur – Voices of Darfur* (July–August 2015), p. 15.

UNAMID, "UNAMID DJSR encourages IDPs sheiks in Kalma IDPs camp to find joint solution to security problems", 2 December 2008.

UNHCR News Stories, "UNHCR to resume protection activities in South Darfur", 23 November 2004. Available at http://www.unhcr.org/cgi-bin/texis/vtx/search?page=search&docid=41a4a8694&query=protection (accessed 20 January 2015).

United States GOA, "Darfur Crisis: Progress in Aid and Peace Monitoring Threatened by Ongoing Violence and Operational Challenges", GOA Report to Congressional Requests, p. 45.

Wallis, William, "President of Sudan's Bid", *Financial Times*, 30 January 2007.

——— "The Black Book history or Darfur's Darkest Chapter", *Sudan Tribune*, 21 August 2004, p. 16.

Warburg, Gabriel, *Islam, Sectarianism and Politics in Sudan Since the Mahdiyya* (London, 2003).

Wax, Emily, "In Darfur, Rwandan soldiers relive their past again", *Washington Post*, 7 August 2005.

Weiss, Thomas G., *Humanitarian Intervention: Ideas in Action* (Cambridge, UK, 2012).

Weiss, Thomas G. and Don Hubert (eds), *The Responsibly to Protect* (Ottawa, 2001).

Welch, Claude E., "The OAU and the promotion of human rights", *The Journal of Modern African Studies* 29/4 (1991), pp. 535–55.

Williams, P. D., "The African Union mission in Somalia: Decision time", *Stockholm International Peace Research Institute,* 10 December 2010.

Wöndu, Steven and Ann Mosely Lesch, *Battle for Peace in Sudan: An Analysis of the Abuja Conferences, 1992–1993* (Lanham, MD, 2000).

Zweifel, Thomas D., *International Organizations and Democracy: Accountability, Politics, and Power* (Boulder, CO, 2006).

INDEX